Yoga inVision 15

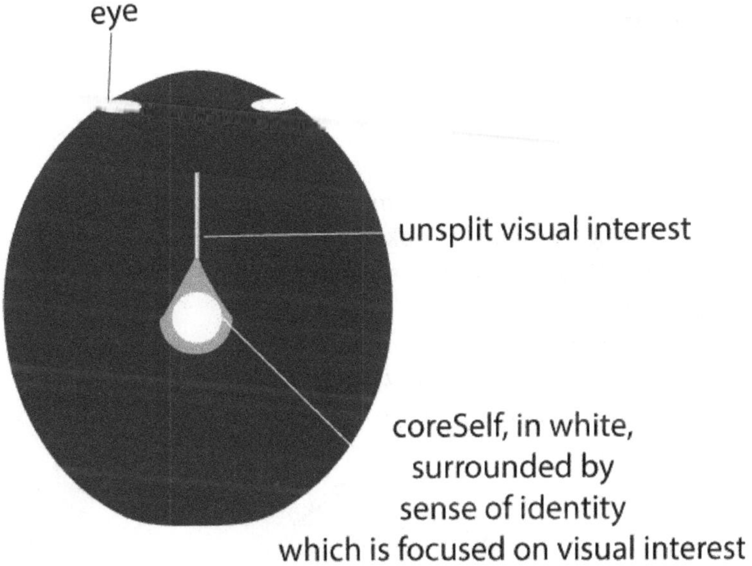

Michael Beloved

Illustrations: Author

Correspondence:
Michael Beloved
19311 SW 30th Street
Miramar FL 33029
USA
Email: axisnexus@gmail.com
michaelbelovedbooks@gmail.com

Paperback ISBN: 9781942887362
eBook ISBN: 9781942887379
LCCN: 2021904465

Mi-Beloved

Table of Contents

INTRODUCTION

This is the fifteenth of the Yoga inVision series. It relates experiences and practices done in 2014. These give beginners ideas of the physical, psychological and spiritual experiences one may have when doing asana postures, pranayama breath-infusion and *pratyahar* sensual energy withdrawal. Beyond that is higher yoga, which Patañjali named the *samyama* procedures. He defined *samyama* as a combination of *dharana* deliberate focus, *dhyana* spontaneous focus and *samadhi* continuous spontaneous focus. During practice, these progress one into the other. If one is expert at *pratyahar* sensual energy withdrawal, one may graduate to *dharana* which is deliberate focus of the attention to a higher concentration force or person. As soon as one masters *dharana* one may slip into *dhyana* which is an effortless focus on a higher concentration force or person. Once you practice *dhyana*, *samadhi* happens as the continuous effortless focus on a higher concentration force or person.

Many persons on a spiritual path feel that they can construct a process as they advance. This idea denotes failure. After all, if the supernatural and spiritual environment, is not already there, no one can create it now. It is either there or it is not. For instance, if one intends to moves to a different country, then of course one will fail if the country intended does not exist. It has to be there prior. Similarly, what you aim for as spiritual life, must be there already, or one will find that the aspiration is incorrect. This is why I speak of a concentration force or person. I could have said concentration person or divine person, or God. I did not because I do not know how anyone's spiritual path will develop.

One may leave an island in the safest boat and still the vessel may sink. One should keep one's mind open and be willing to work with fate. In spiritual development, there is providence too. What one desires to have one may not achieve. What one wishes to see may never appear.

These Yoga inVision journals show how sporadic my course of yoga was. This is after years of practice. It gives some idea of what to expect. Once you get through the lower yoga practice, you will see advancement in a more stable way but it may be incremental, accruing little by little, with bright flashes here and there.

Part 1

Wrong Method ~ Unfavorable Birth

Lahiri spoke of a yogin who has neither the right method nor right birth. He said that much of what passes as kriya yoga is not that and misleads the ascetic. With the wrong method, an ascetic cannot succeed.

To cull the correct method, one should study the *Bhagavad Gita* and the Patanjali *Yoga Sutras*. These books are standard reference. One may also read the *Uddhava Gita* and the *Hatha Yoga Pradipika*. Using that information, one should extract what is practical and what is not, from the methods given by gurus.

The right method is required but one must also have the right birth, where there is ample opportunity for spiritual practice in contrast to social involvement for maintaining the status of a family and to be sure that one is not on the bottom of the social tier, eking out a living by spending many hours in concerns for a livelihood.

The ideal birth is described by Krishna:

प्राप्य पुण्यकृताँल्लोकान्
उषित्वा शाश्वतीः समाः ।
शुचीनां श्रीमतां गेहे
योगभ्रष्टोऽभिजायते ॥६.४१॥

prāpya puṇyakṛtām̐llokān
uṣitvā śāśvatīḥ samāḥ
śucīnāṁ śrīmatāṁ gehe
yogabhraṣṭo'bhijāyate(6.41)

prāpya — obtaining; puṇyakṛtām — of the performer of virtuous acts; lokān — celestial places; uṣitvā — having lived; śāśvatīḥ — many, many; samāḥ — years; śucīnām — of the purified person; śrīmatām — of the prosperous person; gehe — in the social circumstance; yogabhraṣṭo = yogabhraṣṭaḥ — fallen from yoga; 'bhijāyate = abhijāyate — is born

After obtaining the celestial places where the virtuous souls go, having lived there for many, many years, the fallen yogi is born into the social circumstances of the purified and prosperous people. (Bhagavad Gita 6.41)

अथ वा योगिनामेव
कुले भवति धीमताम् ।
एतद्धि दुर्लभतरं
लोके जन्म यदीदृशम् ॥६.४२॥

atha vā yogināmeva
kule bhavati dhīmatām
etaddhi durlabhataraṁ
loke janma yadīdṛśam (6.42)

atha vā — alternately; yoginām — of the yogi; eva — indeed; kule — in the family situation; bhavati — is born; dhīmatām — of the enlightened people; etad — this; dhi = hi — indeed; durlabhataram — difficult to attain; loke — in this world; janma — birth; yad — which; īdṛśam — such

Alternately, he is born into a family of enlightened people. But such a birth is very difficult to attain in this world. (Bhagavad Gita 6.42)

This defines favorable births as being from parents who are either purified and prosperous or enlightened.

But even if one has such a birth, if one does not have the right method there will be failure in higher yoga.

Sensual Energy Withdrawal Success

Yogis should always bear in mind that Patanjali segmented the four higher states of yoga into two processes.

Of the eight stages of yoga, the first four involve physical and psychological activities but the final four processes concern only psychological movements.

Asanas in particular are an obvious physical process. In fact, yoga is known popularly as *asana* postures or as a physical process of disciplining the body to make it supple.

But the higher four stages are anything but physical. These are psychological motions.

- *pratyahar* sensual energy withdrawal
- *dharana* deliberate focus on what is not physical
- *dhyana* spontaneous focus on what is not physical
- *samadhi* continuous spontaneous focus on what is not physical

But Patanjali listed the last three procedures as one sequential process naming it as *samyama* or the complete psychological restraint.

Hence, we have *pratyahar* sensual energy withdrawal and *samyama* complete psychological restraint.

If the yogi does *pratyahar* sensual energy withdrawal inefficiently, the *samyama* complete psychological restraint will not occur or it may be experienced haphazardly. Completion of *pratyahar* sensual energy withdrawal is a must for anyone who wants to do the *samyama* complete psychological restraint successfully.

If possible, or better, if the yogi is lucky, he/she would do *pranayama* practice before sitting to meditate.

Why?

Because *pranayama* breath infusion is the fourth procedure which is followed by the fifth which is *pratyahar* sensual energy withdrawal.

If *pranayama* breath infusion is not done, there is little likelihood that *pratyahar* will occur in an effective way with the senses internalized or de-activated when the yogi sits to meditate.

It is possible to have *samyama* succeed even if one does not do *pranayama* but that does not mean that Patanjali was excessive when he listed breath infusion as the fourth stage. He listed that because it is the reliable method to attain *pratyahar* sensual energy withdrawal.

It is important that when doing breath infusion, the mind be kept within the psyche; that it is not allowed to wander through any of the senses while doing that practice. It should not be interested in or pursuant of anything physical. It should have no interest in or pursuant of any sound. It should not be interested in or pursuant of any odor. It should not be interested in anything which stimulates taste. And it should not be pursuant of and interested in feeling any object which is not in the body or psyche of the yogi.

The mind should be kept in the body of the yogi during *pranayama* practice. That will guarantee a richer *pranayama* breath infusion process which will yield a deeper *pratyahar* sensual energy withdrawal experience, prior to entering the *samyama* complete psychological restraint

Bhagavad Gita gives insight into the attainment of *pratyahar* sensual energy withdrawal:

यदा संहरते चायं

कूर्मोऽङ्गानीव सर्वशः।

इन्द्रियाणीन्द्रियार्थेभ्यस्
तस्य प्रज्ञा प्रतिष्ठिता ॥२.५८॥

yadā saṁharate cāyaṁ
kūrmo'ṅgānīva sarvaśaḥ
indriyāṇīndriyārthebhyas
tasya prajñā pratiṣṭhitā (2.58)

yadā — when; saṁharate — pulls; cāyaṁ = ca — and + ayam — this; kūrmo = kūrmaḥ — tortoise; 'ṅgānīva = aṅgānīva = aṅgāni — limbs + iva — like, compared to; sarvaśaḥ — fully; indriyāṇīndriyārthebhyas = indriyani — senses + indriyarthebhyaḥ — attractive things; tasya — his; prajñā — reality-piercing vision; pratiṣṭhitā — is established

When such a person pulls fully out of moods, he/she may be compared to the tortoise with its limbs retracted. The senses are withdrawn from the attractive things in the case of a person whose reality-piercing vision is established. (Bhagavad Gita 2.58)

Buildings Flying in the Astral World

Last night I was drawn into an astral world where people live out their fantasies which are related to the present digital age. A friend who still has a physical body, wanted me to be with him in that astral place. His subtle form intends to transit to that place after the death of his physical system.

We were in a building which he designed mentally and which appeared in that place with no extra effort on his part, on the basis of his willpower only. Next door where there was a house of another person, a flying building grazed the roof of that place.

We saw the airborne flying buildings. They were similar to airplanes in the large cities on this earth, where they land one after another.

In that astral place there were many flying buildings which were residences but the one which passed over his neighbor's house, actually grazed the roof of his neighbor's place. It was so close that there was no space between it and his neighbor place. He looked at it and smiled because he was proud of the achievement of being able to fly houses and move them here or there or move to another location carrying the house intact without having to sell the place and move the furniture to other locations.

Breath Infusion Extraction

Meditation this morning was part of the progression I had while doing procedures given by Lahiri. These are centered around clearing carbon dioxide from the body and noticing what if any advantage that gives during the meditation which follows.

Lahiri is of the opinion that it is essential to clear the subtle body of all lower astral energy. This view is in contrast to the traditional idea about raising kundalini and then doing meditation after kundalini burst in the head of the subtle form, particularly after it pierced through the crown chakra.

There are two attainments which relate to this. The first is when kundalini pierces through the neck, enters the subtle head and punctures the crown chakra *(brahmarandra)*. Then a person gains special insight into transcendental realms or a person may enter into *satchidananda* spiritual bliss energy. He is washed by transcendental happiness for a time.

The second is where the subtle body is cleared of all lower astral energy by an effective breath infusion. Then instead of having the crown chakra burst, from within the subtle head, there is a transit the person makes to the *chit akash* sky of consciousness. This second attainment is the process I currently use.

Which is better?

That depends on the level of practice. It is not a matter of which is best but rather what is needed at the particular stage of advancement.

I use *bhastrika* and *kapalabhati pranayama* to extract the gaseous pollution from the subtle body. Formerly many yogis successfully used *anuloma-viloma* alternate breathing. Using that *pranayama* however entails hours of practice with steady concentration for the entire time.

Breath infusion for me this morning was more about doing the rapid breathing, then holding off while the accumulated energy was distributed, then doing more rapid breathing, then again checking the distribution, then again and again and again, repeating this sequence, with focus in various parts of the body especially in the extremities and other *hard to reach* places like the thighs, legs and feet.

After that when I sat to mediate, I was in a large chamber which was divided so that the back part of it had a dark black-blue energy in which naad sound resonance blared from a central node which was to the back but slightly to my right. Up front in the subtle head there was another energy which was like when there are grey and white dots on a television screen. But then after a time the entire chamber was filled with bliss energy which was pixels of energy like ice-crystals except that it did not have a frozen feeling. It was a bliss force.

During the extraction breath process, which is a combination of fresh air breath infusion into the subtle body and used-stale air extraction of used energy out of it, there were times when I felt that I completed the extraction. Then soon after I felt that I had to do more. I did more. That confirmed that the extraction was not complete.

Naad Meditative Contact Despite Noise

Hearing naad even when there are loud noises and other aural irritation, is a special skill for a yogi. Keeping connected with naad under most disagreeable situations is essential.

Do you ever reach out to connect with naad just before slumber descends?

What is the last mental event one usually experiences before sleeping?

Recently I meditated in a location where I could hear car tires rolling on a nearby highway. There was also the occasional barking of dogs. There was the hum of a compressor. Still, I hung to the naad. I kept with it, making it prominent to focal consciousness.

If a yogi has to be in a noisy location, can he/she still meditate deeply?

Is it worth the struggle to try when one is in a humbug environment with modern machinery humming, automobile tires roaring, and animals howling?

Rupture of Naad Sound Resonance Meditation

In the *Hatha Yoga Pradipika*, naad sound resonance is said to be the best consciousness transit:

नासनं सिद्ध - सदृशं न कुम्भः केवलोपमः ।

न खेचरी - समा मुद्रा न नाद - सदृशो लयः ॥ ४५ ॥

nāsanaṁ siddha–sadṝśaṁ na kumbhaḥ kevalopama ।

na khecarī–samā mudrā na nāda–sadṝśo layaḥ

nāsanaṁ = na (not) + āsanaṁ (posture), siddha – perfected yogi posture, sadṝśaṁ – compared, na – not, kumbhaḥ – breath retension, kevalopamaḥ = kevala (complete isolation of the core–self) + upamah (best, next, like), na – not, khecarī – procedure for transiting through divine space, samā – similar, equal, mudra – physio–psychic application technique, na – not, nāda – naad subtle sound resonation, sadṝśo = sadṝśaḥ = similar, like, layaḥ – consciousness transit

There is no posture which compares to the perfected yogi pose. There is no physio–psychic application technique which is like the khecarī procedure for transiting through kha divine space. There is no consciousness–transit like focus on naad subtle sound resonation. (Kundalini Hatha Yoga Pradipika 1.45)

Once the yogi becomes habituated to hearing naad sound, the coreSelf becomes immerged in naad to such an extent that a relationship of love and concern develops between the yogi and the sound. This is a personal relationship even though naad is not present as a person.

However, in time after developing a deep love with naad, a love which may be compared to the conjugal love between partners, still there may be a breach of the relationship just as between a lover and a beloved there may be ruptures and heartache due to major or minor disagreements.

Then the yogi must make the next move, but on occasion naad may reach out and take the yogi into its association. When the yogi decides to realign his interest with naad, to re-invest his attention to it, there is some sadness on the part of the ascetic where he/she realizes that the breach was severe. That is regretted but what happened did occur. The yogi must endeavor to reestablish the closeness in love.

A question arises as to why the yogi is distracted from naad. What was the initial activity which caused the breach?

Why, even with the help of a great teacher, a student will suffer a rupture and not hear naad for a time during meditation sessions.

What did the student do which reduced contact with naad?

After keen observation, I noticed that when I sit to meditate, I either reach naad or I do not contact it. Instead, I become involved in other aspects of the psyche. I find myself under the influence of a cruising sequence of thoughts which came from an outside source but which was present in the mind as if it was native to my psyche.

At the time of seeing this, one may or may not know the source of the thoughts. It really does not matter whom the thoughts originated from. Once the thoughts enter into the mind, they derive or express a power, just as bombs have destructive power after they left an enemy aircraft.

Thinking about the enemy planes have some value but the technique required is a way to either neutralize the bombs after they leave the aircraft or have a method so that their explosive impact is nil.

In the ultimate consideration, it does not matter whom the thoughts belong to. Once they enter the psyche, the damage is done.

Wherefrom did they derive the penetrative power?

I noticed that on the way to meet naad, I was pulled to the side by a cruising thought energy so that I never saw or perceived naad in any way. My natural inclination which is to go in the direction of naad was nullified by the pulling and redirecting force of the cruising thought. It tugged until I viewed the fullness of it. Then there was no chance for reaching naad because there was no memory or even a hint that naad even existed.

If I had no idea what influenced me, how could I change it? If the meditation begins with not being in touch with naad, but with being under the influence of a rapidly or slowly developing thought, how can the yogi break lose, especially if he/she has no objectivity about the undesirable influence?

Ocean Sounds Meditation

Ocean sounds, river sounds, hollow sounds in caves, sounds of water falls and hollow sounds in a conch, may serve as mantras for meditation or basis for meditative focus and mind-trash clearance.

Because of the steady repeat of ocean wave, their sounds may be used as a free mantra for focus which would clear the mind of trash ideas, imaginations and even harmful memories which carry a recurring traumatic content.

We have many associations, which bring trauma energies into our psyches. These come from incidences with others whereby their upsets ricochet into our minds and causes waves of emotions which are detrimental to mental peace. It is not just the impulsive habit of nurturing painful emotions but the habits of others as well, which affect us.

As a driver does not have to commit a traffic violation to be killed in an accident, so one does not have to nurture traumatic incidences, to be affected by the trauma energy of others.

If the sound of the ocean can relieve us of much self-inflicted and acquired trauma, why is it that people who sit by the sea do not get such relief?

The answer is that unless one focuses on the ocean sound, the constant crashing of waves, one may not derive the benefit.

- Sit by the sea.
- Put everything aside mentally and emotionally.
- Listen to the crashing sounds of the waves
- Listen intently with full focus.
- Do this for twenty minutes.
- Relax the focus.

When one uses a mantra, one should say the mantra either audibly or non-audibly (mentally). One may generate a feeling towards the mantra, like a feeling of love and devotion to the deity whose name or energy is given in the mantra. After making the effort to intone the mantra, one should listen for it.

In either of these actions, one may be careless. If one is focused one will get more benefit from the recital and hearing of the mantra. If, however one uses the ocean sound as the mantra, one is only obligated to hear it and can do so continuously. The task of generating the mantra is conducted by the ocean, free of charge. Focus does not waver back and forth between intoning the sound and listening to it. Instead, focus is doubly intensified and is continuous and seamless, less jerky.

Yogi Uses the Passionate Force

I practice some experimental procedures for Lahiri. These are systems which some yogis used and were successful with in the past, but which were untested for the culture of our time. By testing these I can report as to whether they gave the same or different result. Because of the changes in the subtle bodies from the time those methods were useful as to now, some practices from before are ineffective in our time. Thus, everything must be tested. Or we will find that people are given kriyas which worked before but which give no benefit currently.

Simply because a method worked in the past, does not mean it will function now. A bonafide method may prove to be ineffective now. Usually, I test a method before recommending it. Even in my case, sometimes the method does not work for another person, who returns and complains that it was useless.

Presently, I practice the lift-hormone kriya along with the lifting of kundalini base kriya. This is a double action of lifting hormone up the front of the trunk of the subtle body and lifting kundalini chakra up the back of the same trunk. When these are effectively lifted and when they are influenced to take the upward instead of the downward routes, everything changes whereby the traditional kundalini system is dismantled.

The hormone system relies on gravity to transport it downward. This is easy because the earth's gravity is ever present. All solids in the body were created from the earth's physicals. An ascetic must either rely on nature or redesign it. This redesigning is done under the supervision of an advanced yogi or deity.

If the natural system is to be disrupted, the ascetic must perform several tasks himself. He/She can no longer rely on kundalini to do everything as it has from ancient times. The convenient and very natural way is to let kundalini do everything automatically, while the coreSelf breezes it through life enjoying whatever the kundalini arranges as it maneuvers through the maze of destiny.

The passionate force is the enthusiasm energy. It is used by the kundalini in the tasks of maintaining the body. The coreSelf, for redesigning the psyche, must use that passion influence in a constructive way. He must harness it and cause it to lift the hormonal and kundalini energies up through the trunk of the body.

preliminary kundalini yoga

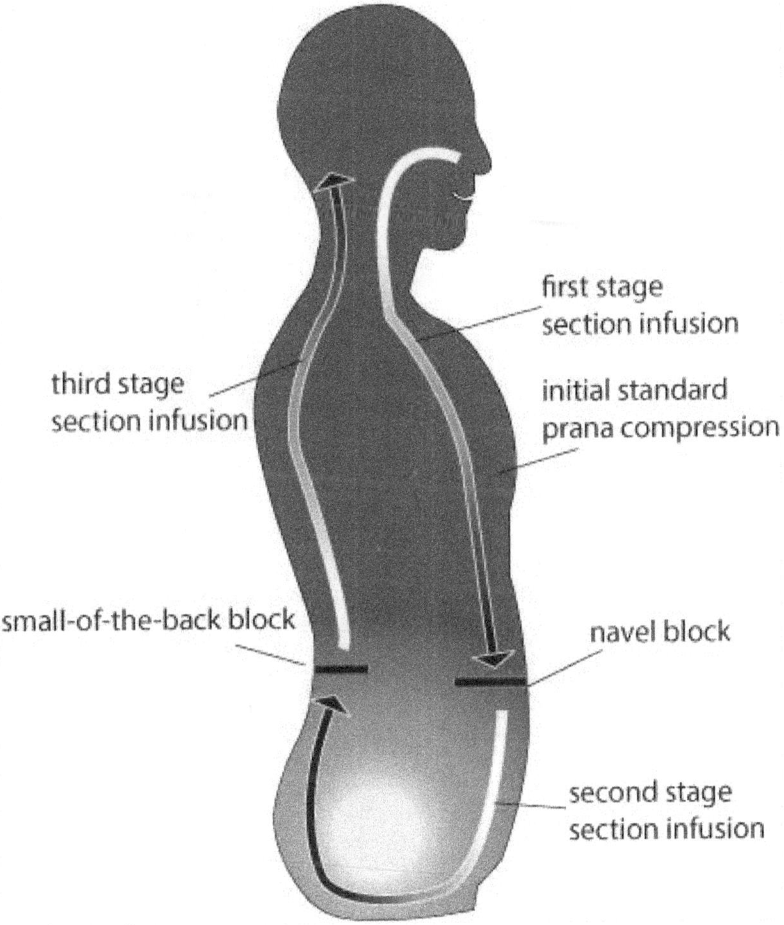

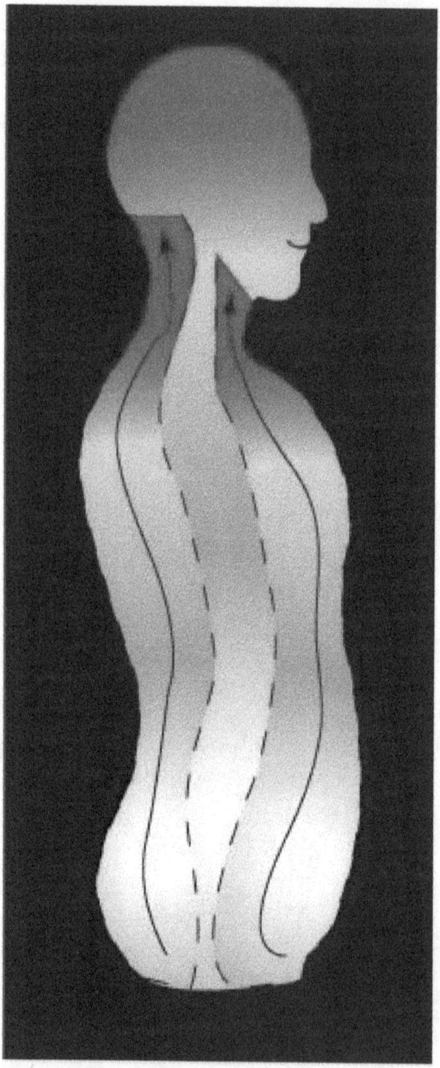

Root Lock

Initially it is difficult to isolate the base locks but if one continues doing it, the time will come when one can do each separately or conjointly as desired.

The application of the locks has different efficiencies according to how it is done by different yogis. The more one does it, the more one should increase its efficiency. Check for the effect in the subtle body, as to whether energy escapes from either of the areas involved.

If one feels that energy escapes from the base chakra, when one applies the anus lock, one should check to see if the escaping energy ceased. If it did not or if it did partially, that means that there is partial efficiency.

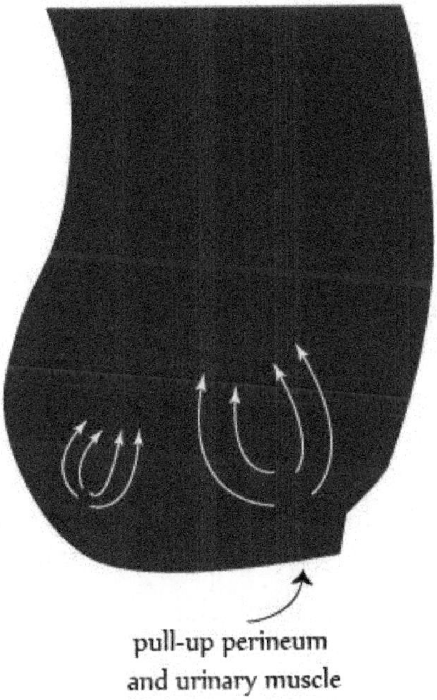

Testing the Effects of Breath Infusion

Sometimes there is the question as to if breath infusion does anything. The breath infusion process I teach using *kapalabhati* or *bhastrika*, involves the use of the *asana* postures in combination with rapid breathing, compression of breath energy and inner focus to track the movements of the infused subtle force.

However, having confidence only in breath infusion is a different matter. In science to understand one factor, they isolate it. They check to see what it does all by itself. This allows researchers to know exactly what that element affects.

There is a way to test breath infusion without multiple postures. To do this one should assume one, two, three or four postures during a session and work steadily to infuse air into the system with those selected postures.

One should check to see the effects. The value of this is that the student can develop confidence about the practice. Students inquire of the benefits of practice. They want me to levy a value for particular actions. One guy whom I showed a series of exercises challenged me. He said:

What is the benefit of that posture?

For breath infusion there are two definite results to observe or anticipate. First, do the infusion for a time in one or two postures. Get the polluted air extracted from the system. If you do rapid breathing that would take at least twenty minutes if not more. For me it takes usually about forty minutes. However even if it is done for only twenty minutes the yogi should experience results.

Physical result:

Prompter evacuation with a surge push when the waste is evacuated. It may be at least 20 minutes or earlier than it was previously and will evacuate much easier, noticeably.

Psychic result:

The meditation which follows immediately after the infusion, will have little or no mental thinking and imaging. The mind is cleared of thoughts and images or some ideas come slow with the ability to terminate them.

Rate of Absorption during Breath Infusion

The absorption rate of fresh air varies from person to person. It depends on the health of the lungs and their genetic attitude which is usually derived from the family in which one acquired the body.

Some family lines have a more efficient absorption as compared to others. There is the individual health of the body, like if for instance, someone had asthma as an infant. Then for the whole life of the body, he may have breath inefficiency and have to live with that limitation.

In either case of high or low efficiency the breath infusion would cause more oxygen to be absorbed and more carbon dioxide to be expelled from the system. The increase of fresh air carries with it one serious problem which is an increase in influenza viruses which are in the air.

All students should know, and teachers should admit it outright, that if there are cold virus in the air anyone doing breath infusion will have more of those organisms ingested through the lungs than anyone else who does not do the infusion. That is the negative aspect of this. But one may use sour fruits, herbs, syrups or pharmaceutical products to counteract such bacteria.

I have colds frequently. Some persons bawl about it and harbor doubts. Some of this is because of the high absorption rate of my body and the vast amounts of bacteria which enter into it because of that. It is a risk I am willing to take. In the physical world everything has advantages and disadvantages.

If there is a large quantity of carbon dioxide in the lower trunk, that will form a resistance. The student will have to endeavor aggressively with the breath infusion to flush that. It is removed over time of practice by pushing down again and again day after day, twice per day for weeks or years or even for lifetimes of practice.

Carbon dioxide resists removal and does not yield easily. Some cells of the body like it. These exert a resistance to its removal.

A student should study the attitude at the cellular level to get some understanding about the resistance in the system to the intake of fresh air. I may do breath infusion day and night but if my lungs and blood cells do not like fresh air, if they prefer pollutants, they will refuse to ingest the fresh air. They will hoard the pollutants.

It is a question of changing their preference.

Pranayama and *Asanas* Combined

In 1970, I began studying yoga under a martial arts master, Arthur Beverford. He was trained by Rishi Singh Gherwal who explained to him that each of the stages of yoga beginning with the *asana* takes twelve years to master. That is if the student's lifestyle is managed by the teacher.

It was the system at the strict ashrams that one served a guru while learning. After about twelve years, one was released to study a higher stage. For that matter the term *Upanishad* suggests serving a guru while learning yoga, philosophy and Vedic rituals. That was the system.

The other thing that we need to know is that women for the most part were not part of the yoga practice. Yes, in the *Hatha Yoga Pradipika* which is the manual for kundalini yoga, it begins with Shiva as *Adinatha* and the first disciple there is *Matsyendranath*. But the legend has it that the instructions which *Matsyendranath* overheard was given to Goddess Durga, a woman. This means that the first student of classic yoga was female. But that is where it ends more or less, because the other names listed in the lineage are males for the most part.

Women yoginis are sprinkled here and there in the *Ramayana, Upanishads, Puranas* and *Mahabharata*. But now in the West yoga classes are female predominant.

Pranayama as far I reviewed it in the current life, cannot be understood or made into an effective practice, if the student has not mastered the postures. I feel that you can do *pranayama* at any stage but I feel that you will not understand its usefulness until you master the postures and extract from them their psychological benefit. Stated plainly if the postures do not bring you to realize your subtle body, or yourself as just psychological energy, then even if you do the *pranayama,* you will not capitalize on it fully.

The *pranayama* which I do is *kapalabhati* and *bhastrika* breath infusion. I follow the method given by Yogi Bhajan initially around 1972. That is a combination of *asana* postures and *pranayama* combined. I find that some *asanas* cannot be exploited fully unless *pranayama* is combined into them and visa versa where the *pranayama* cannot work fully unless *asana*s are combined with it.

In my experience none of the steps of yoga are mastered completely before one advances into its higher stages. One finds that sometimes one has to return and re-practice a lower stage so as to better integrate a higher one.

Meditation: Absence of interest and Thought-Images

As one meditates and keenly observes what happens in the subtle environment, one notices strange things which are rarely described in yoga books and which are unknown to the thousands of people who meditate.

Have you ever heard that meditation is all about a void of mind or a unity with everything, a removal of personality, of individuality?

That may be one kind of meditation but it is not the whole scope. There are other possibilities.

Pranayama practice gives the meditator a huge advantage. It is the jump start on the *pratyahar* sensual energy withdrawal, fifth stage of yoga. When sitting to meditate if you do an effective *pranayama* practice first, for at least say about twenty minutes or more, the meditation will begin at the sixth stage which is *dharana* linkage to higher realities.

What are these realities?

That depends on your level of meditation and on your developed supernatural perception. If you have no supernatural senses, your mind will be blank or void if you complete the sensual withdrawal stage. What is there to see if you have no super-vision.

It was years now since I began practicing the *bhastrika pranayama* breath infusion. After becoming somewhat proficient, I can emphatically say that it causes the automatic completion of the *pratyahar* sensual energy withdrawal fifth stage of yoga, so that if I sit to meditate immediately after doing the breath infusion, the sensual energy has no external interest. No effort is required to pull it into the psyche or to stop it from indulging thoughts and images. There is no display. The frontal part of the subtle head is silent like when a storm ceases and one can hear even a pin drop.

Because of years of meditation, I became increasingly sensitive and what was nothing or what was void or what was merged, is now perceived as a composite with distinct parts or sections.

If you look on a clean glass surface, obviously there will be nothing but that is because the eyes are not capable of discerning what is microscopic. As soon as one puts that surface under a instrument, one may see thousands of micro-lifeforms on the surface.

Void?

What does that mean?

Is that another way of saying that one does not have the required sense perception?

I was once of the opinion that *pratyahar* sensual energy withdrawal was all about withdrawing the sensual energies from their objects but there is much more to it than that. Usually in yoga one begins with a simplistic, naive view of the process. One underestimates the task and feels that it is easy or that an initial accomplishment is the grand finale.

Pratyahar has many parts.

- withdrawal of the senses from the external objects
- withdrawal of the senses from the memory of the external objects
- withdrawal of the senses from internal objects within the psyche
- withdrawal of the senses so that they fold into themselves and become inactive
- withdrawal of the interest of the coreSelf in the senses and their external objects
- withdrawal of the interest of the coreSelf in the senses and the memories which the senses pursue
- withdrawal of the interest of the coreSelf in the senses and the internal objects which the sense pursues

Once these features are attained another development occurs where there is a complete absence of the interest of the coreSelf or where the core suddenly finds itself with a new power, which is that it can close its interest in the frontal part of the subtle head. This is not a mental or conceptual achievement. This is actually a psychic action where a dark psychic lid is pulled like a curtain dropping to stop perception.

This causes the realization that apart from the thoughts and images in the frontal part of the head, there is definitely an interest which comes out of the core but which can be suspended completely and then reactivated as desired.

Elevation of Females

Yogeshwarananda discussed the difficulty he has in elevating women disciples. Apparently, some females, whom he assisted when he used his last physical body, could not sustain the assistance. They abandoned the practice. After he reviewed their condition from the astral world, he determined that much of his assistance was not upheld due to one reason or the other.

However, it is a fact that traditionally yoga as it was practiced in ancient times was a discipline more suited to the hardy bodies of males. Yogesh ran away from home at a juvenile age. He did gruesome austerities which a female would not be likely to perform.

Later when he was recognized for his accomplishments in yoga, people came for instruction. Among these were females. He used what is called power infusement or *shaktipat* to give students a boost but after his demise, when he checked he found that many females whom he assisted were unable to sustain the mystic lift.

What is the reason?

He did not explain. He remarked that to his view it is rather difficult to uplift females in a sustained way.

Recently in a conversation with Gautam Buddha, the subject of women doing the austerities was mentioned. In this case it was the mental and psychological disciplines which Buddha pioneered and shared with his disciples when he used the last physical body.

This buddha person was in a high astral region called the *Tushita* heavens. Roughly that is the equivalent of the *Satyaloka* paradise world in the *Puranas*. He said that so long as a female whom is related to him remains in the *Tushita* heavens, there is no danger for that female to go to a lower plane.

However, we must understand that the body assumed in that place is not a human type. It is not an astral copy or parallel of a human body as we know it. It is an entirely different form which does not have many of the lowering tendencies which are in a human form.

A question arises as to how a female can get that body. The answer is that it is possible by the grace of Buddha or by the grace of one of the buddhas. However, how these buddhas make such selections is unknown.

A female could carefully study the Buddhist texts, the original from the Pali cannon. From that one would get an idea of what one can do to get Buddha's approval. Then one may attract his attention and may qualify for migration to the *Tushita* place.

One cannot instruct a person like Buddha nor influence him. Therefore, it is totally in his hands if he would select one for association. Besides, the Tushita heaven does not lack anything whereby the Buddhas feel that they need something or someone from a lower domain.

Nutrition System Pull-Up

For the past six months I intensely practiced some procedures which are to be tested before I share them with students. I did this work before some years back. In my notes, there are notations, but within the past six months at every opportunity, I worked on the nutrition system.

Lahiri has this idea that if the system was lifted the problem about hormonal influence would be eliminated. The yogi would get a clear pass to a higher dimension either *Siddhaloka* or places beyond that.

The hormonal influence is a drag on the system and keeps a yogi in the physical world involved in one situation or the other, mostly having to do with sexual alliances with members of the opposite sex as enforced by nature in its perpetual survival pursuit.

It was necessary to work with the hormone system but Lahiri thinks that this can be bypassed if one could lift the nutrition energy and thus prevent it from being charged by the hormone glands in a body.

This is grand idea but is it practical?

I tested the process. It seems practical. I can see that the energy of nutrition can be lifted before it is sexually charged. I do not know as yet if others can do this because it requires a tremendous amount of mystic perception and confidence which most students do not have. I will minutely observe this before divulging it to others.

When it is pulled up it appears to the mystic vision to be a type of jell. Sometimes it appears to be a syrup. At other times it appears to be a thick goop which flows upwards as it is pulled by breath infusion in conjunction with the attention energy pull of the yogi. It seems that it pulls up most in the front of the trunk of the body as compared to the kundalini which is a back-centered system mostly and the sexual hormone system which is in the center of the subtle body.

Association Affects Yoga Practice

Despite all the hype about what we can do, and what we are free to do, there are definite effects which deter yoga practice and cause a student to procrastinate. Our expansive self-esteem is no match for negative association which could come even from fellow seekers.

When was the last time you found that you could not rise early for practice?

When was the last time you overslept?

When was the last time you broke the commitment to practice for a set period each day?

Is your positive thinking not working?

Is your oneness, peace and love not enough to spur you?

How about tracing the negative influences which are a drag on practice?

Have you moved recently and found that as soon as you got to that other place, you could not practice?

What makes you think that with millions of human beings sleeping at four in the morning, you will have the strength to awaken?

Do you feel that you are immune to the collective stupor?

Misty Memories

Recently as I practice to lift the nutritional energy, to stop it from going down into the reproduction hormone center. The breath infusion worked to reverse the flow of that energy, so that instead of going down the energy comes up against the pull of gravity. This happens because of the breath infusion lift circulation.

I declare that visualization and willpower, on their own, are useless. When breath infusion is used, willpower gets a grip on the situation and can do something effective. Visualization is for fake yogis. That is my view.

The nutritional energy lift is a process given by Lahiri in the astral world. He explained it for experimental purposes to see if it would help students to reach the *chit akash* within the shortest period of time.

I want to state that in doing this, during the breath infusion session as well as during the meditation which follows, the student should use a blindfold. There is no use telling yourself that you do not need a blindfold because here we do not address you, nor your pride, nor confidence. We do not challenge your ability to remain introverted during practice.

We face the fact that the senses are extrovert by nature. When they are restrained from that they may cease pursuits or become introvert but even then, their disposition remains in the background brooding, so that if you do the practice without a blindfold, you will find that once in a while or frequently, the senses escape from the restraint and charge out of the concentration to do things which are counterproductive.

However, the main reason for using the blindfold is to train the self to remain introverted and to be satisfied with this. That satisfaction is important. In the long run, a student should develop this satisfaction to such an extent that the senses which are usually only satisfied when pursuing their objects, remains satisfied in a disabled condition. Of course, this takes weeks, months, years or even lifetimes to achieve.

During meditation this morning, I experienced a new phase of this practice, something that within the memory of my experiences in this life, I do not recall this experience. In the chest area under the shoulders, I found that there were thoughts and images. These were very scanty, very far and in-between. These did not have the compelling power of the thoughts and images which appear in the frontal part of the head.

These were in a misty psychic environment, a foggy place and were weak in their attractive power when compared to images occurring in the head.

These were from the subconscious stockpile of memories. These scanty thoughts which had little attractive power, went on for about seven minutes. Then as if someone turned it on, I heard naad. Then the images in the chest under the shoulders ceased.

I was relocated into the head of the subtle body, above the neck. There I heard naad and then up front I saw a glow of light.

During the breath infusion session before the meditation, I had several spreads of cell kundalini where there would be a clump of this breath infusion energy which was compressed. Then it would burst like fireworks in the psyche, then I would do more breath infusion and compress that inwards. Then there was a big burst upwards under the shoulders in the chest. That felt like twinkles firing in rapid succession with a bliss aspect to it and lights sparkling like swiftly moving silverfish glowing radioactively on a dark moon night.

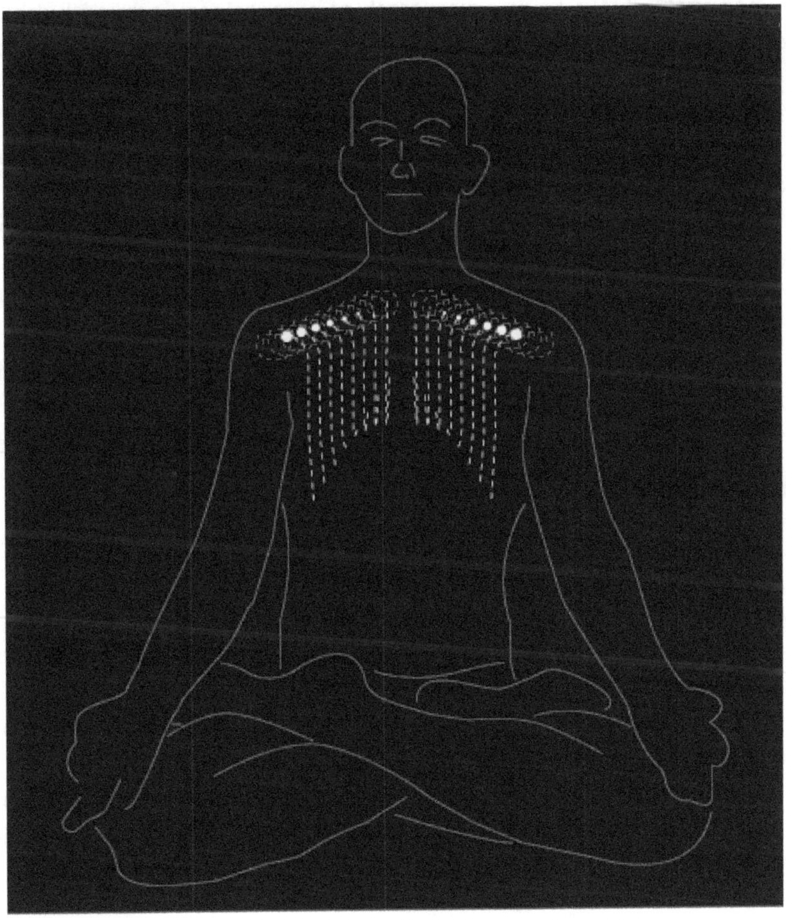

Cell kundalini is different to spinal *sushumna-nadi* kundalini, in that each cell in a particular part of the body, issues a tiny bit of bliss energy which converge with that from nearby cells and form a clump of kundalini. A similar feeling is had in various parts of the body during sex pleasure experience.

Compress or Squeeze Infused Energy

This morning I observed a compression which was a squeeze. This is similar to when cheese is made. Curd is put into a bag which is put into a press which applies pressure. All liquid is pressed through the fabric or gauze. The remaining solid mass forms cheese.

In this practice there is no gauze membrane, there is a muscular and psychic pressure applied from every direction to compress the mass of infused breath energy inwards upon itself. In this experience the location of the mass is in the lower central torso.

At one point in the compression, trickles of energy leaked. These were like when water leaks from a tiny crack of a container, forming bubbles of water which squirt outwards, having a transparent but silvery color. These had sparkling bobs and were a bliss energy. These squirted upward under the collar bones.

Instead of spinal kundalini, this energy emanated from cells which released their kundalini bliss charges which bundled together.

During sexual experience a similar experience is garnished where the cells from various parts of the body yield bliss charges which run rapidly to the sex organ chakras, like messengers who must deliver a message by express routing.

Here, instead of giving their bliss charge to the sex organ chakra, these cells yielded energy to the infused breath compact which was mixed with hormone energy and which upgrades the subtle body as a *yogaSiddha* form.

Celibacy Conservation

Celibacy, in terms of conservation of sexual energy, works if one has a yogic process to distribute the conserved energy so that it does not accumulate and cause masturbation or copulation.

When celibacy means conservation of energy without a method for distributing the conserved energy, it is celibacy with a privacy failure, where the individual either self-stimulates or gets involved in sexual intercourse either on the physical level, the subtle level (dreams) or both.

Without yogic methods which effectively distributes the sexual energy throughout the psyche, celibacy is a farce because the accumulated energy will overpower the person, forcing a masturbation or partner involvement.

This may be seen objectively in the menstrual cycle of human females, where the energy is accumulated. Then it is discharged from the body, then it is accumulated, and then discharged repeatedly. In animals, like a cow for instance this discharge does not take place, except in the urine to some extent. In the body of the animal, the energy is distributed and used. The animal does not have to self-stimulate.

However, we see that bulls are forced to discharge the fluids on fence posts or elsewhere if they do not have ovulating cows available when the fluids accumulate to an intolerable quantity.

This also applies to the subtle body, because the sexually related energies run parallel in the subtle form. This is why we have erotic dreams.

The system I teach is the *bhastrika/kapalabhati pranayama* but in combination with various *asana* postures. One part of it is to train the subtle body to distribute the sexual energy so that it does not accumulate and force the system to self-stimulate or to partner, just for release.

Breath infusion can, if it is done correctly, mop and then mist the sexual energies so that it does not build a strong overpowering charge. The sexual energy can be trained to link to the *muladhara* base chakra where it may strike kundalini, arouse kundalini and with the proper locks *(bandhas)* cause kundalini to remain in *sushumna nadi* and to go into the brain for shifting the coreSelf to insight consciousness.

In sex experience, the reverse occurs where the kundalini jumps across from *muladhara* chakra to the sex organ chakra. That causes the compelling experience of sexual climax pleasure. In kundalini yoga, the direction is reversed where the sex energy jumps to the *muladhara* and goes up through the spine with the kundalini lifeForce energy.

Samyama

This is what Patanjali wrote about *samyama*:
Yoga Sutras chapter 3 verses 1-4:

देशबन्धश्चित्तस्य धारणा॥१॥

deśa bandhaḥ cittasya dhāraṇā

deśa – location; bandhaḥ – confinement, restriction; cittasya – of the mento-emotional energy; dhāraṇā – linking of the attention to a concentration force or person.

Linking of the attention to a concentration force or person, involves a restricted location in the mento-emotional energy. (Yoga Sutras 3.1)

तत्र प्रत्ययैकतानता ध्यानम्॥२॥

tatra pratyayaḥ ekatānatā dhyānam

tatra – there, in that location; pratyayaḥ – conviction or belief as mental content, instinctive interest; ekatānatā – one continuous threadlike flow of attention = eka – one + tānatā – thread of fiber; dhyānam – effortless linking of the attention to a higher concentration force or person.

When in that location, there is one continuous threadlike flow of one's instinctive interest, that is the effortless linking of the attention to a higher concentration force or person. (Yoga Sutras 3.2)

तदेवार्थमात्रनिर्भासं स्वरूपशून्यमिव समाधिः॥३॥

tadeva arthamātranirbhāsaṁ
svarūpaśūnyam iva samādhiḥ

tadeva = tat – that + eva – only, alone; artha – purpose objective; mātra – only, merely; nirbhāsaṁ – illuminating; svarūpa – own form; śūnyam – empty, void, lacking; iva – as if; samādhiḥ – continuous effortless linking of the attention to a higher concentration force or person.

That same effortless linkage of the attention when experienced as illumination of the higher concentration force or person, while the yogi feels as if devoid of himself, is samādhi or continuous effortless linkage of his attention to the special person, object, or force. (Yoga Sutras 3.3)

त्रयमेकत्र संयमः॥४॥

trayam ekatra saṁyamaḥ

trayam – three; ekatra – in one place, all taken together as one practice; saṁyamah – complete restraint.

The three as one practice are the complete restraint. (Yoga Sutras 3.4)

This is the equation:
dharana + dhyana + samadhi = samyama

In practice, however, when one does *dharana*, it may progress into *dhyana* and develop into *samadhi.* There could be a regression, where when one is in a *samadhi*, it digresses into *dhyana* and then into *dharana*.

Samyama is the sequential development of the three higher stages of yoga.

Yogi and Pretty Women

A few days ago, I had the occasion to be at a restaurant in a mall. We sat outside and could see people walking along the pavements. As fate would have it, it was a time when many women were with their teenaged daughters. I took the opportunity to observe them. Some say that I look at pretty women only but most of these females were either ordinary in looks or unattractive. Their bodies varied from not-so-attractive to attractive.

Why would a yogi take the opportunity to look at such bodies? The reason is that whenever possible as decreed by fate, a yogi should learn about this creation, especially about transmigration in and through various species.

While people feel that a yogi looks for this or that reason and they take satisfaction in rash conclusions, the truth is that due to superior insight a yogi, does not perceive in the ordinary way.

There were three special features which I observed:

- body type with deterioration quotient
- body type in terms of which species those human forms evolved from
- body type in terms of attraction potentials based on the environments in which those bodies first appeared

Could you guess that a yogi would be interested in such things?

Does a yogi really see such features or does a yogi see only sex potential but pretends to see those aspects?

The **body type with deterioration quotient** is revealed by nature when it shows what a certain body type is in the height of youth in comparison to what it would be when the elderly years set in. To see this, nature presents opportunities to a yogi to see a young body of a particular type with an elderly body of the same type. The yogi references one to the other to see the deterioration quotient of that particular body. The yogi considers that if someone has a youth's body, it would deteriorate to be like its father, irrespective of his personality.

A yogi checks the minds of others to see if they were affected by the age status of the body. For instance:

Is the personSelf in an older body embarrassed because that body deteriorated?

Is the personSelf in the younger body proud because that body is its youth?

Is the personSelf in the younger body aware that its deterioration potential is the same as that of the elderly relative of that same body type?

Does that personSelf know that it will have to transmigrate from that body to take an infant form, which in turn will reach the height of youth and then deteriorate just the same?

The **body type in terms of which species those human forms evolved from** is an important consideration for a yogi in understanding why certain human beings have propensities which are dissimilar to others. Say, for instance, a human body came up through the line of the big cats, what tendencies of the animals would transfer into the human forms which evolved from those feline bodies millions of years ago? How much adjustment can be made by a personSelf using such a body to change those traits?

Can the personSelf in a body know which traits in that body came from certain lower species?

If the self can identify that, can it alter those behaviors?

How much influence can a personSelf have on the genetic dispositions of a body?

A yogi may regard this and check his body to determine what instinct was from an animal profile and what is due to divine influence.

The **body type, in terms of attraction potentials based on the environments in which those bodies first appeared** competes with the divine influences which saturate human existence. Humanity is between animal and divine, with both influences pressing mankind at every moment. Some aspects of the evolutionary drive are desirable. For instance, was a sleek Egyptian female body adopted initially from a cheetah body or from a divine person?

Was the full breast of a woman derived from a big-breasted species of cow or from a buxom goddess in a higher dimension?

Wonderful indeed are these considerations for a yogi. The next time one sees a yogi looking at a beautiful woman, give these considerations a space in your mind!

Yoga Sutras

In Chapter two of the *Yoga Sutras*, there is this verse:

तपःस्वाध्यायेश्वरप्रणिधानानि क्रियायोगः ॥१॥

tapas svādhyāya Īśvarapraṇidhānāni kriyāyogaḥ

Austerity, study of the psyche and profound religious meditation on the Supreme Lord is the dynamic kriyā yoga practice. (Yoga Sutras 2.1)

Austerity *(tapas)* is restriction of sensual fulfillments.

Svadhyaya (svaad-hee-yaa-ya) is study of the psyche.

Īśvarapraṇidhānāni is profound religious meditation on the Supreme Lord.

This means that meditation on God is part of the process not all of it. There must also be austerity to restrict sense pursuits which otherwise would attract the attention of the ascetic. The yogi must focus on his/her psyche to study how to adjust it.

In India some people who worship Krishna criticized that Patanjali did not stress the profound religious meditation on the Supreme Lord. They are mistaken because Patanjali set out to show the syllabus of yoga. Krishna explained yoga without pushing himself into the picture as being everything about yoga. Look at this verse from Bhagavad Gita:

तत्रैकाग्रं मनः कृत्वा
यतचित्तेन्द्रियक्रियः ।
उपविश्यासने युञ्ज्याद्
योगमात्मविशुद्धये ॥६.१२॥

tatraikāgraṁ manaḥ kṛtvā
yatacittendriyakriyaḥ
upaviśyāsane yuñjyād
yogamātmaviśuddhaye (6.12)

tatraikāgraṁ = tatra — there + ekāgram — single-focused; manaḥ — mind; kṛtvā — having made; yatacittendriyakriyaḥ = yata - controlled + citta — thought + indriyakriyaḥ — sense energy; upaviśyāsane = upaviśya — seating himself + āsane — in a posture; yuñjād = yuñjāt — should practice; yogamātmaviśuddhaye = yogam — to yoga discipline + ātma — self + viśuddhaye — to purification

...being there, seated in a posture, having the mind focused, the person who controls his thinking and sensual energy, should practise the yoga discipline for self-purification. (Bhagavad Gita 6.12)

Krishna explained that the purpose of yoga is *atma vishuddha* which is complete purification *(vishuddha)* of the *atma* (coreSelf). He does not say that he is the purpose of yoga. The involvement with him for yoga has to do with the fact that the yogi must be assisted by Krishna, Shiva or someone who is empowered to aid in the purifications.

The horse cannot remove the bit from its mouth, and without doing so chewing grass is a problem. Thus, the horse gets help from the farmer.

Without assistance, we are not equipped to remove ourselves from this mundane energy. We must take help from higher beings.

To understand the purpose of the *Yoga Sutras* one must understand these Sanskrit terms

- *kevala*
- *samyogah*
- *avidya*
- *kaivalyam*
- *dṛśeḥ*
- *vivekakhyātiḥ*
- *sattva*
- *puruṣayoḥ*
- *śuddhi*
- *svarūpa*

The verses below require serious study with an open mind and without wanting to make Patanjali endorse our preferred methods for enlightenment.

स्वस्वामिशक्त्योः स्वरूपोपलब्धिहेतुः संयोगः ॥२३॥

sva svāmiśaktyoḥ svarūpa upalabdhi hetuḥ saṁyogaḥ

sva – own nature, own psyche; svāmi – the master, the individual self; saktyoḥ – of the potency of the two; svarūpa – essential form; upalabdhi – obtaining experience; hetuḥ – cause, reason; saṁyogaḥ – conjunction.

There is a reason for the conjunction of the individual self and its psychological energies. It is for obtaining the experience of its essential form. (Yoga Sutras 2.23)

तस्य हेतुरविद्या ॥२४॥

tasya hetuḥ avidyā

tasya – of it; hetuḥ – cause; avidyā – spiritual ignorance.

The cause of the conjunction is spiritual ignorance. (Yoga Sutras 2.24)

तदभावात्संयोगाभावो हानं तद्दृशेः कैवल्यम् ॥२५॥

tad abhāvāt saṁyogā abhāvaḥ

hānaṁ taddṛśeḥ kaivalyam

tad = tat – that spiritual ignorance; abhāvāt – resulting from the elimination; saṁyogā – conjunction; abhāvaḥ – disappearance, elimination; hānaṁ – withdrawal, escape; tad = tat – that; dṛśeḥ – of the perceiver; kaivalyam – total separation from the mundane psychology.

The elimination of the conjunction which results from the elimination of that spiritual ignorance is the withdrawal that is the total separation of the perceiver from the mundane psychology. (Yoga Sutras 2.25)

विवेकख्यातिरविप्लवा हानोपायः ॥२६॥

vivekakhyātiḥ aviplavā hānopāyaḥ

viveka – discrimination; khyātiḥ – insight; aviplavā – unbroken, continuous; hānopāyaḥ = hana – avoidance + upāyaḥ – means, method.

The method for avoiding that spiritual ignorance is the establishment of continuous discriminative insight. (Yoga Sutras 2.26)

तद्वैराग्यादपि दोषबीजक्षये कैवल्यम्॥५१॥

tadvairāgyāt api doṣabījakṣaye kaivalyam

tadvairāgyāt = tad (tat) – that + vairāgyāt – from a lack of interest; api – also, even; doṣabījakṣaye = doṣa – fault, defect + bīja – seed, origin, source + kṣaye – on elimination; kaivalyam – the absolute isolation of the self from what is lower than itself, isolation of the self from the lower psyche of itself.

By a lack of interest, even to that (discrimination between the clarifying mundane energy and the self) when the cause of that defect is eliminated, the absolute isolation of the self from its lower psyche, is achieved. (Yoga Sutras 3.51)

सत्त्वपुरुषयोः शुद्धिसाम्ये कैवल्यमिति॥५६॥

sattva puruṣayoḥ śuddhi sāmye kaivalyam iti

sattva – intelligence energy of material nature; puruṣayoḥ – of the spirit; śuddhi – purity; sāmye – on being equal; kaivalyam – total separation from the mundane psychology; iti – thus.

When there is equal purity between the intelligence energy of material nature and the spirit, then there is total separation from the mundane psychology. (Yoga Sutras 3.56)

तदा हि विवेकनिम्नङ्कैवल्यप्राग्भारञ्चित्तम्॥२६॥

tadā hi vivekanimnaṁ kaivalya prāgbhāraṁ cittam

tadā – then; hi – indeed; viveka – discrimination; nimnaṁ – leaning towards, inclined to; kaivalya – total separation from the mundane psychology; prāg – towards; bhāraṁ – gravitating; cittam – mento-emotional force.

Then, indeed, the mento-emotional force is inclined towards discrimination and gravitates towards the total separation from the mundane psychology. (Yoga Sutras 4.26)

पुरुषार्थशून्यानां गुणानां प्रतिप्रसवः कैवल्यं स्वरूपप्रतिष्ठा वा चितिशक्तिरिति॥३४॥

puruṣārtha śūnyānāṁ guṇānāṁ
pratiprasavaḥ kaivalyaṁ
svarūpapratiṣṭhā vā citiśaktiḥ iti

puruṣārtha – the aims of a human being; śūnyānāṁ – devoid of; guṇānāṁ – of the influences of material nature; pratiprasavaḥ – reabsorption, retrogression, neutralization; kaivalyam – separation of the spirit from psychology; svarūpa – own form; pratiṣṭhā – established; vā – thus, at last; citiśaktiḥ – the power of pure consciousness; iti – that is all.

Separation of the spirit from the mento-emotional energy *(kaivalyam)* occurs when there is neutrality in respect to the influence of material nature, when the yogi's psyche becomes devoid of the general aims of a human being. Thus at last, the spirit is established in its own form as the force empowering the mento-emotional energy. (Yoga Sutras 4.34)

The object of Patanjali is not the Supreme Lord. The object is the person-self, the *atma* or *jivatma* as termed in Sanskrit. This self is also termed as a *purusha*. Patanjali uses special terms for this self.

- *swa*
- *swami*
- *draṣṭā*
- *dṛśeḥ*
- *ātmā*

See these verses:

द्रष्टा दृशिमात्रः शुद्धोऽपि प्रत्ययानुपश्यः ॥२०॥

draṣṭā dṛśimātraḥ śuddhaḥ api pratyayānupaśyaḥ

draṣṭā – the perceiver; dṛśi – perception, consciousness; mātraḥ – measure or extent; śuddhaḥ – purity; api – but; pratyayaḥ – conviction or belief as mental content; anu – following along, patterning after; paśyaḥ – what is perceived.

The perceiver is the pure extent of its consciousness but its conviction is patterned by what it perceives. (Yoga Sutras 2.20)

तदर्थ एव दृश्यस्यात्मा ॥२१॥

tadarthaḥ eva dṛśyasya ātmā

tad = tat – that; arthaḥ – purpose; eva – only; dṛśyasya – of what is seen; ātmā – individual spirit.

The individual spirit, who is involved in what is seen, exists here for that purpose only. (Yoga Sutras 2.21)

स्वस्वामिशक्त्योः स्वरूपोपलब्धिहेतुः संयोगः ॥२३॥

sva svāmiśaktyoḥ svarūpa upalabdhi hetuḥ saṁyogaḥ

sva – own nature, own psyche; svāmi – the master, the individual self; saktyoḥ – of the potency of the two; svarūpa – essential form; upalabdhi – obtaining experience; hetuḥ – cause, reason; saṁyogaḥ – conjunction.

There is a reason for the conjunction of the individual self and its psychological energies. It is for obtaining the experience of its essential form. (Yoga Sutras 2.23)

तस्य हेतुरविद्या ॥२४॥

tasya hetuḥ avidyā

tasya – of it; hetuḥ – cause; avidyā – spiritual ignorance.

The cause of the conjunction is spiritual ignorance. (Yoga Sutras 2.24)

तदभावात्संयोगाभावो हानं तद्दृशेः कैवल्यम् ॥२५॥

tad abhāvāt saṁyogā abhāvaḥ

hānaṁ taddṛśeḥ kaivalyam

tad = tat – that spiritual ignorance; abhāvāt – resulting from the elimination; saṁyogā – conjunction; abhāvaḥ – disappearance, elimination; hānaṁ – withdrawal, escape; tad = tat – that; dṛśeḥ – of the perceiver; kaivalyam – total separation from the mundane psychology.

The elimination of the conjunction which results from the elimination of that spiritual ignorance is the withdrawal that is the total separation of the perceiver from the mundane psychology. (Yoga Sutras 2.24)

सत्त्वशुद्धिसौमनस्यैकाग्र्येन्द्रियजयात्मदर्शनयोग्यत्वानि च ॥४१॥

sattvaśuddhi saumanasya ekāgra indriyajaya
ātmadarśana yogyatvāni ca

sattva – being, nature, psyche; śuddhi – purification; saumanasya – concerning benevolence; ekāgra – ability to link the attention to one concentration force or person; indriya – sensual energy; jaya – conquest; ātma – spirit; darśana – sight, vision; yogyatvāni – being fit for yoga or abstract meditation; ca – and.

Purification of the psyche results in benevolence, the ability to link the attention to one concentration force or person, conquest of the sensual energy, vision of the spirit and fitness for abstract meditation. (Yoga Sutras 2.41)

Patanjali speaks of breaking off the unity (*samyogah*) or complete (sam) fusion (yogah) between this personSelf (*puruṣayoḥ*) and its affiliate psychic nature (*sattva*). Then he mentions the reunification of these when both achieved purity.

The value in this of the Supreme Lord, the God, is that he instructs for this. Without his direction we cannot implement this. By ourselves, we lack the means of doing so.

Here is the related verse:

स पूर्वेषामपि गुरुः कालेनानवच्छेदात् ॥२६॥

sa eṣaḥ pūrveṣām api guruḥ kālena anavacchedāt

sa = sah – He; eṣaḥ – this particular person; pūrveṣām – of those before, previous authorities, the ancient teachers; api – even; guruḥ – the spiritual teacher; kālena – by time; anavacchedāt – unconditioned.

He, this particular person being unconditioned by time, is the guru even of the ancient teachers, the previous authorities. (Yoga Sutras 1.26)

The primary object of meditation focus is the personSelf as a contaminated spiritual entity, a specific person who has liberation potential, and who is required to segregate itself from its psychic equipment which came from the subtle physical nature *(sattva)*. Once it achieves this split, it can work for its purification and the purification of the subtle physical nature. When this is achieved it can become reunified with that nature and function as a liberated self.

Because God is perpetually in the liberated state and is not afflicted by the *kleshas* or traumas which the contaminated spiritual entity must deal with, God is not the object. The contaminated entity will not become God and cannot assume the nature of God in full either. It can assume some of God's aloof and antiseptic status if it follows and completes the instructions in the sutras.

From a contaminated state, one cannot focus on God in real terms. God is not within range of the contaminated vision. First the perception must be elevated. Then there could be focus on God. Once the contact with God is made, the instruction of what one should do to clean the individual psyche, is given.

Rebirth Potential Energy

I lapsed on posting reports over the last three weeks. This is due to time constraints. Meditation progress is made step by step on a daily basis despite the ups and downs which are due to non-yogic association. Somehow or the other, a yogi must keep pushing and keeping tallying the spiritual progress, even when there seems to be none and when he is overwhelmed by non-yogic associations.

One day last week I had an astral visit from Yogeshwarananda but in the distance behind him was *Atmananda*, one of his gurus. When the senior teacher was forty feet near me, he hit a wave energy which he was scared of. He retreated and disappeared. I knew what it was. I regretted that it was there but at the time I could do nothing to remove it. Yogeshwarananda came through the energy and checked the condition of my subtle body.

Miraculously, there was a dimensional switch, where I was in the presence of both gurus. Atmananda said this,

"Too important to fail. Failure cannot happen in your case. Let me see. Let me see. Ah, here is the problem, a small impediment. Push on. Push on. I rely on you."

They left after this.

The wave of energy which he was scared off is the rebirth potential energy which each creature in the physical existence, carries in the subtle body. Presently my subtle body has that energy. Great yogis, who removed it from their subtle forms, avoid contacting those who still have it because that energy is like a virus which can invade subtle forms.

One must recognize this rebirth potential. Then one must learn from a great yogin how to remove it. One should remove it while using the physical body but if one fails to do so, one may remove it hereafter if one is lucky. Those who remove it when having a physical body are called *jivanmuktas* or persons who are liberated even while using a physical form.

Failed Yogi

There are many methods for reaching *chit akash* but the one which is most popular and which is well known and fabled is the one through the third eye brow chakra. This one is mentioned in many books, even in the *Bhagavad Gita*. However, there are other methods. As a yogi practices, he may discover other procedures. He should take note and inform others.

The frustration modern students will get, when trying to reach the *chit akash*, is that even if one reaches it, it will be for a moment or two and no more. This will happen infrequently.

It is not just a matter of sitting and staring at or through the third eye.

It is not just a matter of having a guru touch your head.

It is not just a matter of chanting *gayatri* mantras.

It is not just a matter of visualizing a spiritual sky.

It is not just a matter of holding the breath for long periods.

It is not just a matter of doing alternate breathing.

It is not just a matter of chanting a confidential mantra which was whispered into one's ear by a brahmin.

What is the secret?

The first part of the secret is to realize that one was conned. One got a method which does not give the intended result. One tried it day after day. One pretended that it was successful but one never got the *chit akash* experience, not even for a moment. Your friend said he got it. He described what happened but how can you tell if he did.

Once you realize that you were conned, the next step, the second part, is to admit that this is not easy. The *chit akash* for whatever it is, will not give itself without much effort with the right method. At this point one should make a decision to continue the practice or abandon it.

The third part is to pray sincerely to Shiva for help, for anything which will show the way, a book, a teacher, a voice from the sky, an inspiration, anything. Otherwise, one is lost in the jungle called Bogus Yoga, False Idea Yoga, and Ineffective Process Yoga. Any hint of where to go will do.

The fourth part is to check with authoritative books like the *Yoga Sutras* and the *Bhagavad Gita*. Map the process. Assess where you were when you realized that you made no progress.

There are eight procedures to be mastered, according to Patanjali.

Did you master yama moral restraints, niyama approved behaviors, *asana* postures, *pranayama* breath infusion, *pratyahar* sensual energy withdrawal, *dharana* deliberate focus into non-imaginative higher dimensions or deities, *dhyana* spontaneous focus into the same and *samadhi* continuous spontaneous focus?

Chit Akash Discovery

I discovered a *chit akash* light which comes from the back overhead. This happens during the listening of naad sound resonance. There is a *chit akash* light which is in the frontal part of the subtle head, which opens through the third eye area. There is another one up front which is overhead, which comes from behind a shadow area which is overhead in the frontal part of the subtle head.

The one I discovered last week comes from the back when listening to the naad sound resonance which is heard at the back top. This happened while I did a practice which Lahiri introduced. This is where just after doing breath infusion and filling up the subtle body with fresh astral energy, one sits to meditate. At first one hears naad sound in the top back of the head. Then one should enter deeply into that resonance. It may seem at the time that there is a shaft of sound which is like a narrow metal bar which is about one quarter inch wide. One should get near to this sound shaft, as near as can be. Then one should move down with it through the neck down into the trunk of the subtle body.

This is a special practice for shifting naad resonance to various parts of the subtle body, so as to energize and change the vibrational content of those areas.

After doing this for a time, suddenly there may be a dark area overhead, dark-grey. Behind that, coming forward, will be a shimmering light which has a bliss aspect and which gives one a sense of absolute security. It will illuminate a sky overhead.

This may last for a few seconds only or for longer if the yogi is lucky.

When I asked Lahiri about keeping this *chit akash* light in view, he said this:

"It cannot be kept in view by keeping it in view. It is kept in view by studying the state of consciousness the psyche is in when it is perceived, then going back into that state and keeping the self there continuous. It is not the light which the yogi must control but the state of consciousness which he experienced when he perceived it. Let him control what he can control. The light is beyond his control but it exists in that dimension at all times. It can be reached there if his consciousness is configured suitably."

Yoga + Drugs

Those who do yoga and who take psychoactive drugs, should know that to really test to see if yoga works, one should do yoga alone without drugs. I suggest ceasing the use of drugs for one year while doing yoga. In this way one can make a conclusion as to its effectiveness.

Many students who approach yoga come with a drug use background of marijuana, a hallucinogen drug or a narcotic like cocaine or heroin or some other substance. These habits are hard to renounce especially if the person got some spiritual insight while using the drug.

Over the years, some students who approached to learn yoga and who were already familiar with marijuana or some other drug, would state that the drug brought them to spiritual life. This is because of having increased psychic perception under that influence.

However, to really test yoga, it has to be done without drug use. I recommended ceasing the use for a time, for at least a year. The difficult with this instruction is that the drug may not be easy to renounce. Usually, students say that they will renounce it but then for one reason or the other they are unable to.

Baby Attraction

Another thing that holds my interest other than teen girls and their mothers at the mall, is babies and their parents. Sometimes you see a mother and child, or more frequently now in public in the developed countries, a nanny and child. In Manhattan, New York City, one regularly sees nannies on the streets pushing proms with infants. The nanny is plain to identify because of her race or ethnicity which is variant from the child.

Where is the Mother?

Who is the father?

What are their professions?

My interest in this is even stronger than my interest in girls and moms at the Mall, because after all if I have to take another body, and that is likely to happen if nature has the upper hand, will I be in the same predicament. At least those kids in those proms on Fifth Avenue in New York City are in expensive proms. Their nannies are paid above minimum wage. They live in deluxe apartments with luxurious surroundings. They may attend Columbia University.

Where will I be?

Somewhere in a dumpy daycare with other kids of questionable ethnicity?

As an infant where will my father be late at night in the wee wee hours of the morning?

At a club checking the scanty-clad ladies?

Will my mother be leaving in the morning in high heeled shoes and form fitting gabs to whatever career she feels she should develop?

That next life?

Right now, it is a puzzle, that much I see!

Up-through-Neck Cell Kundalini

I completed the cell kundalini practice which Lahiri required. I have not seen him for a while. When he returns, he should notice that the assignment is complete. Even though I got the hint from him about it, the hint is given big-time in the psyche during sex experience and during some traumatic experiences when the psyche becomes involuntarily involved in an incidence.

Students may never get a yogin like Lahiri to give them that hint. I give it and say that it can be taken from the experiences one has in life, especially from sex experience where the emotions or pleasure feelings come from everywhere in the body and converge at the genitals.

Of course, these emotions and pleasure feelings, so long as one sees them or feels them as such, are near impossible to analyze, but a student can on the basis of confidence in what I declare, gain a grip on this. The pleasure feelings from every cell here, there and everywhere in the psyche is the kundalini of that particular cell. It expresses itself and is revealed during sex climax experience.

Thus, there is a practice in kundalini yoga to directly access these micro-kundalinis of the individual cells. One is introduced to that in advanced kriya practice. Then, the value of the genitals is drastically reduced.

Think of it in this way:

Which is preferred:

One rich man in a city, who taxes from everyone else who are paupers?

Or all fairly wealthy persons in a city who are not taxed by anybody?

As nature would have it, there is one rich man in the city which is the sex organ chakra which taxes the rest of the body for energy. This chakra takes the kundalini charges from every cell or micro-cell. It also taxes the main kundalini which is like the Central Bank in a city.

Do you want the psyche to remain in this configuration?

Today during breath infusion, I pulled all hormonal energy from the lower trunk. At a certain point the pull took hold of the energy. It caused an up flow through the chest, through the neck into the head. It was like a striated panel of energy moving electrically through the chest and then through the neck. It had a bliss aspect.

Cell Kundalini Light-Green Energy Release

This morning during breath infusion some cells in the lower part of the abdomen compacted and were infused. After they were infused again and compressed inwards, they released a bliss energy which went upwards through the front of the chest in long strands of light-green striated energy wavering up and around.

After this happened and to arrest this energy and move it up further, up through the neck, I did another infusion session but with holding this energy where it was in compression. Then it moved through the flesh parts of the neck.

When I sat to meditate, there was naad sound but I was not as close to naad as I was some months ago. Still, it was close. I entered naad and realized that there was a narrow rectangular rod of energy in the center. At that place there was no sound. There was a yellow tinged light around the rod. The rod itself was about one-eighth of an inch across and the yellow light emanated from it for about one quarter of an inch.

I tried to move naad down into the trunk of the subtle body but was unable to. It did not budge. I decided to stay in naad and not make the attempt to move it. I felt a switch up front and looking forward saw that there were no thoughts or memory images anywhere. The mechanism for thought production was absent.

I remained in naad for some time. After a while, about thirty minutes, I found myself as a subtle body in the subtle dimension which is parallel to Trinidad. Some people whom I knew there some fifty years ago spoke of our association at that time. Not one of these persons made spiritual progress. It is amazing how a person can go through an entire lifetime and not have a deep spiritual interest and be totally satisfied with physical existence and with identifying the self as the physical body.

Prana Lift Assistance

Based on recent evaluation and in retrospect from when I began doing the *pranayama* breath infusion practice in this lifetime, I could state conclusively that the *apana/prana* mix of energy, cannot be fully lifted from the lower trunk unless one gets some grace energy from an advanced yogi, who is in the *siddha* category. Part of it can be lifted without assistance but not all.

I reviewed this every which way and can find no way around this requirement because it appears that the strength of lift one can generate is not enough to make a complete suction upwards of the hormone energy which falls into the pubic floor. This is valid even if one uses *vajroli* or *amaroli* lifting suction technique.

The energy is held in the lower trunk by the gravity of the earth and also by the psychological influence of the lifeForce which is at the *muladhara* base chakra. If one endeavors in earnest, one can lift some of it. However as soon as one attracts a *siddhaGuru*, he can if he is so inclined give one the assistance which is necessary. If a car runs into a gorge or ravine, it cannot reverse even if it has the most powerful engine. The driver may be willing to drive it but still there is not enough power and traction in the vehicle to affect its own rescue. But if a rescue truck released a strong cable, then once that was hooked to the vehicle, it would be pulled out of the ravine.

Urdhvareta in the traditional sense means driving the sexual hormonal energy around the pubic floor into the *muladhara* base chakra, where when it strikes the kundalini, that force will try to move and if the locks are effectively applied, it will go up the spine.

However, the kundalini reestablishes itself at the base chakra. That is its tendency. Gravity pulls it down. Eventually according to the Chinese Taoist system, the hormone energy is pulled up directly from the *kanda* bulb storage psychic container. However, beyond that is the complete lift. One can get the power to do it if one gets help from a *siddha*.

Frontal Light Absorption

This is a procedure from Lahiri. It is a part of a process which I develop for him, which if it works in completion will be described as a process of reaching *chit akash* sky of consciousness.

In this procedure the lists of required actions are:

- Do a session of thorough breath infusion.
- Sit to meditate.
- Tune to naad sound resonance.
- Check to see what is in the frontal part of the head.
- If nothing is present, no thoughts or images, proceed.
- Terminate all interest in frontal part of head. Be sure there is no interest. To do this, check to see if any vision energy goes to the front. If any energy leaks from the back half of the head, it should be arrested.

- Once there is no leakage, wait in the naad resonance, until you are sure the leakage stopped and it requires no effort to keep the quiet situation.
- Look forward. If there is nothing in the frontal part, no thoughts or images, open the vision interest to the front. Notice scattered light there.
- Close the vision interest to be sure that when it remains closed, it should have no interest or urge to act.
- Again, open the vision interest. This will be like opening a wide double door and seeing some dim light like when it is a half-moon night when it is neither bright nor pitch dark.
- Let the vision interest absorb scattered bits of lights.
- Maintain the absorption. Be sure to keep the self braced into the naad resonance which is heard behind the coreSelf.

Part 2

Careless Usage of Mantras

Mantras to deities should not be used whimsically nor without permission of those deities or their empowered agents. In India originally one could not hear certain confidential mantras if one was not born in a brahmin family. A man was killed by Rama because someone reported that the offender chanted Vedic mantras and did yoga in the forest. He was shot and beheaded by Rama after Narada Yogi explained that the man did this and it caused the death of a brahmin's son. When Rama questioned the man, the man said that he chanted because he wanted to absolve his unfavorable destiny. Still Rama killed him.

Even today some pundits will ask a bhajan group to begin singing as soon as the pundit begins chanting the puja mantras. This is a strategy to shield the sound of the mantras so that the public cannot hear the confidential sounds.

The *gayatri* mantras are confidential declarations which are not to be used whimsically and not to be used congregationally or casually. They are special call prayers.

You cannot reach the President of a country merely by dialing his phone number. There are security issues which will not allow you to even get the number. If you get it, your call will be routed to an agent or to a message system which will deny access.

The point is that there are confidential mantras. If they are divulged, we may question the authority of the person who shared it. Suppose I work for the Office of the President. I know the president's number. I get this idea that it should be given to everyone; because I feel that everyone should have equal access to the person who governs the country. We are citizens. Why should anyone be barred from talking to the person whose actions affect us nationally?

I gave the number to a newspaper publisher. He publishes it on the first page of the daily paper.

What will happen?

What do you think the President will do?

Will he take calls from the ordinary citizens?

Will he dismiss me from the Cabinet?

Will he change his number?

I know many people who saw or heard confidential mantras. They used those mantras, chanting them day and night, and feeling that they are in touch with the deities or vibrations of those sounds. Some are confidential mantras which use terms like *shreem* and *kleem*.

I know people who use such mantras in meditation or who chant on beads or do silent murmuring.

Is this beneficial?

If you do not have a direct connection to the deity or an agent of the deity, if the deity or the agent did not approach you personally and gave the mantra, it is best to not use the sound.

Is there danger in using a mantra if one does not have contact with the deity or agent?

If someone gets the confidential number of the President of the country and repeatedly dials that number, sooner or later there will be an investigation by the government security. The caller may be inconvenienced by law enforcement.

As for deities, they are not ordinary people. They are supernatural beings. There is no telling if they will take an action which would stifle the offender's spiritual progress.

There are many stories in the *Puranas* of people calling deities with ulterior motives and then being disciplined in some way by the deity. The case of *Shambuka* being killed by Rama was cited above. It is from the *Valmiki Ramayana*.

Ask some questions before using a Vedic mantra, especially a confidential one which is a call prayer for a deity or a *gayatri* mantra which is a confidential glorification of a deity:

Did you get the mantra from the deity?

Did you get the mantra from someone who claimed to be an agent of the deity?

Does the deity expressly say to you that he/she wants your audience?

Did the deity say to you that you should murmur or chant the prayer?

To be fair however, I will mention a mantra as well as the agent of the deity who shared it.

A mantra is not secretive. What is secretive is the connection between the chanter and the deity. If you can get that connection the mantra can be activated, otherwise you will use a sound which either has no potency or which will have a reverse potency where it will corrupt your spiritual life.

Everybody who is anybody in yoga, knows the popular mantra for Shiva which is

Om Namo Shivaya

The actually mantra is this:

Om Namah Shivaya

This sentence is well known. People say it here, there and everywhere. Yet this is a confidential mantra used by the greatest of the yogis.

Just as there is an active ingredient in every pharmaceutical product, so there is a confidential relationship in each mantra. If that relationship is absent, the mantra is useless or worse, it is harmful.

Recently about two years ago, I got that mantra from Lahiri. He said that I should chant it at a certain time during a certain special meditation. After saying this he left. When he instructed the mantra, it had an energy in it where I could reach a supernatural territory where Shiva resides.

Mind you, it was not for reaching Shiva but only for reaching a certain supernatural territory and only during a certain specific introspective meditation. This mantra was not to be used in the physical world even, or to be chanted by the physical tongue. In the meditative state, the physical body is inactive.

Inside the mantra package-energy, there was a permission from Lahiri which gave me legitimate access to that place, because if I reached that place and did not have that permission, I would develop a progress demerit which would upset my practice.

Sensual Energy In-Stream

Some progress was made this morning in the system of meditation which Lahiri wants me to test and perhaps develop and divulge. This morning I worked with the same process of being braced by naad resonance in the back and then looking forward into the frontal part of the subtle head which is already cleared of ideas and images by the breath infusion session which was done immediately prior to the meditation.

A new development occurred where I checked and knew for sure that the intellect was absent.

Where was it?

I do not know. It was not there in the dimension I was in, even though it resumed its place, which means that its disappearance does not say anything about its non-existence. It continues to exist but somewhere else. It resumes its functions as soon as one enters the dimensions in which it is prominent.

It was totally absent during that meditation. Its location was blank.

A new development occurred where instead of having scattered pixelated light up ahead in the frontal part of the subtle head, there was an energy streaming but it was only inside the subtle head. It made no attempt to peer or transit outside.

When I checked this energy closely, I realized that it was the sensual energy. It was inside the subtle head from about one-half inch inside the membrane of the subtle head. It streamed back to me for about two and one-half inches, as it had an interest in me, a mild not a passionate interest.

As soon as I noticed this energy, there was a message from Lahiri for me to be absorbent in naad and let the sensual energy keep streaming to me, letting it focus on me as the core.

I did this for some time.

How long?

That I do not know but it was for a time.

Some developments happen once and then never again. Most of this process of Lahiri happens repeatedly until that part is integrated and develops to a more advanced stage.

It is interesting how it feels to have the sensual energy streaming to the coreSelf when that energy was not pulled to the coreSelf or forced to abandon its conventional interests. It has a neutral feel without a pleasure sense or bliss aspect; like if you did not know someone, as if someone whom you met was a total stranger who had no interest in talking or holding a conversation, but who kept staring at you anyway.

In the natural configuration of the subtle body, for the most part, the sensual energies follow instructions from the kundalini lifeForce. Those energies are not concerned with the needs of the core. This new development allowed me to see what the sensual energies were before they came under the influence of the lifeForce and its accessory powers, where those sensual energies were colored or prejudiced with preferences.

In this way a yogi gets direct insight into what the sensual energies were before they were expressed, when the universe was first generated, and everything was new and unused.

While on the causal plane, the energy has potency, like a jar of concentrated dye which will be diluted into various colors; the sensual energies initially have no potency only a neutral beaming energy which later becomes prejudiced as influenced by the kundalini lifeForce. However, the coreSelf, silly as it is, is apt to assume that it is the primary motivator while in fact it is the least of the influences.

Experiencing the sensual energies in this way without them having their supports from the kundalini lifeForce causes the yogi to ponder on the power of the senses, because here they are stripped of their empowerment. They have neither attraction nor compulsion, nothing. They are like when a celebrity is found on a street corner as a dirty disheveled beggar.

People will then question,

"Are you such and such? I cannot believe what happened. Where is your fame and glory? Where is the luxury and money?"

Reconfiguring the Energy Distribution system

This morning, Lahiri explained the accumulation of tiny droplets of bliss force during the night while the body sleeps. This substance is legendary among the yogis and is mentioned as something which is nectar and which drops in the middle of the subtle head.

However, Lahiri said that this is similar to what happens in a bee hive where one bee in thousands brings nectar from a flower and deposits that in a cell within the hive. Other bees fan those cells to dehydrate the nectar converting it into honey concentrate.

During the night, the body processes nutrients from the food eaten. It deposits those energies near particular cells. Because the body sleeps and many of the cells are dormant, this energy is parked outside the cells.

In the morning the cells notice the delivery of energy which was stocked during the night. The cells use that energy as the body moves when it is awakened. Some energy is kept as a reserve. Part of that is sent to the genitals, while the other part is held in reserve and is sent to the genitals during sexual pleasure experience.

However, a yogi can change this system of delivery and usage by rising early and doing breath infusion, where the stored energy which is parked outside the cells is confiscated by the yogi who uses the infused breath energy to arrest it. As instructed by the yogaGuru, the yogi distributes the energy thus disrupting nature's convention which is to store, distribute, and use the energy in the struggle for survival and in the system of reproduction which is exploited as sex desire.

If the yogi is successful, the energy which usually drops and which is later experienced as sex pleasure, accumulates instead in the head of the subtle body and is experienced as consciousness nectar but without affiliation with the sex organs.

Naad Love Embrace

There is a naad-embrace sensual energy pull practice which I observed when doing a meditation development for Lahiri. This is when one does a thorough breath infusion while focusing on pulling polluted energy from the psyche and displacing it with fresh astral force.

Once the yogi extracts the pollutions, something happens to the subtle body where it cannot function in the normal way, where it serves the purpose of yoga as defined by Patanjali, which is that the mento-emotional energy ceases its conventional thought/image display.

The yogi does the infusion. He sits to meditate. As soon as he sits, he becomes aware of naad sound and moves into association with it in a confidential way. This is like when a person sees someone whom he/she loves and naturally goes closer to that person. The yogi perceives naad, which is close to him but he gets the feeling that he should get closer. Being in the arms of naad resonance, being embraced by it on every side, squeezed lovingly, the yogi becomes aware of the shutdown perception which is like when a person lost interest in something where there is no energy from him going to that object.

The yogi then opens the perception of the self, which in fact is its sense of identity energy which surrounds the core. Then since there is no conventional activity of thinking and imaging, there will be an energy which is quiescent, which has no agitation or compulsion. This energy should be drawn towards the core so that it streams into the core. In some sessions this energy will not stream. It will remain like a silent sky on a dark moon night.

The yogi should be confident that this procedure will eventually cause access to the *chit akash* sky of consciousness. He should wait patiently while doing this practice.

Woman as a Motive for doing Meditation

There is more than one story in the Pali cannon literature of the life of Gautama Buddha which put to question the opinion that he was an atheist and that he did not accept the Vedic system of deities. One such story is that of Nanda, the Buddha's cousin.

Buddha's maternal aunt had a son named Nanda who in a huff and a puff under social influence took to the life of the monks, abandoning social duties in the traditional way of the clan.

After a time, *Nanda* became disillusioned and wanted to return home. He was a prince of the same royal family as Buddha. Nanda confided in some monks that he would return home to live by convention. They in turn reported what he said to the Buddha who requested that Nanda should come to discuss it.

During the conversation, *Nanda* told the Buddha that since he left the home life for the way of the monks, he could not forget the look of a girl who asked him to come back when he was about to leave for the monk life. This girl was named *Kalyani*.

After he said this, Buddha in a split second, disappeared from the earth and appeared in *Trayastrimsha* heaven, the realm of deity Indra who is also known as *Sakka* (*Shakra*-Sanskrit). According to the Vedic pantheon of deities, this Indra rules the *Swarga* angelic world where qualified performers of Vedic sacrifices go for a time after the death of their physical bodies. Arjuna of the *Bhagavad Gita* as well as his four famous brothers and their wife Draupadi were seen in this heavenly world after they abandoned their physical bodies. This is described in detail in the *Mahabharata*.

A famous Vedic king of the name of *Yayati* fell from this heavenly world after his pious merits were exhausted

When Buddha arrived there with *Nanda*, some five hundred celestial beauties were in attendance to Indra. Buddha asked Nanda how *Kalyani* compared to these celestial females. *Nanda* said that in reference the earthly girl was like a monkey with her nose and ears cut off. He said that the heavenly women were infinitely more beautiful and comelier.

Buddha then told *Nanda* that if he would remain as a monk, he would be guaranteed five hundred of these females hereafter. *Nanda* then agreed to be a monk.

The question is:

If Buddha did not believe in the Vedic deities, why did he go to this heavenly place of Indra which is famous in the Vedic literatures?

Why did he take a disciple there?

It is also interesting that Buddha used celestial women in that instance as a way to convince his cousin to be a renunciant.

Was that a worthy trick?

Nanda did eventually attain the status as an Arahant or realized soul. At the time he lost interest in the celestial females and explained that he released Buddha from the promise to supply him with five hundred such nymphs.

For all his seriousness, Buddha was a humorous person. He is a lovely individual who is worthy of affection as a dear father of the living entities.

Breath-Infusion Hormone Lift

After one consistently raised kundalini through the *sushumna nadi* central passage, on a daily basis with a reliable method, the central passage remains open continuously and does not clog or have deposits of heavy astral energy.

Kundalini may still be stationed at the *muladhara* base chakra but even so, it has free access and spreads its glory through the cleared *sushumna*. This means that visually there would be a clear atmosphere in the passage. The kundalini shines through the passage from the *muladhara* chakra continuously. It is not in an arousal situation as when kundalini flashes like lightning through the spine into the brain but it will be that its diffused light spreads through the central passage into the brain.

If somehow or the other, the yogi can get his lifestyle under control, and this would happen if the grace of providence is on his side, then kundalini will disconnect from the *muladhara* base chakra and float through the spine into the brain. It will do this now and again until at last it does this permanently, and clings to the bottom back of the brain as stub kundalini.

Once this happens, the yogi's kundalini yoga process changes because he can no longer hit kundalini at the *muladhara* chakra. The body itself changes because with kundalini no longer resident at the base, the energies in the trunk are forced to realign themselves to the new reality. These energies will search for kundalini but will be unable to find it. They will make an effort to find kundalini by sending detection rays through the neck but since the neck was not cleared by the yogi, since it has dense energy except for the *sushumna* central passage which passes through it, the energies will find that their detection rays fail to locate it. They do not have the power to bore the *sushumna nadi* and the rest of the neck having dense astral energy prohibits the penetration.

It is at this point that the yogi must get help from a *siddha* who is familiar with a more advanced procedure.

The method is to clear the neck so that it has no dense energy in any part, not even in the fleshy portion. If that is done the cells which could not find kundalini, will locate it and get themselves reoriented thus breaching nature's evolutionary system of using kundalini as a survival-reproduction mechanism.

So long as the yogi is in a social circumstance and is not isolated, he must participate in whatever providence produces but that will not interfere with his record of austerities. His subtle body will retain the progress even if the physical body is involved in the conventions of fate.

Instead of wasting time fighting reality, a yogi should let fate have its way while he keeps focused on the yogaGurus and the methods of advancement which they introduce and inspire into his mind.

Secretly and silently, ignoring critics and others who badger him, the yogi should maintain the practice, especially on the subtle side of existence. He should not be occupied defending himself and proving anything to human beings because ultimately, they are of little consequence. What is achieved in the subtle body is the vital key to this.

The purpose of this practice is to exit the course of evolution, not to master it, not to change it, not to prove anything in relation to it, not to show human society how one will exit. Thus, a yogi should remain focused. He should heed the advanced teachers.

Yoga for Health

There is no statement in the *Yoga Sutras* or the *Bhagavad Gita* defining yoga as a cure for bad health. There are books about yoga, as for instance the *Hatha Yoga Pradipika*, where the health benefits of yoga are mentioned but these books do not define yoga as being the cure for bad health. Its benefits for health are to facilitate its practice.

People sometimes get this idea that a yogi is healthy because of doing *asanas* postures and/or breath infusion. When their health wanes they call the yogi to ask for a cure.

They ask:

What posture can I do to fix this?

What about breath-infusion, which method will correct this?

But yoga is not for health. Its purpose is to sort what is the coreSelf?

What are the psychic accessories?

What is the best method for regulating the relationships between the components of consciousness?

Fixing the physical body by yoga, when it becomes unhealthy, and then casting yoga aside as soon as the body resumes comfort, is an abuse of yoga.

Lust-free Bliss Energy

Today, Atmananda, who is the guru of Yogeshwarananda, said that the loop around system for driving kundalini out from its lair at *muladhara* base chakra, does not affect what is processed in the gut of the yogi. He was of the opinion that the rigid austerities designed by Gorakshnath were meant to deal with this issue but many yogis are so satisfied if they can raise kundalini by any which means, that they feel that is the culmination of the practice, even though in a sense it is preparatory.

The loop around system is the compaction of fresh air into the front of the trunk of the body, then forcing that pass the navel and around the pubic loop where it then seeks out, targets and fuses into the kundalini at the base chakra. This causes the kundalini to move but since the locks are applied by the yogi, kundalini has no alternative but to move upwards through the *sushumna nadi* central passage.

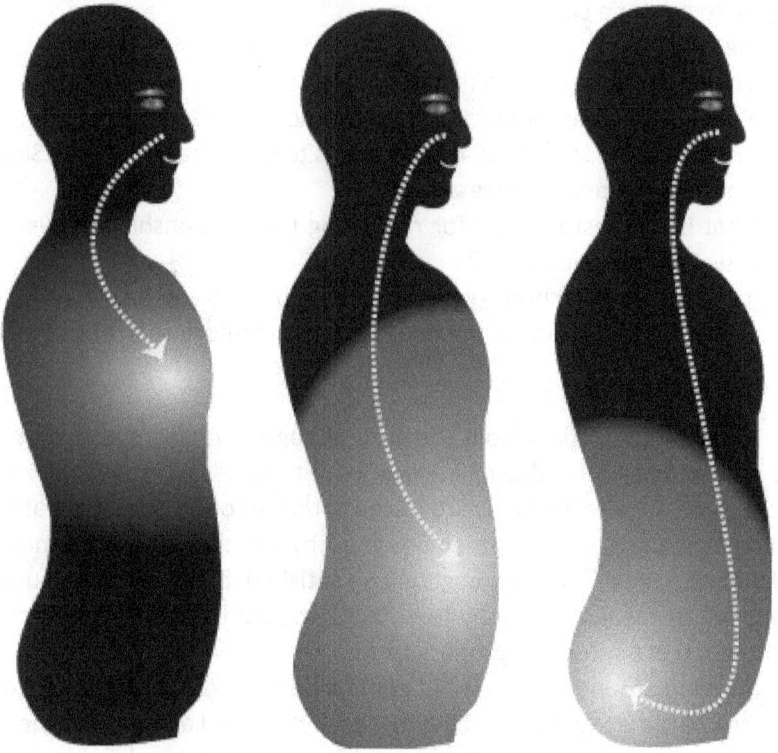

This causes kundalini to enter into the head of the subtle body, where when it first emerges there, it looks for an objective. This is similar to a snake, which comes up from an underground burrow into full sunlight where it is blinded by the light initially and has to adjust to get a sense of direction, except in this case kundalini is the one which produces the light and it sees while the other adjuncts and even the coreSelf may be blinded by it.

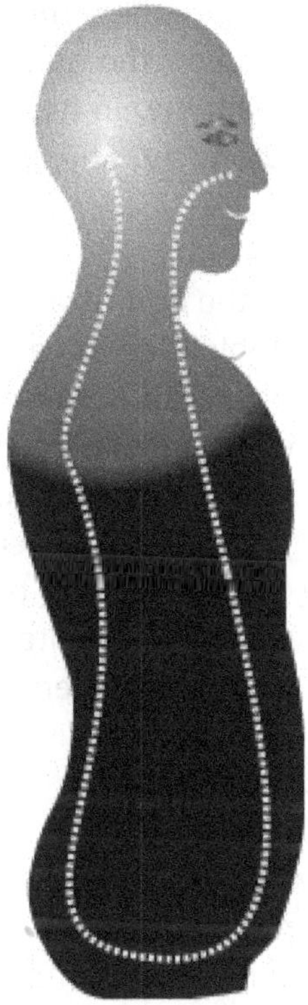

That would be like when a snake emerges from its hole at midnight and then suddenly because it is a magical snake; it shines a bright light from its head and blinds all other creatures. Then it strikes one creature which it sees, even before that stunned animal can understand what happened.

Once kundalini enters the brain, and looks around, it makes a decision to either attack the intellect orb, the third-eye or crown chakra *brahmrandra*. In some instances, it avoids these psychic adjuncts and focuses on the coreSelf. Or it may penetrate through the back of head and exits from the subtle body into the astral dimension which is suited to its aroused condition. In some instances, it subsides back to the *muladhara* base chakra.

Because the kundalini has vast powers and is rated by yogis as being a supreme goddess, the coreSelf is afraid of this psychic accessory. By logic there can only be one supreme goddess but kundalini is termed as a supreme goddess because in each body, the specific kundalini rules as the goddess of that individual psyche.

The core which may rate itself as a buddha or as a potential buddha, or as a Shiva or as God or as the sum total of what exists, is still afraid of the kundalini psychic mechanism which it must rely on for many services in maintaining both the physical and astral bodies.

When asked as to if it can replace the kundalini lifeForce, the self becomes silent and does not answer the question. It believes that it is the equivalent of a god. In the meantime, in its own psyche it is a serf of the kundalini. It does not have autonomy. Still, in its little mind, it idolizes an image of itself as being God.

When asked point blank:

Can you the coreSelf make the body evacuate?

It runs away with its hands blocking its ears.

When kundalini enters the brain, the core becomes afraid because kundalini threatens to deprive the self of objectivity which is something that the self must have to maintain whatever little control it has over the body.

If the self did not prepare for kundalini's entrance before hand, if it did not run for cover by focusing the intellect orb properly, then when kundalini strikes, the core will lose objectivity in a white out, black-out or gold-out. It will lose consciousness and be either in a mental fog in a lost condition or be in nothingness as nothingness, or be in a bliss energy as bliss consciousness with no reference of anything anywhere.

When the influence of kundalini subsides, it will resume some objectivity and wonder where it is and what happened.

However, the issue still remains that even though the yogi successfully attacked kundalini and caused its arousal into the brain of the subtle body, many other parts of the psyche remain untouched. These areas still have heavy astral energy and pollutants of various sorts.

Right above the pubic loop is energy which is not charged by the sex organ chakra. This is a relatively lust-free energy. This energy should also be charged with fresh air energy during breath infusion practice.

Can the yogi appreciate lust-free bliss energy?

How enjoyable is that when it is breath-infused as compared to lust-charge energy which is breath-infused?

Is the yogi condemned forever to deal with only lust-charged bliss energy either in sexual intercourse or in kundalini's passage through the *sushumna* central channel into the brain?

What is the difference in the pleasure energy when it is sexually charged and is used by kundalini to bore into the brain and when it is used via the genitals?

This morning in lifting the lust free bliss energy which floated above the pubic loop, I noticed that it flashed and then released wriggly rays which came up like dangling twinkies, squirming like ring worms shivering up, on and on, in a shallow pond. When this energy was compressed into itself, it fired under the shoulder blades and released lust-free bliss pixels.

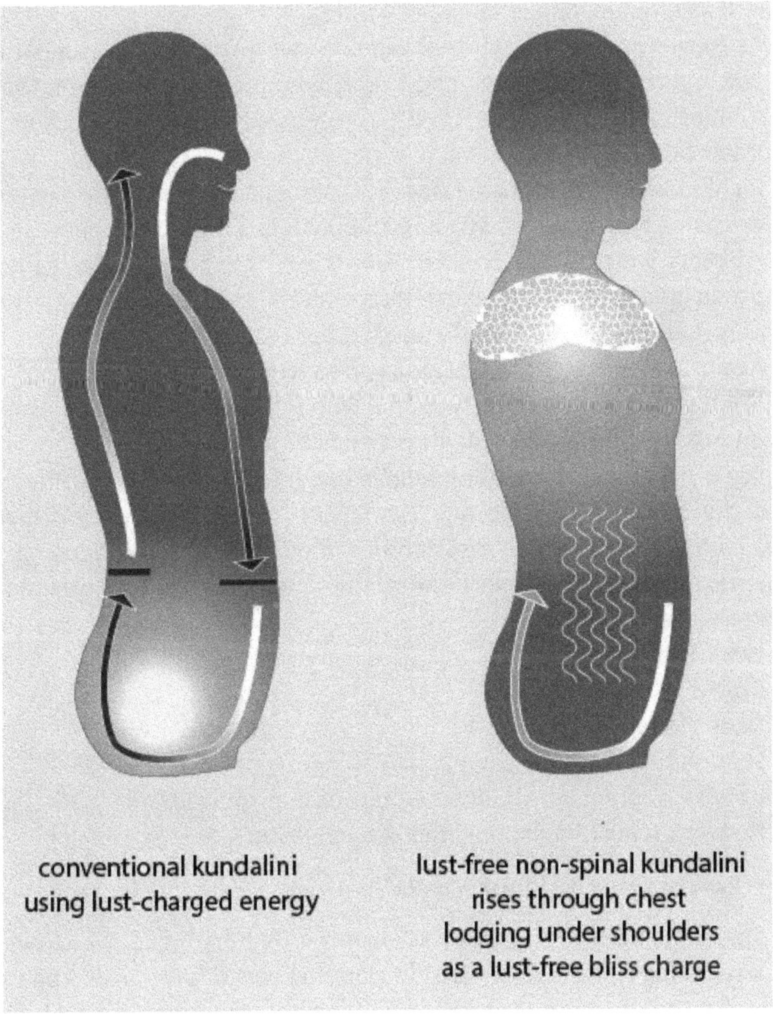

Supernatural People

Today during breath infusion practice, I heard some supernatural beings arguing. These were eight persons, four with one argument, and four with the opposing view.

It went like this:

One group:

"He should be left alone."

The other group:

"He should be harassed and harnessed"

They discussed as to whether I should be allowed to do austerities in some remote place. In this life I made more than one attempt to do this. So far, each attempt failed.

As they argued I realized that the ones who said I should be harassed won the argument. They remained to talk with me but I told them that my only request was that some time be reserved for me to proceed with austerities bit by bit.

Right now, I abandoned hope that I could complete the austerities before leaving this body. It is still possible but it is not probably because of so many factors which hinge on fate. Fate is not reliable in so far as it may support an individual. No one but a mad man will think that fate will sponsor his interest above everything else which it has to take into account.

Again, and again that issue comes up as to who owns the body.

Is it owned by supernatural people who argue about its usage as if they were in a casino betting over the throw of dice? We hear in the *Mahabharata* that some negative supernatural beings had a talk with some positive ones about the situation of *Nala* and *Damayanti*. Subsequently *Nala* married *Damayanti* and then lost her association immediately after the wedding. Both of them lived condemned lives because the supernatural people were against their marriage.

Who owns the body?

Do the relatives?

Does the government?

Who should the body serve?

At whose command should the body be transported?

How much austerity should the body perform?

Sex --- Expulsion for Buddhist Monks

There is an interesting story of how the Buddha made it a stipulation about sex being a cause for expulsion from the Sanga for monks. Apparently for the first thirty years after his enlightenment, there was no such formal rule.

Actually, it was an undeclared rule but it was not formally announced because the various sects which the Buddha entered before enlightenment were sects in which ascetics could not be married even though there always were superior teachers who were married and who were rated as rishis. These rishis may have had more than one wife. Some had extramarital affairs.

There was no need for a declaration about monks not having sex once a person entered the Sanga and declared that he abandoned the home life. Once for the sake of having heirs to carry on their family, a monk by the name of *Sudinna* was induced by his mother to impregnate his abandoned wife. This monk left his wife and entered the monk life before begetting children. When his mother asked him to impregnate his wife, he agreed.

The literature said that in the woods, he had intercourse with his former wife thrice, resulting in a pregnancy. Other monks got to know of it. They told Buddha who became annoyed. He condemned *Sudinna* and even said that it would be better if the offending monk had put his organ into the mouth of viper.

Buddha then called the assembly of monks and made a rule that if any monk should be sexually involved, he should be expelled from the Sanga.

The callousness of Buddha towards family life and even towards assisting ancestors with rebirth is clearly shown in this discourse which is mentioned in the book, *Life of Buddha* by *Bhikkhu Nanamoli.*

Buddha himself left aside his wife and son permanently and did nothing to support them financially. He showed no interest in their social well-being. His son joined the Sanga because when the son was advised by Buddha's abandoned wife to approach Buddha for an inheritance, Buddha influenced the boy to become a monk.

This hostility to family life is part of the reason why Buddhism was pushed out of India. To an extent the Indian system takes into consideration the need for ancestral accommodation through family life.

In the Buddhist system as Buddha initially established it, there was no middle ground where one could proceed with a strong practice and be a family man. The yogi had to do what was called 'go out of the home life'. In fact, a term which is used for Buddha which is *Tathagata* (Tut haa Guh-tuh) means a person who went (*agata*) out of (tatha) the family into the life of being a bachelor ascetic.

In the Vedic system one may be a family man and still be in the disciplines. Or one may be a bachelor and do the same with the understanding that those who were bachelors were likely to excel others. When a person takes the monk status it is accepted that he would excel others because he will not have to spend time raising a family which includes relationship with women and children. But the Vedic system accommodated family men who were serious ascetics and who agreed to help the ancestors to get bodies.

Buddha was disinclined to having women monks but under pressure from his aunt who served as a wet nurse when he was an infant, he ordained women as monks, but with stipulations that they were to offer respect to male monks, even to newcomers, and that they could not sit with the males at any time.

Buddha: Sanskrit Meter Banned

At one time Buddha prohibited that the explanation of his teachings be put in Sanskrit meter. This is interesting because the most reliable literature about his life is in Pali which is hybrid Sanskrit. The occasion was this:

Two well-trained brahmin monks named *Yamelu* and *Tekula* who lived at *Savatthi* told Buddha that the monks *(bhikkhus)* were of various names, races, born variously and being from various types of ethnic and racial families. They explained that this spoilt the word of Buddha because everyone repeated the stories using their local language. They asked the Buddha for permission to compose everything in Sanskrit meter which was the official way to speak about sacred people and things.

Buddha chastised the two brahmins saying that they were misguided and should not ask to put his words into classical meter. He said that if this was done it will not arouse faith in the faithless. It would keep the faithless without faith and harm some of the faithful followers even.

Buddha then called the assembly of monks and said that his words should not be put in Sanskrit meter and that it should be in a person's local language.

This may be considered to be one of the reasons why Buddha alienated the brahmin caste of India. Sanskrit is a monopoly language whereby only certain families learnt it in the time of Buddha. Even today it is not easy to learn Sanskrit and even if one does, there is yet a completion to master, which is to learn the rituals which accompany the recitation of the language. The meters are mathematically, musically and syntaxly adjusted in such a precise way that one cannot master it without being instructed. Usually, this information passes from father to son. In other words, it is a caste restricted education.

Apparently, Buddha did not think that Sanskrit had anything to do with the kind of enlightenment he achieved.

Narcotics / *Muladhara* Base Chakra

I was in a hospital today to see a relative who had knee surgery. This is someone whose body is over sixty years of age. I glanced at the lists of medications. Two in particular were of interest. These were:

- hydromorphone
- oxycodone

These were listed on the sheet as narcotics with these effects:

- dizziness
- sedation
- constipation

- nausea

After a while, the patient told me that he was constipated. He was depressed mentally. This person knows that I practice and teach yoga. He wondered if I could provide relief by giving him a posture. However, his knee surgery prohibited most of the *asanas* because he cannot move his leg or thigh without severe pain.

He wanted to know if *pranayama* would help with pain management. I suggested that he be of a sober mind instead of asking such questions.

I wanted to share this experience for another reason however, which is to point out that pain killers, opiates and the like, usually affect the *muladhara* base chakra. They cause this chakra to assume it densest dark condition. Once that happens the colon and anus cease their peristaltic operations which means that food waste will be stationary and will dehydrate, getting denser and denser. That is the physical part. The psychological part is worth considering.

Dizziness and sedation are mentioned in the list of effects which means that the narcotics affect the third eye and crown chakras. They affect the intellect orb in the subtle body.

Does it matter?

Could this have an effect on a person's awareness?

There is one other thing. After being in the hospital for about thirty minutes, I realized that I ingested many drugs by breathing the air in the room. The place was toxic from the gases which were released from the pores of the patients and from various dispensing machines. I feel bad for the nurses and other professionals who work in these places for hours on end. Their bodies must be laden with the chemicals used in the drugs.

As a *pranayama* yogi, my body is sensitive to air quality. After I left the place, I could taste the chemicals in my saliva. I did not drink or eat anything there. It entered my body through the most efficient and constant entry point which is the mucus membrane and lungs.

Practicing Yoga Alone

Initially yoga was a lone practice under supervision of an accomplished yogi. The teacher was either a lifelong celibate like one of the four *Kumaras*, or as a family ascetic like *Vashishtha*.

Bhagavad Gita is the speech of a householder named Krishna, except that he declared himself as the Supreme Person. It was written by one *Dwaipayana Vyasa* who was a family man.

Of the sons of Brahma, some were bachelors. Some were householders. Each was a yoga expert as was Brahma.

Two things are required in yoga.

- practice
- persistence

Personal persistence with practice

Practice Alone

One needs a teacher to practice yoga. This however, is a generalization which applies to most students. There are exceptions. For instance, Buddha was an exception. He began by learning from teachers. When he exhausted the realization potential of their processes, he struck out on his own and pioneered a method.

In his case, it is clear that for yoga practice, the student must do it alone either under superior guidance or by effective self-direction.

There are two types of self learning.

- One is when one sits alone with a teacher and learns methods.
- The other is when one sits alone and practices what one was advised to do by the teacher.

One can learn alone even in a group session. When one is alone with the teacher, one can hear specifically what is for one's benefit. Some students like to get cozy with a teacher. Others have other motives such as being able to boast that they were alone with the teacher and got special instructions. Some others like to be alone with the teacher just for the concern expressed, so that whatever the teacher says is not taken seriously. They soak up the affection of the teacher and ignore the advisories. Instead of being put to use by the teacher, some students make an effort to employ teacher. They ask for a personal meeting and then demand that the teacher answer certain questions or relate in an affectionate way.

For practice one needs to be alone, otherwise one may be distracted. However, some students like to be in a group. They feel lonely and isolated if they are put to meditate separately.

It is a fact though that unless one mediates alone, one cannot advance in kriya yoga which is for self-investigation in isolation within the mind or psyche. Unless one turns about in the mind and becomes completely introspective, one cannot discover the components of consciousness and will never sort what exists on the internal plane.

Some students come to the teacher with a compassionate nature, where they feel that they can learn a skill of yoga and share it with others. These are not students in the real sense. They are like retailers who purchase items cheaply at a wholesale outlet, and who sell the products for a profit to people who have no wholesale access.

Some come to a teacher with a kindness nature, where they think, "I am a good person. This teacher has assets which could be serviceable to mankind. I will learn from him. I will show others what they can do to help themselves."

This kind of person goes with a good motive to the teacher. Still this person cannot learn because yoga is not for satisfying the kindness nature of a human being.

Some students stick with a teacher for a long time, tolerating even an irritable insultive teacher. They claim not to have a motive and to be free of resentment. However, as nature would have it, and as history folds out, this student eventually becomes despondent if ever the teacher teaches something new to any other person. It is then that this person thinks:

"O well! Look at this. I served this teacher for many years. I did it selflessly. I never asked for anything in return. He regards me as nothing. A new student got teachings which were never explained to me."

This student then becomes disgruntled, sour, and resentful. He/She goes away.

Practicing alone is important but few can do it effectively. This is because there is little excitement and reference in such practice. Long sessions of meditation do not necessarily pay off. One may sit for long periods with a blank mind or with a mind which is fully of thoughts and images, and not make progress. This can go on for months.

Imagine what it would be like if you read a book by a great yogin or about one, with fantastic tales about bliss and *samadhi*, and then when you sit to mediate none of it becomes your experience. You are left with a blank or partially blank mind. Or worse, your mind is ridden with images and thoughts, which you can neither control nor dismiss. Or imagine if you have a glimpse of spiritual happiness for three seconds only, in say an hour of meditation.

What is Kundalini?

Kundalini is the psychic lifeForce in a creature's body. It is not a physical principle but it uses physical stuffs for some of its operations. It may be compared to fire which is not a solid physical but which uses a solid physical like a block of wood for feeding itself.

Because it is not a physical principle, it cannot be defined with physical proof except indirectly. I will give three proofs for kundalini which are:

- involuntary actions
- sexual climax
- astral projection

Of the three, the first two are basic physical incidences. The last is psychic. The last one is useless if one does not have developed psychic perception.

Forget whatever you heard about kundalini. In ordinary existence everyone is a physical body. Each has or had a mother and father. We find ourselves to be these current physical bodies. We also found that these bodies act on their own with us as only the observer on occasion. I heard a gunshot. I ran from the sound. After thirty seconds of running, I realized that I was in flight. I slowed but I kept running. When I was three blocks from the sound, I stopped.

The initial running action was involuntary because I did not think of it. I did not give a willpower command to do it. Some other principle in my body activated it.

This something, whatever it is, is the kundalini.

The second feature listed is sexual climax experience. This is perhaps the most sensation, extreme and expressive use of the kundalini.

What is it?

One has to engage in that experience and be observant in the psyche to make the evaluation. It is within the feelings and within the mind, confidentially, only the experience describes how it feels. If someone could get to the inside of what happens during the sexual climax experience, the mystery of kundalini would, for the most part, be understood.

The third and last feature is astral projection.

Did anyone become objectively aware in a dream or in an experience, where he/she is fully conscious, sober, just as objective as one usually is when the physical body is awake and sober? If one has, kundalini can be understood as the psychic mechanism which separates the astral body from the physical one. Better yet, it is the system which causes the re-unification of the two forms, so that after an astral projection the person can awaken in the physical form as that sleeping body.

If one was ever in an astral projection and something scary happened, or the physical body detected danger, one would experience a sudden and abrupt end to the astral projection, with the self awakening as the physical body in a split second. The psychic feature in the sleeping body, which pulled the astral form into fusion with the physical one, is the kundalini.

Where does it exist in body?

Traditionally kundalini is said to reside at the *muladhara* base chakra, which is at the end of the spinal column. It is said to have three and one-half coils. The bottom coil is the base chakra; the second tier is the sex chakra (not the sex organ chakra). The third coil is the navel chakra (not the navel). The remaining half coil is the lung-heart complex of energy.

Besides information from yoga texts, a yogi can investigate to find kundalini at the base chakra. To do this, one should use *pranayama* breath infusion.

Is it physical existence or imagination?

Kundalini is a psychic or supernatural energy which has primal instincts or emotional intelligence. It knows how to procure physical bodies, how to survive as these bodies and how to leave these bodies and procure other physical forms.

Kundalini is not a physical existence but it develops for itself a physical form. It maintains that until the form dies. Then it jumps into a parent form and creates another form for itself.

Kundalini is not virtual imagination. It transcends imagination. It is a supernatural energy.

Is it possible for a human to arouse kundalini?

Someone can activate kundalini by using *pranayama* breath infusion and by other methods.

Presently using *kapalabhati/bhastrika* breath infusion, I can raise kundalini. I do this practice twice per day. By studying the movements of kundalini during sexual climax experience, I noticed that kundalini arcs across from the base chakra to the sex organ chakra (not to be confused with the second *svadhishthana* sex chakra on the spine). It does this. That is interpreted by a human being as intense sexual pleasure.

Using breath infusion however, a yogi can generate a charge of breath energy in the sex organ chakra (not the sex chakra on the spine). This charge will arc to the *muladhara* chakra, striking kundalini which then attempts to move. To control its movement, the yogi must apply the locks *(bandhas).* Then kundalini feels trapped and can only ascend the spine (*sushumna nadi*). This experience of kundalini rushing through the spine into the brain is similar to sexual climax experience except for the location in which the experience is felt.

In sexual climax experience the pleasure is focalized in the genitals, while in the breath infusion method, it is focalized in the spine and brain. In sexual experience there is fluid discharge but in breath infusion kundalini arousal, there is no physical discharge even though there are energy bursts on the psychic or subtle planes.

After sexual experience a male is usually exhausted while after kundalini arousal up the spine, he is energized and shifts to a higher plane.

Buddha / Fish-Meat Allowance

When Buddhism became popular in the USA in the 1960s and 1970s, it hailed as a religion of nonviolence. Hardly any hippie who admired it ever read any original book or reliable translation about Buddha. Many left aside their Christian flesh-eating background, shunning it, and became proud vegetarians.

But what exactly was nonviolence for Buddha?

In the *Life of the Buddha* by *Bhikkhu Nanamo*li (page 266), there is a story where Buddha had an argument with one of his wayward followers named *Devadatta*. This person wanted to split the *Sanga* into two groups, one being led by him. At first, he wanted to kill Buddha and confiscate the *Sanga* but since that did not work because of Buddha's supernatural power, he decided to create a schism where he would take half of the sanga collective of monks under his directorship and the other half would be with Buddha.

In a conversation with Buddha, where *Devadatta* wanted to establish certain austerity rules for groups of monks, Buddha explained how he ordained monks. One of the stipulations had to do with diet, where Buddha said this:

"I allowed fish and meat which is pure in the three aspects -- when it is not seen or heard or suspected to have been killed for one, personally."

This is interesting because it means that whatever nonviolence meant to Buddha it did not include being strictly vegetarian. It involved eating fish and meat provided that the monk who ate it, did not ask that it be prepared for him specifically. In other words, it had to be taken on the alms round of a monk without the monk influencing the household who prepared it.

Nanamoli, the translator, does not state what meat from what animal carcass. However, it is a far cry to Vedic considerations about eating fish or animals where the butcher, the cook, the diners, everyone involved, are considered to be part of the violence *(karma).*

In those Buddhist sects where vegetarianism is a principle for monks, it would be interesting to know which Buddhist teacher introduced that and how he established a diet which was variant to Buddha's.

Depression Dips

Any type of drug, even mild ones like caffeine, causes depression which drive the user to use the drug. Addiction to these substances does not have to be grotesque, it could be mild and hardly noticed but still it is an addiction.

The extreme drugs like marijuana, cocaine and the opium, regardless of if they are medically prescribed or taken without that supervision, chemically pure or otherwise, cause depression dips in consciousness. At first the drug gives a high which varies from just a slight lift or stimulant to a big rise or euphoria. The larger the rise, the bigger the depression dip which occurs after. There is no way around it. It may be postponed but it will swing downwards later.

Even sugar and pepper are stimulants with a depression dip and a call for more usages by the cells which are afflicted by it.

In yoga there is talk about balance, in consciousness, about sober highs, about clean bliss which is not forced or primed with herbs or drugs. How is that done because in our atmosphere we have moon phases, sun flares and so many incidences of high and lows in every way? Even in our bodies, there are hormones maximums and minimums.

Is nature all about highs and lows?

What is your drug?

How much marijuana have you smoked in the past month?

How many cups of coffee do you take per day?

How many pounds of sugar have you taken in various covert forms in the past month?

Addiction to food and drink transfers from one life to another. I noticed that even though my children were raised vegetarian with never a taste of meat, fish or eggs, it does not hold up in every case that they continue in that tradition.

I was raised as an average human being eating just about everything. When I got on my own, I stripped away the flesh foods and eggs. It took some time to do it because the cells of the body resisted change. They did not give in without a struggle. Eventually I brought them to order to do as desired. Now I witnessed the reverse, where someone who was raised with a higher habit goes to a lower one, partially on the basis of their having lived with that behavior in a past life. We worry in the developed countries over addiction in the current life but do we take into account addiction which is transferred from a previous life?

Recently I did research into naad sound in terms of the inability to either hear naad or to hear it and be unable to be in tune with it positively. Some persons hear naad easily but they have little or no affinity for it. Others do not hear naad ever, or they hear it every so often, by chance, with no idea how to contact it on demand.

For those who hear naad but who have little or no affinity to it, there are ways to improve this. Even if you have to force yourself to do so, spend more time listening to it. Emerge yourself in it in meditation. Stay with it. If you drift from it, as soon as you realize the breach, go back to it. Do this over and over, until you feel that you developed a kinship, where it is friendly and welcoming to you.

For those who hear naad, by chance, infrequently, or who do not hear it ever, they should draw the conclusion, that since senior yogis attested to it, naad is there. They should feel that it is in their interest to detune from other sounds which cause deafness to naad resonance.

Those who feel that they can meditate successfully without hearing naad, should drop the quest to tune into naad and complete the meditation method of their choice.

For those who feel that they must get in touch with naad, for whatever reason, they should sit silently in meditation, close the eyelids and listen internally for any sound which arises in the mind.

Press on the ear lobes to close the outer air canal. Listen to sounds inside the head. Listen for as long as you can, then release the ear lobes and see which sounds remain. Keep listening day after day. Eventually one should contact naad.

Naad is a shrill sound which is a combination of micro-sounds. It is usually heard in the back or side of the head. It is continuous

For those who listen frequently but who do not have a cozy relationship with it, they may improve the situation by detuning from other sounds during meditation. They should reduce the attention they give to the voices of others during normal social dealings.

A low-quality mind content causes naad to be distant from the yogi. Any valid method of mind content upgrade causes an increase in quality of naad hearing and causes a cozier relationship with it. A yogi can be romantic with naad. This would result in his gaining access into the *chit akash* sky of consciousness.

Physical Body / Subtle Body

The genetic situation supersedes our preferences to a greater degree. There are small adjustments we can make but that will not budge or put a dent in nature with its kundalini which runs the genetic code in the physical bodies.

If one has a monkey body, how much can one alter that form if one was shown a yogic technique. We hear that Rama expressed wonder and surprised at a monkey-man who composed and spoke fluent Sanskrit. This means that such a feat was unusual. That monkey-man got his inferior body adjusted so that it could learn and express itself in a language with a complicated syntax.

But the subtle body is the area where we can make adjustments. However, even that is not simple. Once years ago, I was in a spiritual society from India. The guru of the sect said that if anyone would chant the mantra which he swore by, and if anyone would follow the lifestyle he had, that person's subtle body would be changed instantly. It was untrue as was shown years later when many of his leading disciples, some of whom he said were pure people as a result of the process, were found to be deviant in their principles, and resumed their former undesirable habits.

Some said that by mantras the subtle body is changed but the evidence for this is hard to come by. What we have is belief in this with no permanent change.

The subtle body has impulsions. Some of its desires coincide with what the physical system is aligned to. Some other desires are contrary to what the physical body is inclined to do. There are disputes between the two operations, that of the subtle body and that of the physical one.

Because it is complicated, there is no one-two-three punch to settle this. It varies from person to person. There are two evolutions happening. One is the evolution of the physical system. The other is the upgrade of the subtle body.

One should aspire to remove from the subtle body, the tendency for using a physical system. So long as this tendency is there, we must take physical bodies no matter how great we rate our circumstance.

Buddha: Full Dedication

I had some contact with Buddha through his deity when I was in South Korea some years ago. Yesterday however I had astral contact with him during an exercise session. He looked at the breath infusion practice and some of the meditation process which I currently do. He made an important remark.

We discussed the process he used in contrast to the method I developed. He said this:

> *No matter what method is used, if it is an effective procedure, the intensity of it and the full engagement in it will be required, otherwise it will fail. People should review themselves and check to see which materialistic activity they liked the most. Whatever that may be, they should check to see how industrious they become when doing whatever that is. For some it may be sexual indulgence, or merchandising, or ruling others, or hunting animals, or competitive sport or cheating others.*
>
> *It does not matter what it. The student should check on the enthusiasm he/she has when doing that activity. This same degree of impetus should be applied to the liberation method. In my time, we as princes, used to sit and play a game which is similar to chess. We studied the moves intently. It represented conquering other rulers and taking their lands and peoples.*
>
> *But the other vocations also have their particular focuses to gain mastery. In every respect each living entity applies himself/herself to some area. Transfer that persistence to the practice.*

When I began studying under teachers, that is what I did. I quickly came to the full potential of their methods. Then I shifted to something higher. I sat down and pioneered a way to go even higher. It took full dedication, full research, full occupation of my energies.

Buddha: Cause of Death

There is a controversy as to what cause the death of Buddha's body. The issue is cleared in the book, *Life of The Buddha* by *Nanamoli Bhikkhu*. Based on the Pali cannon information, it is explained that during the last year of his life, Buddha ate the food of an aristocratic prostitute named *Ambapali*.

This may sound outlandish because everyone in the area knew that this woman was involved in sex business and was wealthy. Why did someone who claimed to be an especially enlightened person, greater than even the Brahma deity, eat her food?

We may bear in mind that at the time the custom was for monks to accept food when they were invited by lay people. It was considered an honor of the lay people to get a monk, especially a recognized leader to take food.

During the last year of his life, Buddha passed through the area of *Vesali*, a countryside inhabited by a clan of people known as *Licchavis*. Somehow Buddha and many of his monks accepted an offer to live in a mango grove of the wealthy courtesan named *Ambapali*. When the woman heard that he was there, she ordered coaches to be prepared. She mounted one and went to Buddha. She circumambulated him as was customary for respected religious leaders.

After the greetings, Buddha lectured her about the process which he introduced. After some time, she asked him if she could prepare food. He was silent, which as custom would have it, meant that he agreed.

The woman then left. On her way home she met some members of the royal families which governed the area, but she did not instruct her coaches to stand aside for the royal entourage to pass. They questioned her about this insubordination. She told them that the Blessed One, Buddha, accepted her invitation for meals on the following day. Everyone was struck with wonder hearing that Buddha did this.

Ambapali must have been of royal family herself because she would not have had such status to have coaches prepared for her journeys and the royal families would not have taken it lightly that she did not instruct her coaches to stand aside.

The royal families asked her to allow them to do the meal for the price of one hundred thousand but she refused, saying that she would not trade the opportunity even if they were to offer their lands. They admitted that they were superseded by the mango woman.

After this they went to Buddha and asked him if he would accept their food the next day but he told them that he was already committed to the courtesan.

However, the next day she had the meals prepared and served. Then she sat and was given more instructions. Buddha stayed in that mango grove for some time and then instructed *Ananda* that they should depart. Right after Buddha took that first meal, the courtesan offered the mango grove as a permanent sanctuary for the monks.

After staying at that grove for a while, Buddha went to a place called *Beluva*. There he had a severe sickness and used mystic power to stave it off. But it cannot be said that this sickness occurred immediately after the meal was provided by the courtesan. At the time his body was some eighty years of age. Buddha then went to *Jeta* Park where he heard about the death of his two main disciples, namely *Sariputtra* and *Moggallana*

After this they moved from place to place for a while, until Buddha requested to go to *Pava* where he was approached by a goldsmith's son named *Cunda*. This person requested the honor of preparing meals for them. It is said that this person prepared meals but one of the preps was hog's mincemeat.

Early that morning, Buddha went to *Cunda's* house and told him to serve the hog's mincemeat only to Buddha and no other monk. *Cunda* agreed. Then Buddha said to him,

"If any of the meat is left over bury it in a hole. I do not see anyone except the Perfect One in this world, with its deities, *Mara* devils, Brahma creators, in this generation of humans with its monks and brahmins, with its princes and men, who could digest it if eaten."

Cunda agreed

This is not the first time. In fact, repeatedly, Buddha distinguished himself from everyone, even from the Vedic deities like Brahma, as being the Perfect One. Going through the literature I found not one single instance where he rated anyone else to be a Perfect One. However once when *Sariputtra* his main disciple wanted to declare Buddha to be the only Perfect one in all the eons of the creations, Buddha questioned *Sariputtra* as to the source of that information. This caused *Sariputta* not to make that declaration. I state this to clarify the idea that Buddha gave the impression that others, his disciples included, were his equal in any way. It is important to get this clear if one approached Buddha in the astral or spiritual existence. He acclaimed himself as *the* Perfect One not as *a* Perfect One. He singled himself even from the deities like Brahma.

In my dealings with Buddha in the astral world and also in the supernatural dimensions which transcend even the astral world, I find him to be humorous. Everything he says has humor in it, even the most serious opinions. But it is a humor which a materialistic person may find to be cutting and sarcastic. He is very caring and loving like an endearing father. I never had occasion to ask him about the *Perfect One* declaration, because usually in those places, I am one of his sons only. The relationship never has room for questioning. As rain does not fall in the Sahara Desert so in those places such questions never surface in the mind. One never thinks that one is or could be at any stage his equal or that one could develop his degree of perception and insight. The feeling one gets in his association is that if one can stay in it, one will not have to deal with adversity. One will have no responsibility, no stress, no problem. One will not have to face existence all alone as a limited infinitesimal being.

It is interesting how people have some other idea about Buddha, even Buddhist monks who live in established temples. Once in a temple in South Korea, when I asked about a large Buddha statue, a monk was quick to say that the statue had little meaning and that it was the monk's buddha nature which counted. This is amazing but in many Asian countries, even the monks have not read the literature carefully and have beliefs and opinions which the literature deny.

After Buddha ate *Cunda's* meal, a severe pain was felt. There was a flux of blood with violent pains. Buddha tolerated it without compliant, mindful and fully aware. Then he instructed *Ananda* that they should travel.

Thereafter Buddha instructed *Ananda* that in the future no one should blame *Cunda* for Buddha's death. He said that anyone who offered meal to monks, as *Cunda* did, had great merit for the result of it.

Anger Revisited

ध्यायतो विषयान्पुंसः
सङ्गस्तेषूपजायते ।
सङ्गात्संजायते कामः
कामात्क्रोधोऽभिजायते ॥२.६२॥

dhyāyato viṣayānpuṁsaḥ
saṅgasteṣūpajāyate
saṅgātsaṁjāyate kāmaḥ
kāmātkrodho'bhijāyate (Bhagavad Gita 2.62)

dhyāyato = dhyāyataḥ — considering; viṣayān — sensual objects; puṁsaḥ — a person; saṅgas — attachment; teṣūpajāyate = teṣu — in them + upajāyate — is born, is created; saṅgāt — from attachment; saṁjāyate — is born; kāmaḥ — craving; kāmāt — from craving; krodho = krodhah — anger; 'bhijāyate = abhijāyate — is derived

The act of considering sensual objects, creates in a person, an attachment to them. From attachment comes craving. From this craving anger is derived. (Bhagavad Gita 2.62)

क्रोधाद्भवति संमोहः
संमोहात्स्मृतिविभ्रमः ।
स्मृतिभ्रंशाद्बुद्धिनाशो
बुद्धिनाशात्प्रणश्यति ॥२.६३॥

krodhādbhavati saṁmohaḥ
saṁmohātsmṛtivibhramaḥ
smṛtibhraṁśādbuddhināśo
buddhināśātpraṇaśyati (2.63)

krodhād = krodhāt — from anger; bhavati — becomes (comes); saṁmohaḥ — delusion; saṁmohāt — from delusion; smṛti — conscience + vibhramaḥ — vanish; smṛtibhraṁśād = smṛtibhraṁśāt = smṛti — memory, judgement + bhraṁśāt — from fading away; buddhināśo = buddhināśaḥ = buddhi —discerning power + nāśaḥ — lose, affected; buddhināśāt = buddhi — discernment + nāśāt — from loss, from being affected; praṇaśyati — is ruined

From anger, comes delusion. From this delusion, the conscience vanishes. When he loses judgment, his discerning power fades away. Once the discernment is affected, he is ruined. (Bhagavad Gita 2.63)

रागद्वेषवियुक्तैस्तु
विषयानिन्द्रियैश्चरन् ।
आत्मवश्यैर्विधेयात्मा
प्रसादमधिगच्छति ॥२.६४॥

rāgadveṣaviyuktaistu
viṣayānindriyaiścaran ।
ā tmavaśyairvidheyātmā

prasādamadhigacchati (2.64)

rāgadveṣaviyuktais = rāga — cravings + dveṣa — disliking + viyuktaiḥ — discontinued; tu — if, however; viṣayān — attractive objects; indriyaiścaran = indriyaiḥ — by the senses + caran — interacting; ātmavaśyair = ātmavaśyaiḥ — disciplined person; vidheyātmā — a well-behaved person; prasādam — grace of providence; adhigacchati — gets

If, on the other hand, cravings and dislikings are continued and the attractive objects and senses continue interaction, a disciplined person who is usually well-behaved, gets the grace of providence. (Bhagavad Gita 2.64)

Please note my translation of the first verse again:

The act of considering sensual objects, creates in a person, an attachment to them. From attachment comes craving. From this craving anger is derived.

I went to the *Bhagavad Gita* this morning because of seeing a two-week old child in its anger when its mother did not hold it to her body. The infant screamed. His face beamed with anger. I concluded that anger is a perpetual reality. I decided to not listen to anyone who says that anger is unreal and that it is easy to eliminate it.

Looking at the Gita verse, anger is not an original anything. It is sourced in craving which is sourced in attachment which is turn is sourced in considering sensual objects.

This one statement of Krishna about the origins of anger runs directly parallel to what Buddha said about how to end suffering.

For anger to be unreal, we must prove that its source, which is considering sensual objects, is unreal. In the case of the infant, its mother was the sensual object. It developed an attachment to that. When that attachment developed further it became a craving, when the craving was not fulfilled, the craving energy converted into anger which the infant vehemently expressed as nuisance crying.

Anger then is a potential form of the contemplation of sensual objects. In the case of this infant, its mother is the sensual object. When the mind is barred access, its thinking or feeling desire for the mother converted into anger. This is like the difference between milk and yogurt. If it sits there, in time, milk will convert into yogurt. If a sensual object is considered, thought about or imaged in the mind, if no access is granted to the object, there is the likelihood that the consideration energy will convert into anger.

If anger is superficial as some people suggests, then how is the infant to control it, or is it that adults only are capable of that. Can the infant from within its mind cease the buildup of attachment which later converts in anger when the attachment is not fulfilled.

Nutrition Bliss Micro-Droplets

Recently due to practicing to lift nutrition bliss micro-droplets, I did not file reports. Events occur. Progress is made. However, it is abstract, as if nothing happened. It is hard to verbalize. I enter no man's land, a place where novices would not like to be and cannot appreciate. They want sensational events. They cannot make an observation unless it is obvious or objective.

Nature trained us to perceive sensations. When we become yogis, we have that need even though we try to transfer it to what is transcendental. Unfortunately, much of what is subtle is slight or non-sensational. We miss much because many events in meditation are not obvious and yield no pleasure.

Currently I practice a project for Lahiri. It consists of lifting the micro-droplets of nutrition energy from digested food. This energy has a bliss aspect which is not intense and which can hardly be detected. If I directed students to do this, they would become discouraged because the bliss aspect is slight as to be non-existence to a person who can only sense concentrated energy.

If you ride in an oxcart, it will rattle as you travel on a gravel road. You will not hear earth tremors. You will not feel them. It will be to you that they do not occur but you will feel the shaking and bumpy ride of the oxcart as something you are accustomed to.

If there is an earthquake however you will be aware of that and will take notice. Novices in yoga miss everything which is subtle and abstract but in the advanced stages that must be meticulously noted.

I reported to Lahiri, that in the early morning the micro-droplets of nutrition energy have more concentration and are larger; while in the afternoon, they seem diluted. It will be difficult for students to use this method because they are conditioned to be observant of sensational experiences. They do not appreciate events which lack excitement.

Students dislike yoga practice when they cannot get an excitement from it which matches, or rivals, whatever excitement they got from physical nature, in whatever way and in whatever activity, they engaged in.

To lift the nutrition bliss micro-droplets, one must first get rid of kundalini by drawing it into the brain on a consistent basis so that its energy is longer lodged at the *muladhara* base chakra. Kundalini acts as a magnet, pulling the nutrition energy. Once it is moved from the base chakra, that energy will float freely instead of having a downward movement.

Missing from the energy as well will be the reproductive charge which it usually got by the original design of the psyche. This will cause that nutrition bliss energy to have a mild bliss charge which does not have the lust potential in it. The yogi must be accustomed to this change in the energy and must learn to be satisfied with this new configuration.

The method of pulling the nutrition bliss micro-droplets is *kapalabhati/bhastrika pranayama*.

Part 3

Buddha: Women in the Sanga

Initially there were no women in the Sanga, the association of monks which Buddha created. The cultural at the time was that women were part of the family life. Thus, persons who joined Buddha were considered to be going away from the domestic situation which means leaving aside their ancestry, property and family. Family meant associating with women, children and elderly persons.

Buddha's aunt, *Gotami,* is the one who first went to Buddha to ask that women be awarded monk status. Buddha refused to hear anything of it. He asked his aunt not to say anything about it. This aunt was his wet nurse, as the sister of his mother who passed soon after Buddha's birth.

Once she realized that he was determined not to include women, she approached Buddha's personal assistant monk who was also a relative of his. This was *Ananda*. After *Ananda* heard what happened, he took it upon himself to request that women be allowed to take monastic vows.

At first Buddha told *Ananda* to back off but then as *Ananda* persisted, Buddha gave permission saying that the sanga would last for one thousand years if there were only males but only five hundred years if females were allowed.

Soon after women were allowed in the sanga, but with restrictions. For instance, they had to bow to any male. Once *Gotami* asked Buddha that new male monks should bow to female nuns who were elderly and were senior. Buddha would have none of it. He stressed that any and every female monk was to bow to any and every male monk regardless of the relative time of practice of either.

In terms of what happens today, these stipulations were brutal. However, in the culture of the time in India, this was normal. For us to get a better idea of what really happened, there is a discourse in the *Life of The Buddha* by *Nanamoli Bhikkhu*, where it is explained that at the end of his life, when he was questioned about the rules for women in the sanga, regarding how the male monks should treat the nuns, Buddha said,

"Do not see them *Ananda*."

Ananda pressed on, asking that if the nuns were seen anyway, how should they be treated.

Buddha stated:

"Do not speak to them *Ananda*."

Ananda then pressed on again saying,

"Lord, say that we do address them, then how should we treat them?"

Buddha stated:

"Mindfulness should be maintained."

There is a one small detail from which we may cull an important point which is that the word for Lord usually given is *Bhagavan*.

But that is a Sanskrit term which is used frequently in books like the *Bhagavad Gita* which means Lord or personGod.

If his teachings are non-theistic, we wonder why Buddha was addressed in that way. Why did he not object to being addressed in that way? What was the meaning of that word for the people who used it?

Memory - Bodies

The two lower bodies are:

- physical *(deha, sharira)*
- subtle *(sukshma sharira)*

These systems run parallel.

coreSelf is different.

It uses those bodies and relies on their respective abilities to retain or not to retain memory.

coreSelf *(atma)* for all it is, cannot transmigrate without using the subtle body.

It does not have the ability to do so independently.

Memory is not transferred from the body to the soul after death.

Memory which is in the physical system as brain neuron information, stays with the physical body at death. It cannot be extracted ever.

Memory which is in the subtle body as impressions *(samskaras)* goes with that body at the death of the physical one. After death, the self in the subtle body may or may not have access to those memories which exist side by side with it in the subtle body.

The soul does not have free access to memory, or we would not forget past lives and be ignorant of them when we assume an embryo.

Naad Meditation: *Dharana/Dhyana*

A few days ago, Lahiri explained that naad resonance should be a waiting room for the students, the place where the students go in the psyche to wait for the *chit akash* sky of consciousness to open. The student does not have to stare between the eyebrows unless that activity is non-tiresome and relaxing. If it is strenuous, the student should simply wait in the naad sound for the mind-sky environment at the frontal part of the subtle head to change in quality, where it becomes a transcendental energy which has an uplifting feel to it.

Naad meditation has various stages, some of which he explained. He spoke of two distinct features:

- *dharana* naad
- *dhyana* naad

These use the terms of Patanjali for the sixth and seventh stages of yoga but these are applications of those stages to naad listening saturation. To better understand, the student should learn the difference between the two.

The best way to understand this is to study what happens when one falls asleep. In some sleep approaches, the person wants to sleep even though the body has no interest in resting. The person then goes to a dark quiet place, reclines and closes the eyelids. Then there may or may not be a sleeping condition. That is like *dharana* naad. It is deliberately done by the person where he locates the naad sound and then puts his interest into it. He may or may not continually focus his interest. Just as when trying to fall asleep, a person may find that his mind does not relax, so sometimes when a person deliberately tries to go into naad, he goes in for a split-second and finds himself relocated out of naad time and time again. This is the *dharana* phase. It requires effort to hold the self in naad, and even with effort the self may fail to remain in naad once the sound is contacted.

The second phase which is *dhyana* is comparable to when a person wants or does not want to fall asleep but he sits up. He is not reclined. He finds that he falls sleep even from a sitting position. He tries to sit up, as for instance someone who waits at a train station on a bench, and who has to guard the baggage from thieves. Even though he wants to be alert, he finds that he falls asleep even from a sitting position. When a student finds that in meditation, he finds his interest in the naad sound even though he did not deliberately place it there or even if he did deliberately do it, then that is *dhyana* naad. The student realizes that besides his willpower and desire, some other force causes his interest to be in naad. Even when he loses interest, still he finds that he is in naad being held there by another force besides his desire and willpower.

Lahiri said that a student should not go into meditation feeling that naad is omni-directional. One should be open minded and find the location nodes of naad and adhere oneself to the most forceful, most pronounced one.

In summary, the difference between *dharana* and *dhyana* naad is that in *dhyana* naad the student remains in naad without effort on his/her part, while in *dharana* naad the student only remains in naad by a sustained effort. Usually, a student cannot access the *chit akash* sky of consciousness from a *dharana* naad because that is not stable. It consists of being in naad and then being thrown out of naad, then making the effort to be in naad and then being hurled from it again. From that erratic condition, one cannot access the *chit akash*.

In contrast, in *dhyana* naad, the student makes no effort. In that stage the student finds himself/herself in naad, being held there by some other force. Because no effort is required that is a stable state from which access to *chit akash* may be granted.

Whenever there is *dhyana* naad, the student should regard it as being in a waiting room. The student should wait for the *chit akash* to open in the frontal part of the subtle head.

Naad is usually heard in the back of the subtle head. Irrespective of where it is heard, there should be a node or concentration of it in the resonance. The student enters or goes as close as possible to it.

The method of kriya yogis to stare at the center of the eyebrows should be practiced without strain or pin point focus even. The student should focus forward waiting for the *chit akash* to be available. From this side of existence, it cannot be grasped. It cannot be pried. Any effort to force it may delay access.

Since *dharana* naad is useless for causing *chit akash* sky of consciousness to open, it may be concluded that it should not be practiced. However, that is not the case.

Students who have no affinity for naad, who do not find themselves in naad as soon as they sit to meditate, have much to benefit by doing *dharana* naad. That is their method of eventually being graced with natural attraction to naad. After such a student deliberately and painstakingly focused on naad for days, weeks, months or years, he/she will find that *dhyana* natural focus in naad occurs spontaneously.

In addition, even those fortunate persons who easily go into *dhyana* spontaneous naad, should know how to do *dharana* naad because there will be times when naad is non-spontaneous. During those meditations, the student should apply *dharana* deliberate focus on naad.

Buddha: Deities

It is amazing in a way how a system of realization like Buddha's which at a glance seems to be nihilistic and atheistic, has so much information about deities and heavens.

What did Buddha think about deities?

Did he describe that there were heavens and hells hereafter?

On the last day of his life, Buddha was on the move. He was accompanied by an assistant, *Ananda*. They went to a place called *Kusinara*. There Buddha instructed *Ananda* to make a couch between two *Sala* trees. The instruction was that the couch was to be positioned with the head of the bed to the north.

Was Buddha superstitious because in the Vedic literature there is much about sleeping with the head to the north? That was part of the Vedic belief of the time. *Ananda* got the couch made between the *Sala* trees. Buddha reclined there in the lion's sleeping pose on his right side with one foot overlapping the other. He was mindful and aware.

The twin trees were littered with flowers even though it was not the season. The text says that these trees scattered its blossoms over the Blessed One out of veneration for him. In addition, heavenly *mandarava* and heavenly sandalwood powder fell from the sky and were scattered and sprinkled and shrew over him out of veneration. Heavenly music played and heavenly songs were sung in the sky out of veneration for him. This is all related in detail in *"The Life of The Buddha"* by *Nanamoli Bhikkhu*.

Buddha told *Ananda* that these natural and supernatural offerings were not the proper way to honor a Perfect Person. He said that a male monk, a female monk and the lay followers should honor him by living according to the *Dharma*. Incidentally this use of the Sanskrit term *dharma* does not mean righteous life style according to the Vedic definitions. It means the method of conduct and austerity which was recommended by Buddha.

What happened next is strange. There was a monk named *Upavana* who fanned Buddha. Buddha summarily dismissed the junior monk saying to him bluntly,

"Go away *Bhikkhu*. Do not stand before me."

Ananda noticed what happened. He felt sorry for the dismissed monk. *Ananda* thought in his mind,

"The venerable *Upavana* long served the Blessed One, fanning him. Now the Blessed One chased him away at this last period of the Blessed One's life."

Ananda then went to Buddha and questioned about it.

The reply is amazing:

Buddha said:

"*Ananda*, most of the deities from the ten world systems came to see the Perfect One. For twelve leagues around the *Sala* tree grove there is not a place the size of the pricking of a horse-hair's tip not occupied by deities. They said in protest,

"We came from afar to see the Perfect One. Every now and then Perfect Ones arise in the world, accomplished and enlightened. Tonight is the last watch. The Perfect one's attainment of final *Nibbana* will take place. This eminent *bhikkhu* stands in front of the Blessed One obstructing us so that at the last moment we will not see the Perfect One."

"These Deities were protesting *Ananda*."

Ananda then said,

"But Lord, which deities does the Blessed One have in mind."

Buddha mentioned three types of deities:

- Those who are percipient of earth in space
- Those who are percipient of earth in earth
- Those who are free from lust

There were other occasions when Buddha mentioned the presence of other types of deities.

Buddha: Heavens/Hells

In conversations, Buddha mentioned both heavens and hells. He rarely mentioned hells but on occasion he would describe a hell, which on the basis of criminal acts, someone may transfer to after leaving the body.

Heavens were mentioned frequently. Bodhisattvas were said to come from the *Tushita* heaven, the paradise for the content living entities. The Sanskrit word *tosha* has a prefix as *santosha*, which means contentment.

In his notes in the book entitled *"The Life of The Buddha," Nanamoli Bhikkhu* wrote that the cosmology of time describes many heavens, notably six paradises in which the pleasures of the senses are enjoyed, and above those there are twelve Brahma heavens or worlds of high divinity, where consciousness is quite purified of present lust, though not of future potentiality for it, and where (according to the commentary), material form is rarefied by absence of the three senses of smell, taste and bodily touch and of sex.

Beyond these are four formless states of infinity where all perceptions of material form and of difference are transcended. These are listed as:

- infinity of space
- infinity of consciousness
- nothingness
- reduced perception of nothingness

Buddha stated that rebirth in any of these is impermanent and is followed by renewed birth unless *nibbana*, the Unformed, is attained

In the Brahma heavens, there are the pure abodes which are the higher part of those realms. These are inhabited by what Buddha termed to be the non-returners, who are reborn there at their physical death, and who live there without returning to any other world till they attain final *nibbana*.

Question is:

Does this tally with the Vedic information from the Puranas or from even the *Mahabharata*?

The other question which only the New Age experts can answer is this:

If there are no heavens and everything besides physical existence is imagination, what is Buddha's description of these realms? There were many incidences where after a monk died, Buddha would describe that the person transfered to a heaven.

Was it all in Buddha's mind?

In his doctrine of *anatta* (Sanskrit *anatma*) where it is reported that Buddha established that there is no self, how is that idea reconciled with his description of a certain monk going to a heaven.

If there is no self or atma, how is that self transfered to another dimension?

Some Buddhist monks explain the paradox of no-self by stating that Buddha was practical and spoke as we conventionally do. However, that explanation avoids the contradiction.

The biggest part of the paradox of no-self is that after he reached enlightenment, the person who extolled it distinguished himself from others. If I have no self, it makes no sense that I should distinguish myself as being the only this or the first this in the history of the world.

Kundalini Control

Today Lahiri informed me about the nutrition situation, saying that it is the last frontier for yogis. That is why it was necessary to do *haṭha* yoga as that was defined by *Gorakshnatha Mahayogin*.

As nature would have it the nutritional energy in the body is pulled from the intestines. This gives a constant feed of energy to the body. It mixes with the air energy from the lungs. For high power activities, hormones are manufactured by special glands. This concentrated energy is used to power certain physical and psychological operations.

The system operates on the principle of using gravity to pull the nutrients into the reproduction apparatus for creating a hormone concentrate which is used to reproduce more bodies and to operate other functions.

When the yogi sets out to change this system, he is in for a tough fight. Nature resists all changes it did not plan on creating. The yogi should study the system and figure a way to change it toward the objectives of yoga. Since this requires special intelligence and insight, it took a person like *Gorakshnath* to introduce it. People like Patanjali and *Swatmarama* wrote about it. They give hints for the accomplishment.

At first, one should endeavor with nature, learning about it and making small changes here and there. Eventually as one gets some control, one sees that a major overhaul is necessary, a complete redesign. Every step of the way effort must be made because nature is resistant to any change which is not coded into its program.

The yogi begins by tracking the nutrients to see how they are extracted, where they are stored and distributed and which organs take and concentrate them even further.

At first with *pranayama* breath infusion, the student must work with the system as it is, just as a horseman at first must ride a horse, the way the creature is inclined to trot and sprint. The yogi must utilize the system by infusing air into the lungs, forcing that air through the navel chakra, mixing that forced energy with the reproductive hormones and then arcing that to the *muladhara* base chakra.

Once breath energy is fused to the kundalini at the base chakra, the yogi should apply the locks so that kundalini goes through the recommended route upwards through the *sushumna* central spinal passage into the head of the subtle body.

When this is done consistently there will be the advantage of first getting used to fusing with kundalini and riding with it just the way a horseman gets familiar with a wild horse. As the horse will become more and more responsive to the horseman, so kundalini will cooperate with the yogi but only to a certain extent.

Just as there is a limit to what the horseman can do with a horse which is subjugated, so there is a limit to what the yogi can do with the kundalini even after long practice.

Once the *sushumna* central spinal passage is permanently cleared of dense astral energy, the yogi will find that there is no sensational arousal of kundalini through the spine, because it will radiate its energy through the central passage continuously. Because there will be no dense astral energy in the central passage, it will not hold a charge which is restricted to the base chakra.

At that stage of practice, the yogi will be advised to deal with the nutritional energy, to lift it before it is charged by the hormone producing glands. This means that the lust charge which the reproductive hormones usually have, will not be there, because the yogi will lift the nutrition energy before it goes to the reproductive glands. This will produce a lightness, a lack of heavy energy at the reproductive chakra, which will in turn cause energy from the thighs to float away from the groin area.

This floating energy will be evaporated or lifted to mix with the infused fresh air, creating a bliss aspect force that is lust-free.

Anatta - Anatma - No-Self

I repeatedly heard the term buddha-nature as the aim of a person who wants to be enlightened like *Shakyamuni* (*Gautam* Buddha). However, definitions of the terms are hard to come by even in the Buddhist texts.

In the *Comprehensive Manual of Abhidhamma*, which is based on the original Buddhist scriptures, there is a description of Buddha which is interesting (page 24):

Buddha is called the fully Enlightened One because he is the one who fully understood the ultimate nature of all phenomena both in their particular and universal characters. The term *sammasambuddha* implies the direct knowledge of all realities, gained without help from a teacher.

The Buddha is called the peerless one *(atula)* because his qualities and attributes cannot be matched by any other being. Though all Arahants possess the distinguished qualities of morality concentration and wisdom sufficient to result in liberation, none possess the innumerable and immeasurable virtues with which a supreme Buddha is fully endowed, the ten *Tathagata* powers of knowledge, the four grounds of self-confidence, the attainment of great compassion and the unobstructed knowledge of omniscience. Hence the Buddha is without peer among all sentient beings.

As it is said:

There is one person, *bhikkhus*, who is unique, without a peer, without counterpart, incomparable, unequalled, matchless, unrivalled, the best of humans -- the *Tathagata*, the Arahant, the Fully Enlightened One.

On reading this I can see no possibility, where a Buddhist can explain that anyone is or can be the equivalent of Buddha. Buddha's exclusiveness is either totally false, and is said as superficial praise for a leading ascetic or no one can attain a status that is like this individual.

Which is it?

The other problem with this is that it kills the very idea that Buddhism says is absolute, which is that of *anatta (anatma)* non-self; that there is no self.

If there is no self why is there this particular someone which the sect itself highlights.

The Pali word *sambuddha* is from the same in Sanskrit. With the *sam* prefix, it means whatever Buddha is to a complete degree. It reads the complete or total Buddha. That excludes others. Unless it is a superficial title as is frequently used in the Vedic literature, where the leader is praised as this and that, just as a formality and in some cases as flattery.

In Buddha's case it was neither, because he himself insisted that he was to be addressed like this. Initially just after his Enlightenment after he was convinced by the Brahma deity to teach the method which he pioneered,

Buddha on approaching some ascetics whom he used to practice with, chastised them for addressing him as a friend and said that he was the fully Enlightened One who should be given special respect.

Once his chief disciple, Sariputta, explained to another monk, that Buddha was special because he realized everything by himself without a teacher, and because no one else can realize those things without Buddha's help.

If we are potentially Buddha, why do we need his help?

Whatever has the same potentially should do exactly the same as the first reference.

Here we are told that even though they are enlightened beings, Arahants, still this person has the complete enlightenment which no other enlightened being may have. What is the meaning of no-self if this Buddha is distinguished?

How can there be a supreme person, or a person who excels others, if there are no selves, even if such selves will disappear after the enlightenment or after the death of the body used by the illusion-self?

If there is no-self, there must be admitted that in conventional usage, there is an illusion-self before enlightenment. How is it that the illusion-self needs to be enlightened just so it can be liberated so that it can become a no-self?

Imagine that you are an illusion. You feel you have a self but actually you have no-self. Then as the illusion-self you need to work to become enlightened to realize that you are a no-self. Then once you become enlightened, you, as the illusion-self, will vanish to what or to where?

To top it off, just before your death in the life when you would be fully enlightened, I want to remind you because after that death I cannot reach you because you as the illusion-self will be gone forever, I want to remind you that there was this one person who was unique, without a peer, without counterpart, incomparable, unequalled, matchless, unrivalled, the best of humans.

That is the last thing I request you to think of just a moment before your enlightened-self passes from the last physical body.

Naad/Third-Eye Kriya

This morning during meditation Lahiri showed a kriya technique which is secret. Yesterday I did a commentary on a verse from the *Hatha Yoga Pradipika*, chapter 4 text 39, which I translated.

तारे जयोतिष्हि संयोज्य किञ्चिदुन्नमयेद्भ्रुवौ ।
पूर्व - योगं मनो युञ्जन्नुन्मनी - कारकः क्षणात् ॥ ३९ ॥

tāre jyotiṣhi saṁyojya kiñcidunnamayedbhruvau |
pūrva–yogaṁ mano yuñjann unmanī–kārakaḥ kṣaṇāt

tāre – radiant, jyotiṣhi – spiritual light, saṁyojya – linking focus, kiñcid = kiñcid = a little, unnamayed = unnamayet = should raise, bhruvau – visual focus between the eyebrows, pūrva – as before, yogaṁ – yogic state, mano = manaḥ = mind, yuñjann = yuñjan = practicing, unmani – devoid of ordinary mental content, kārakaḥ – producer, kṣaṇāt – instantly

Applying the linking focus on the radiant spiritual light and raising the visual focus to between the eyebrows, with the mind in the yogic state as mentioned before, this will instantaneously produce a state devoid of ordinary mental content. (Kundalini Hatha Yoga Pradipika 4.39)

There are a series of verses which deal with naad and focus on supernatural or spiritual light during meditation. In writing commentaries, one must draw from one's experience. One should avoid speculating or guessing. For some commentaries where I am not currently experienced in the methods, I get help from an astral yogaGuru.

In terms of this practice, it appears that there is much misleading, speculative information. Some was experienced by meditators but in a flash which did not last but for a few moments. However, the yoga process is definite.

Some students feel that if they drop the false ego, sit and be positive about everything, have an elevated self-esteem, rate themselves as being as good as any other yogi, know that they are potentially God, then they do not have to do the austerities and rigors of ancient yogis. They can attain this by the flick of willpower.

Lahiri showed a positional kriya for third eye meditation. He said that because of misinformation they receive from senior teachers and books, most students do this incorrectly.

To understand what he showed, I must explain that I did the following before this instruction was given:

- I had the minimum physical, mental and emotional non-yogic association.
- I did a full session of *kapalabhati/bhastrika pranayama* breath infusion which lasted for fifty minutes. I used a blind fold and kept infusing air into various parts of the body with kundalini rising as a bliss energy in various parts. I used various postures and mudras (body/hand gestures and jerk movements).

- Assuming an easy sitting posture and using a blindfold, I sat to meditate where immediately, I as the coreSelf in the head of the subtle body, was located in naad with no special effort to link into or to emerge into it. Naad was at the back of the subtle head. The moment I sat with the blindfold, I discovered myself to be with naad. As soon as I realized I listened. Naad sound resonance increased in frequency. It was heard more distinctly.

Lahiri took control and positioned me smack center in the back of the head with naad behind and to the sides. He said to look forward but not to move to the front as I looked. I found that when I looked there was a gap passage from where I was located in naad to the center of the eyebrows. He said that was the process.

The gap passage was there like an oval-slit tunnel. It existed there. It was not visualized and did not depend on my mental input. I let my attention flow through it to reach the center of the eyebrows. In the distance beyond the center of the eyebrows was *chit akash* sky of consciousness but I did not reach it.

At that point Lahiri left. I broke from the meditation and made notes. It is important to know that the idealess imageless state of the mind with the naad sound was due to the breath infusion effects on the subtle body (*sukshma sharira*). If I had not done that, this meditation would not have begun with emergence into naad sound. Breath infusion is the magic formulae, the active ingredient in this process. It saves hours of futile efforts, or illusory visualizations, when doing meditation.

Buddha: Teacher of Supernatural People

Heavenly worlds cannot be an illusion in Buddhism unless the earth is also an illusion as well as whatever Buddha was, did or said. In the "*Comprehensive Manual of Abhidhamma*" by *Bhikku Bodhi,* there is information about the *Tavatimsa* heaven. This is the highest of the heavens which are ruled by *Sakka*. This is directly adapted from the Vedic pantheon of deities and their corresponding worlds, where *Tavatimsa* is the *Swargaloka* heavenly place and *Sakka* is *Shakra* or Indra, the supernatural being who governs those celestial locales.

Buddha repeatedly mentioned heavens and hells, astral places of great comfort and horrible discomfort. There is information about him teaching people in the heavenly places while he used the physical body on earth, teaching humans.

In the book on page 10, the writer explained that according to the tradition given in the Pali commentaries, Buddha did not teach the *Abhidhamma* to his disciples but to the *devas* or gods in the *Tavatimsa* heaven, where he was seated on the *Pandukambala* stone at the foot of the *Paricchattaka* tree, for the three months of rains he taught the devas from the ten thousand world systems.

Buddha made the chief recipient of this teaching, to be his deceased mother, *Mahamaya-devi*, who was reborn in that world as a goddess *(devi)*. The reason given for his teaching the *Abhidhamma* there, was that for a complete grasp of the information it has to be given to a single audience for the time of the rainy season of three *months*. Only *devas* and Brahma deities could receive it in unbroken continuity, for only they could remain in one posture for that length of time.

During the discourse however, to sustain his earth body, Buddha descended each day to the human world to go on alms round in the Northern *Uttarakuru*. After collecting food, he would go to the shore of *Anotatta* Lake to take a meal. Then the elder disciple *Sariputta* would meet Buddha there and get a synopsis of what was told to the *devas* for that sitting of Buddha.

The Sanskrit for *Paricchattaka* is *Parijata* which is a jasmine flowering tree which is said to grow only in the heavenly place of the Indra *devata*. In fact, it is mentioned in the story of the life of Krishna in the Srimad Bhagavatam, where a consort of Krishna named *Satyabhama* asked Krishna to bring it to the earth. Supposedly Indra, the lord of those heavenly places objected. He was intimidated by Krishna who took the plant and brought it to Krishna's capital city, Dwaraka.

It is interesting too that Buddha's mother who died soon after his birth, took an appearance in the heavenly world of Indra, because that is not a birth as a baby as we humans do. It is rather just an appearance in a heavenly body in that celestial world. Elsewhere it is said that this woman came from the *Tushita* heaven before her earthly birth as Buddha's mother but that *Tushita* place is higher than this *Swarga Tavatimsa* place. It may be that she returned to the *Tushita* place but descended to the *Swarga* place, to hear what Buddha explained. As elsewhere some persons regretted being in the heavenly place and not having human bodies as disciples of Buddha who could benefit from his association on earth.

When Buddha first achieved enlightenment, he regretted the death of some ascetics whom he knew before and whom he felt could become liberated quickly if they knew the method he discovered. He felt sorry that they passed before he reached enlightenment and were not present on the earth to get his instructions.

The hereafter is so hairy scary, shifty, and flimsy, that even though most of it is higher than the earth place, the stability of the physical body gives the advantage of steadiness of form for some years. If one can apply this physical body to the right method, one could surely attain liberation or at least set into the subtle body, the strong tendency to seek liberation wherever it may be.

The issue of having no-self *(anatta, anatma)* comes up again. As to how a person who has no self could go to one location, even to an abstract place, a heaven, which to many people today does not exist except in the mind, and then come back to his earth body and then return to that heavenly location, meet people, teach them a detailed and very abstract system of meditation research, which the average Buddhist today cannot apply because of it subtlety.

If there is no self why is one self teaching another, even another who is an earthly body or another who is a heavenly body. Why would Buddha's deceased mother get involved if she was a no-self.

Buddhism versus Patanjali: Seer/No-Seer

On a close examination, instead of a superficial assessment, I find that many Eastern doctrines and philosophies run contrary to one another. Practically every culture has a food mix, where many different foods are cooked together to make a blend which is neither this nor that. In the Western countries there is this trend which runs on and on, which is to label it all as being the same, and to mix it and serve it as Oneness.

In Patanjali yoga sutras, there is a seer and there is perception equipment used by the seer. The seer is supposed to split from the perception equipment so that it can realize itself and curb the affiliation with the equipment.

In Buddhism this is not so. For clarification *Bhikkhu Bodhi* in his "*Comprehensive Manual of Abhidhamma*" (page 27), wrote that in relation to the word *citta*, the Buddhist thinkers point out that it is not a self that performs the act of cognition but *citta* or consciousness. This *citta*, he wrote, is nothing other than the act of cognizing, and that act is necessarily impermanent, marked by rise and fall. He stated further that in the case of *citta*, its characteristic is the knowing of an object [*vijanana* - (Sanskrit *vijnana*)]

This is a solid statement to support the idea of no-self, *anatta, anatma*.

However, Patanjali gives the converse view. To put these philosophies together in the Oneness concept shows ignorance of the ideas and a tendency to distort and misuse them to support totally different concepts.

Here are some verses from Patanjali.

परिणामैकत्वाद्वस्तुतत्त्वम् ॥१४॥

pariṇāma ekatvāt vastutattvam

pariṇāma – transformation, change; ekatvāt – singleness, uniqueness; vastu – object; tattvam – essence, actual composition.

The actual composition of an object is based on the uniqueness of the transformation. (Yoga Sutra 4.14)

वस्तुसाम्ये चित्तभेदात्तयोर्विभक्तः पन्थाः ॥१५॥

vastusāmye cittabhedāt tayoḥ vibhaktaḥ panthāḥ

vastu – object; sāmye – in the same; citta – mento-emotional energy; bhedāt – from the difference; tayoḥ – of these two; vibhaktaḥ – separated, divided; panthāḥ – ways of viewing, prejudices.

Because of a difference in the mento-emotional energy of two persons, separate prejudices manifest in their viewing of the very same object. (Yoga Sutra 4.15)

न चैकचित्ततन्त्रं वस्तु तदप्रमाणकं तदा किं स्यात्॥१६॥

na ca ekacitta tantraṁ ced vastu
tat apramāṇakaṁ tadā kiṁ syāt

na – not, nor; ca – and; eka – one; citta – mento-emotional perception; tantraṁ – dependent; ced = cet – if, otherwise; vastu – object; tat – that; apramāṇakaṁ – not being observed; tadā – then; kiṁ – what; syāt – would occur.

An object is not dependent on one person's mento-emotional perception. Otherwise, what would happen if it were not being perceived by that person? (Yoga Sutra 4.16)

तदुपरागापेक्षित्वाच्चित्तस्य वस्तु ज्ञाताज्ञातम्॥१७॥

taduparāga apekṣitvāt cittasya vastu jñāta ajñātam

tad = tat – that; uparāga – color, mood; apekṣitvāt – from the expectation; cittasya – of the mento-emotional energy; vastu – object; jñāta – known; ajñātam – unknown.

An object is known or unknown, all depending on the mood and expectation of the particular mento-emotional energy of the person in reference to it. (Yoga Sutra 4.17)

सदा ज्ञाताश्चित्तवृत्तयस्तत्प्रभोः पुरुषस्यापरिणामित्वात्॥१८॥

sadā jñātāḥ cittavṛttayaḥ tatprabhoḥ
puruṣasya apariṇāmitvāt

sadā – always; jñātāḥ – known; citta – mento-emotional energy; vṛttayaḥ – the operations; tat – that; prabhoḥ – of the governor; puruṣasya – of the spirit; apariṇāmitvāt – due to changelessness.

The operations of the mento-emotional energy are always known to that governor because of the changelessness of that spirit. (Yoga Sutra 4.18)

न तत्स्वाभासं दृश्यत्वात्॥१९॥

na tat svābhāsaṁ dṛśyatvāt

na – not; tat – that; svābhāsaṁ – self-illuminative; dṛśyatvāt – for it is due to being something to be perceived.

That mento-emotional energy is not self-illuminative for it is rather only capable of being perceived. (Yoga Sutra 4.19)

एकसमये चोभयानवधारणम्॥२०॥

ekasamaye ca ubhaya anavadhāraṇam

ekasamaye – at the same time; ca – and; ubhaya – both; anavadhāraṇam – of what cannot focus.

It cannot execute the focus of both at the same time. (Yoga Sutra 4.20)

चित्तान्तरदृश्ये बुद्धिबुद्धेरतिप्रसङ्गः स्मृतिसङ्करश्च॥२१॥

cittāntaradṛśye buddhibuddheḥ
atiprasaṅgaḥ smṛtisaṅkaraḥ ca

cittāntara – dṛśye = citta – mento-emotional energy + antara – another person + dṛśye – in the perception of; buddhi-buddher = buddhi – the intellect organ + buddheḥ – of the intellect organ; atiprasaṅgaḥ – absurd argument, unwarranted stretching of a rule or argument; smṛti – memory; saṅkaraḥ – confusion; ca – and.

In the perception of mento-emotional energy by another such energy, there would be an intellect perceiving another intellect independently. (Yoga Sutra 4.21)

चितेरप्रतिसङ्क्रमायास्तदाकारापत्तौ स्वबुद्धिसंवेदनम्॥२२॥

citeḥ apratisaṁkramāyāḥ tadākārāpattau svabuddhisaṁvedanam

citeḥ – of the spirit; apratisaṁkramāyāḥ – not moving from one position to another; tad – tat – that; ākāra – form, aspect; āpattau – turning into, changing, assuming; sva – itself, oneself; buddhi – intellect organ; saṁvedanam – perception.

The perception of its own intellect occurs when it assumes that form in which there is no movement from one operation to another. (Yoga Sutra 4.22)

द्रष्टृदृश्योपरक्तं चित्तं सर्वार्थम्॥२३॥

draṣṭṛ dṛśya uparaktaṁ cittaṁ sarvārtham

draṣṭṛ - the perceiver; dṛśya – the perceived; uparaktaṁ – prejudiced; cittaṁ – mento-emotional energy; sarvārtham - what is all-evaluating.

The mento-emotional energy which is prejudiced by the perceiver and the perceived, is all-evaluating. (Yoga Sutra 4.23)

तदसङ्ख्येयवासनाभिश्चित्रमपि परार्थं संहत्यकारित्वात्॥२४॥

tat asaṅkhyeya vāsanābhiḥ citram
api parārthaṁ saṁhatyakāritvāt

tat – that; asaṅkhyeya – innumerable; vāsanābhiḥ – subtle impressions; citram – diversified; api – even, although; parārthaṁ – for another's sake; saṁhatya – because of it; kāritvāt – activity, force, factor.

Although the mento-emotional energy is diversified by innumerable subtle impressions, it acts for the sake of another power because of its proximity to that other factor. (Yoga Sutra 4.24)

Patanjali feels that the idea of no-self, no objective individual who uses the *citta* for special cognizing, is absurd, especially if the view is that the *citta* can perceive on its own.

He is diametrically opposed to the Buddhist view.

The question then is:

Which is the fact?

While *Bhikkhu Bodhi* established that the Buddhist thinkers proved that it is not a self that performs the act of cognition but *citta* or consciousness, Patanjali stated that the *citta* or mento-emotional energy is diversified by innumerable subtle impressions, and it acts for the sake of another power because of its proximity to that other factor. That other power is the *atma* or self which the Buddhist doctrine vehemently denies.

This leads to the question as to what becomes liberated or what attains *nibbana (nirvana)* in the Buddhist doctrine?

Buddhism: Liberation When?

There are four high levels of attainment mentioned by Buddha which are given by *Bhikkhu Bodhi* in the book *"Comprehensive Manual of Abhidhamma."*

These are:

- Stream-Entry
- Once-Returning
- Non-Returning
- Arhantship

The first of **stream entry** applies to someone who entered the path given by Buddha and who must complete the process. The term stream (*sota* in Pali) refers to the Noble Eightfold Path.

The stream-entry monk is one who cannot turn back and must become liberated because of his destiny after accepting the path. A person who got the experience of stream entry is assured of reaching final deliverance in a maximum of seven lives and of never being reborn in any of the woeful planes of existence.

In this path three fetters are cut off which are:

- personality view or wrong views of the self
- doubt about the Triple Gem (the Buddha, the *Dhamma* and the *Sangha*)
- clinging to rites and ceremonies in the belief that they lead to liberation

It also cuts off: greed, hatred and delusions which are strong enough to lead to a sub-human rebirth

The second level of **once returning** attenuates the grosser forms of sensual desire and ill will. The person who reached this stage will be reborn in this world at most one more time before attaining liberation,

The person on the third level of **non-returning**, will never again be reborn in the sensuous plane. If that person does not reach Arahantship in the same lifetime, he will be reborn in the fine-material world (subtle existence) and there attain the goal. This course cuts off the fetters of sensual desires, ill will and hate.

The fourth level of **Arhantship** is a fully liberated person who destroyed the enemy consisting of the defilements. This is the destruction of the five subtle fetters of desire for fine-material and immaterial existence, conceit, restlessness and ignorance

Regarding Stream-entry, the Sanskrit is *srotya* (*sota* - Pali). The suggestion is that this person entered the flowing stream of the Noble Eightfold Path and will flow in it till the end, just as a river, with no reversal, keeps flowing until it reaches the sea.

This four-tiered categorization of serious monks whom Buddha is committed to could be listed in this way:

- one who will be liberated within seven births
- one who will be liberated in the next birth
- one who is liberated in the subtle world hereafter
- one who is liberated in the same birth

Buddhism: Death Visions

Every religious system in the world has something to say about death. Buddhism is sometimes said to be a non-religion which means that it is a system without faith

Usually, religion is defined as having two things for minimum

- faith
- deity

This is interesting because on a close examination of the original system of Gautama Buddha which he called the Middle Way, there are many stipulations of moral principles or what can and cannot be done. In Buddha's time, monks were ostracized from the sect when they broke the rules.

Secondly, to join as a monk during Buddha's time, one had to give allegiance to three factors which were

- the Buddha himself as the particular enlightened unique person
- the Dhamma or process of discipline for realization which he laid out
- the monks, who were his disciples, as one collective institution.

Was this allegiance a form of faith?

Was Buddha as the unique founder and leader and the undisputed proponent, a covert deity?

No dissention was allowed in the group during Buddha's time. One either accepted his method or one had to depart. There is not a single case of anyone who had a variant view to Buddha's who successfully stayed with the sect. It was not like today where people say that it is all the same, Buddha's way or Christ's way or the Hindu way or whatever.

In the book *A Comprehensive Manual of Abhidhamma*, *Bhikkhu Bodhi* wrote about the object of door-free consciousness. This he said (page 138), is generally identical with the object of the last cognitive process in the immediately preceding existence.

He wrote that when a person is on the verge of death, in the last phase of active consciousness some object will present itself to the cognitive process, determined by previous *kamma* and present circumstances. This object, he wrote, can be one of three kinds:

- It can be a *kamma*, a good or evil deed performed earlier during the same lifetime.
- It can be a sign of *kamma*, that is, an object or image associated with the good or evil deed that is about to determine rebirth or an instrument used to perform it. For example, a devout person may see the image of a monk or temple. A physician may see the image of patients. A butcher may hear the groans of slaughtered cattle or see an image of a butcher knife.
- It can be a sign of destiny, that is, a symbol of the realm in which the dying person is about to be reborn. For example, a person destined for a heavenly rebirth may see celestial mansions. A person heading for an animal rebirth may see a forest or fields. A person heading for a rebirth in hell may see infernal fires.

From an enlightenment system in which there are proposals of not having a self, this is interesting. The question as to what will be going either to a heaven, a hell, a human or animal rebirth, is hanging in the air. If there is no self, what will experience this. Will the mind which is not a self, be subjected to this. If it will, what will be liberated in the end?

Putting aside the no-self issue and pretending that there is a self, we are left with the time of death having three types of mento-emotional presentations which are possible for the one who is on the verge of being deceased. These are:

- vision of a previous faulty or meritorious action
- vision of an indication of a previous faulty or meritorious act
- vision of the physical or astral realms which will be the habitation hereafter

A question arises as to what determines if an action is faulty or meritorious. In the real world back in physical existence, the deceased person had to face government determination of what was right or wrong. He had to deal with religious authorities who said this was right and that was wrong. He was censored by relatives and friends who applied approvals and disapprovals. But if there is no God anywhere, where is the reference coming into his mind about what was right or wrong which will cause him to go for a particular type of rebirth.

Suppose he was a good man who raised a family and gave money in charity, a person who professed unity and love, but supposed he becomes destined for a hellish place hereafter, what determined that? Was it his mistake in thinking, his lack of positive outlook or the failure of his imagination?

Is it that only in the physical world there are courts and laws which can contravene one's creative idea of what is right or wrong?

Are there astral lands where there are established societies with social rules, where my view of what is right, may be contravened?

Trace of Anger

I had the opportunity recently to observe the behavior of a two-month-old infant. I noticed that when the child did not get what it desired, it became angry and expressed itself with annoyance. It would stop from time to time, listen for a response and then with more emphasis began the annoyance again.

This infant did not contrive the anger. It was spontaneous.

There are many theories about why anger occurs and about how it should be eliminated but I took a closer look at what Krishna said about it.

ध्यायतो विषयान्पुंसः
सङ्गस्तेषूपजायते ।
सङ्गात्संजायते कामः
कामात्क्रोधोऽभिजायते ॥२.६२॥

dhyāyato viṣayānpuṁsaḥ
saṅgasteṣūpajāyate
saṅgātsaṁjāyate kāmaḥ
kāmātkrodho'bhijāyate (2.62)

dhyāyato = dhyāyataḥ — considering; viṣayān — sensual objects; puṁsaḥ — a person; saṅgas — attachment; teṣūpajāyate = teṣu — in them + upajāyate — is born, is created; saṅgāt — from attachment; saṁjāyate — is born; kāmaḥ — craving; kāmāt — from craving; krodho = krodhah — anger; 'bhijāyate = abhijāyate — is derived

The act of considering sensual objects, creates in a person, an attachment to them. From attachment comes craving. From this craving anger is derived. (Bhagavad Gita 2.62)

क्रोधाद्भवति संमोहः
संमोहात्स्मृतिविभ्रमः ।
स्मृतिभ्रंशाद्बुद्धिनाशो
बुद्धिनाशात्प्रणश्यति ॥२.६३॥

krodhādbhavati saṁmohaḥ
saṁmohātsmṛtivibhramaḥ
smṛtibhraṁśādbuddhināśo
buddhināśātpraṇaśyati (2.63)

krodhād = krodhāt — from anger; bhavati — becomes (comes); saṁmohaḥ — delusion; saṁmohāt — from delusion; smṛti — conscience + vibhramaḥ — vanish; smṛtibhraṁśād = smṛtibhraṁśāt = smṛti — memory, judgement + bhraṁśāt — from fading away; buddhināśo = buddhināśaḥ = buddhi —discerning power + nāśaḥ — lose, affected; buddhināśāt = buddhi — discernment + nāśāt — from loss, from being affected; praṇaśyati — is ruined

From anger, comes delusion. From this delusion, the conscience vanishes. When he loses judgment, his discerning power fades away. Once the discernment is affected, he is ruined. (Bhagavad Gita 2.63)

From this explanation, we can deduce that anger is not an original energy. It develops from something else, from craving, which in turn develops from attachment, which in turn comes from considering a sense object. The word for considering is *dhyāyataḥ* in the Sanskrit, which comes from *dhi* which also is the root sound for the seventh stage of yoga which *dhyana*.

Some early writers translated *dhyana* as contemplation. Others said it was concentration. I say that *dhyana* means the linkage of the person's attention to an object or environment. In *ashtanga* yoga it means a higher object or environment. Some say it means mergence or becoming one with some other superior reality or with the whole existence, but that is confusing because any mergence which is reversible is a farce.

Some teachers say that *dhyana* is similar to when a salt crystal is put in water. The crystal disappears. Everyone can see that it merged into the water. However even though that is a clear incidence, still it is misleading because when Jim or *Ananda* sits to meditate, even if he feels merged into some energy or some whatever, he must unmerge and become the individual self to function in society. He has no choice in the matter. There is not a single case of anyone who merged and who did not resume individuality to serve in society, except those whose physical bodies died. Even then even though the method in India is to declare that the guru merged, no definite proof is provided to show how he did. For all we know, he was resumed individually in the astral domains as himself.

When a salt crystal merges, it really does merge at least until the time when the sun will bake planet earth and all the water will be forced to become steam leaving the salt crystals to resume crystalline forms.

How should Krishna's idea about how anger is generated be applied to the infant because we know that the infant cannot contrive as an adult would?

Right after birth there can be no question of the infant considering a sensual object like milk, because the body of the infant never tasted that and has no memory of it. Even if the subtle body of the infant has memories from the past lives, the physical one with its new un-programmed brain, has no recall.

The only way the brain of the child would require milk based on a memory, would be its memory of getting food through the placenta of the mother while it was in the mother's system. The lack of that nourishment may produce a feeling of want which mentally would be manifested as considering the lack of nourishment, which in turn would generate an attachment which could develop into a craving, which if not fulfilled would generate or transform into anger.

In meditation, I transited to the time when I was an infant, to experience those moods.

I saw the following:

First there was a need to look down into the gut of the infant body.

A blank space in the abdomen was seen. It was like a dark cavern with a noticeable central grey space.

There was a shift of attention back into the head of the infant form

Then again there was a need to look down, except that the second time, it did so with a feeling of disbelief, as if something should be there but was absent.

Again, there was a check in the gut. Again, the cavern was perceived. The infant eyes opened and looked to see if there was anything or anyone who could deal with the cavern, anyone who could fill it.

When no one was seen a crying impulse began but this crying impulse was not anger. It was calling someone, checking to see if someone responded.

After about three cry songs, the crying stopped. Again, there was a feeling of disbelief.

Then again this happened and the feeling of disbelief increased. This converted into anger. At which time the sound of the crying changed to one of abject irritation.

Let us return to what Krishna explained:

The act of considering sensual objects, creates in a person, an attachment to them. From attachment comes craving. From this craving anger is derived.

It may be said that in the case of an infant the anger is justified but that is not the issue. Here I am concerned with its formation, regardless of whether it is approved or disapproved. The psyche of the infant considered its nutrition needs. Then an attachment for those needs developed. From that a craving for milk developed. When that craving was not fulfilled, anger was derived.

Even if the infant was filled to the throat with milk, it would sometimes cry for the beverage anyway, and it would do so with anger. In that case the anger was not justified but it developed in the same way as when its stomach was empty.

Killing the body

Yogeshwarananda whom I have not seen for some weeks, appeared today during the afternoon breath infusion session. He wanted to discuss the killing of the body, which is a system of end-of-life yoga, some advanced ascetics perform.

He said that because he had so many disciples at the end of his life, he was unable to complete this procedure properly but he wanted me to consider doing it. I told him that I did not think I could do it because of the circumstances of my own life, where I am not in isolation due to cancelation actions of providence which prohibit that I go into seclusion, something I tried to do unsuccessful some years ago, which some deities prevented.

He did not accept the argument and said he felt I could do it because I will not be bogged with a big mission, and institution, due to my resistance towards the same.

Of course, that can change overnight as it did in his life where after years of isolation, he was circumstantially established as a lineage guru.

Anyway, before I knew it, he poured some energy through the top of my head through the brahmarandra chakra, saying that he had to get rid of the energy for killing the body because he did not use it and also because he will not take another body to demonstrate it.

I then told him that under the situation, I will keep the energy but I also may not use it and then later I may pass it to another yogi.

This all happened during the breath infusion practice.

When I sat to meditate, I tried to locate the package of energy which he poured into my head but I could not detect it. I went down into the trunk of the body. I could not find it. In the trunk there was this whitish yellowish translucent energy. It was like diving through a light grade viscous oil but I found nothing in it. I again came into the head of the subtle body to meditate.

At that time, he sent in a message telling me to chant a mantra which he chanted and to take a certain position in the subtle head while chanting. The mantra was the *Savituh gayatri* mantra. I chanted it. I found that it did not affect my usual connection with naad sound resonance.

He said that he wanted me to chant it for him. I agreed. After that he left and went into the astral dimensions.

Recently, a kriya student, who took instruction from *Hariharananda*, wanted me to explain the killing-of-the-body kriya. I told him I could not give him that method, because it is really not a method. It hinges on fate which in turn hinges on the summary practice of the yogi up the point of when he is to pass from the body.

There are usually two or three escape holes which open for a practicing ascetic. He can use one of these. If he fails to do so, he is held back in the physical body and evicted from it in one way or the other when the body dies and the lifeForce leaves in a panic if it can. Sometimes the lifeForce cannot leave in a panic because the body may be in a coma. In that case the lifeForce leaves in a mist of unconsciousness, and then over time, say for about half hour or for some days after, it finds itself in the astral existence without a body and with a feeling that something went terribly wrong. It feels misted and broken up like when a granite ball falls to a hard surface from the top of a tall building.

People want some kriya to use but the kriya for yogic passing from the body is a matter of taking one or two of the escapes which become evident to the ascetic just before the body dies.

What happens is that at the time before the body dies, there will be an opening in time, a gap-event in consciousness where the yogi can focus as the coreSelf and escape from the body. If the yogi uses that gap the body will silently die. The yogi will be gone, being disconnected permanently from the physical form. This departure really means departure of the subtle body out of the physical one from the last time, as compared to the nightly departures during sleep which carry return potential.

The reason why a yogi may not recognize or may not take the opportunity of escape through the gap is his attachment to disciples, or to his institution or mission as a guru. Any type of attachment like that, to anyone, even to one's family members or to one's followers will cause a yogi not to take the opportunity.

The person who inquired of me about this is very devoted to his family. He cannot utilize the advantage of the gap. He may not see it. Even if he sees it, he will not have the power to use it.

An example of this is a bird which was kept in a cage for years. We experience sometimes that such a bird will not fly away when the cage is opened. It will look at the open door of the cage and not realize what that opening means. Or it may find that opening to be an unwelcomed opportunity.

There was a case which I knew of, where in South America, a man kept a parrot in a cage for some time. After some years, he decided to free the bird. He opened the door and wired it in the open position so that it would never be closed again. At first the bird did not trust the opening and stayed away from it. But then over time the bird got familiar with it and used to handle the wire around the opening with its beak.

After a time, the bird slowly stepped out of the cage but the bird never flew away. It stayed in the house of the man and would go into the cage to sleep regularly. I questioned the man about this because I was interested to study how we become conditioned.

Every person will be given hints about death. These are called portents. Like for instance there was a time about a year ago when I got some portents where many people who were deceased whom I knew came to see me astrally and wanted to greet me favorably. This is like when one is to migrate to another country and some person from that other place comes and greets one and begins to support one and give one confidence about the upcoming transition.

However, when the body is to die there will be indications in the body itself, both in the physical and in the subtle bodies. But on the psychological level there will be an opening in time, where one can go outside of the summary energy influence of this particular life, and fly away.

If, however one is distracted by association with family or with disciples who are obsessed with their physical bodies, one will either not recognize or recognize and not use the opportunity.

There are many people who profess to be spiritual or to be ascetic or to be a yogi. Most of them are phonies. They mean well but they do not qualify. They have no intentions of giving up material existence but they speak as if they are interested but it is just a way of conversation. If their lifestyles are closely checked we will discover that their interest in yoga is purely superficial. Or they intend to use it to support the status in physical existence.

Meditation: Naad / *Chit akash* Reach

Procedure for this:

- Do thorough breath infusion
- Sit to meditate in a position where the spine is tilted back slightly and is braced by a wall or chair-back. Set the feet so that they will not cramp and demand attention
- Close eyelids. Use a blindfold. This is important because otherwise the eyelids may open on occasion. That will interrupt the meditation.
- As you settle in the subtle head to meditate, make a note about the location and focus.
- If your attention is not on naad sound or is not in the back of the subtle head, if it is with conventional thoughts and images, this meditation is over. You should do some other meditation but do not proceed any further with this.
- Provided you find your attention on naad or in the back of the head without random thoughts and images, solidify yourself in naad or in the back of the head as in the diagram.

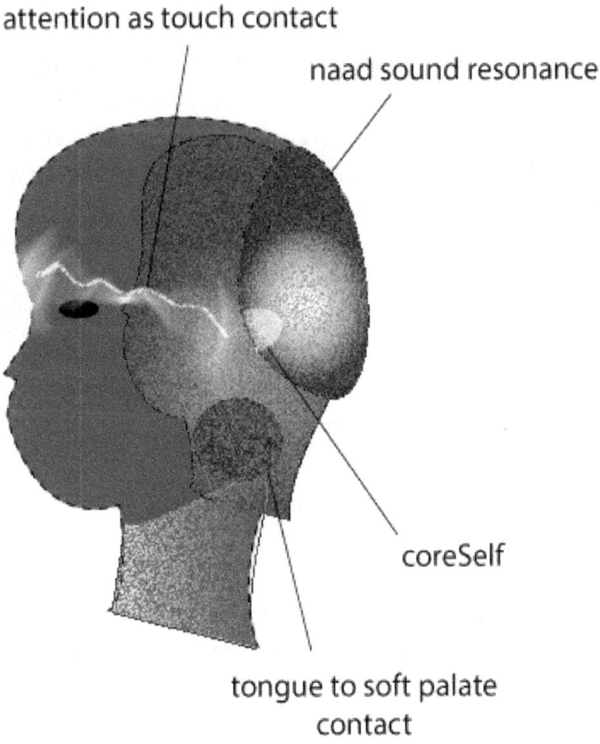

- Check to see if the tongue is rolled back so that the tip of it is implanted in the soft palate. If it is not, direct the tongue into that position.
- Check again to see how you are positioned in reference to naad. Are you still embedded in naad?
- If you are not embedded, this meditation is over, continue meditation in some way but do not proceed with this instruction.
- Provided that you were embedded in naad, being held in naad spontaneously without special effort to remain there, check to see if you are in sound contact with naad. If you are in sound contact check to see if you are in vibration contact with naad.
- If you have both the sound and vibration, contact with naad, check to see if you have a touch contact with the soft palate. If you have that check to see if you have a taste contact with the soft palate.
- If you have both a touch and taste contact with the soft palate, return to where you are positioned in naad. This will be as if someone reached forward and downward from sitting in a chair without actually leaving the chain. The person retracts his hand and sits with his hand close to his body.
- As soon as you accomplish this, send an energy forward to the center of the eyebrows on the inside of the subtle head. This should be a touch energy. It should not be a visual energy. If you find that a visual energy attempts to move forward to do this, stop. Substitute touch energy.

This is a method which I tested for Lahiri for giving something definite which will work for reaching the *chit akash* from within the subtle head of the yogi. This practice was months in developing bit by bit. I am still to take it to the final stage but I released it because Yogeshwarananda gave an addition action. I wanted to at least report on this before applying his addition.

Special Note:

Contact with naad in this process is twofold:

- sound
- touch

The sound contact is through hearing naad. The touch contact is through sensing naad resonance as a vibration rather than as a sound.

Contact with the soft palate is made by rolling the tip of the tongue up and back, pushing it back as far as you can into the soft palate at the back of the mouth. There are two contacts with this:

- touch
- taste

First there is the touch contact. Then there is a taste contact which feels neutral.

Contact of the coreSelf with naad is locational. It is all about where the coreSelf is located in naad. This is a touch contact which the mind may interpret as feelings.

Contact with the place between the eyebrows is a touch contact only. However usually this is a visual energy contact, but in this meditation, the visual energy contact is absent. If one uses it, one will ruin this meditation.

It will be used later in this meditation after the *chit akash* sky of consciousness becomes available. A yogi cannot force this to happen. If he uses the vision to see that before it is manifested, he will ruin his chances of gaining access.

Buddha: His Concept of Time

There is information about what Buddha said about cosmic ages or aeons. *Bhikkhu Bodhi* in *"A Comprehensive Manual of Abhidhamma"* listed Buddha's ideas about time.

We know that some philosophers and spiritually minded people from the East and West profess that there is no time.

Bhagavad Gita attests to the reality of time, with Krishna declaring himself as Time when he displayed the apparition of his Universal Form. Arjuna got nervous and asked Krishna about his intentions. This was because of the threatening stance of the supernatural people who were in the form. Here are a few verses.

आख्याहि मे को भवानुग्ररूपो
नमोऽस्तु ते देववर प्रसीद ।
विज्ञातुमिच्छामि भवन्तमाद्यं
न हि प्रजानामि तव प्रवृत्तिम् ॥११.३१॥

ā khyāhi me ko bhavānugrarūpo
namo'stu te devavara prasīda
vijñātumicchāmi bhavantamādyaṁ
na hi prajānāmi tava pravṛttim (Bhagavad Gita 11.31)

ā khyāhi — explain; me — to me; ko = kaḥ — who; bhavān — respected person; ugrarūpo — ugrarūpaḥ — of terrible form; namo = namaḥ — homage; 'stu — astu — may it be; te — to you; devavara — best of the gods; prasīda — have mercy; vijnātum — to understand; icchāmi — I want; bhavantam — Your lordship; ādyaṁ — primal person: na — not: hi — indeed; prajānāmi — I know; tava — your; pravṛttim — intention

Explain to me who You are, O respected Person of terrible form. I gave my homage to You, O best of gods. Have mercy! I want to understand You, O Primal Person. I do not know Your intentions. (Bhagavad Gita 11.31)

श्रीभगवानुवाच
कालोऽस्मि लोकक्षयकृत्प्रवृद्धो
लोकान्समाहर्तुमिह प्रवृत्तः ।
ऋतेऽपि त्वा न भविष्यन्ति सर्वे
येऽवस्थिताः प्रत्यनीकेषु योधाः ॥११.३२॥

śrībhagavānuvāca
kālo'smi lokakṣayakṛt pravṛddho
lokānsamāhartumiha pravṛttaḥ
ṛte'pi tvāṁ na bhaviṣyanti sarve
ye'vasthitāḥ pratyanīkeṣu yodhāḥ

śrī bhagavān — the Blessed Lord; uvāca — said; kālo — kālah — time-limit; 'smi = asmi — I am; lokaksayakrt — loka — world + ksaya — destruction + kit — causing; pravṛddho — pravṛddhaḥ — mighty; lokān — worlds; samāhartum — to annihilate; iha — here; pravṛttaḥ — appeared; ṛte — without; 'pi = api — also; tvāṁ —you na — not, cease; bhaviṣyanti — they will live; sarve — all; ye — who; 'vasthitāḥ = avasthitāḥ — armored; pratyanikeṣu — on both armies; yodhāḥ — warriors

The Blessed Lord said: I am the time limit, the mighty world-destroying Cause, appearing here to annihilate the worlds. Even without you, all the armored warriors, in both armies will cease to live. (Bhagavad Gita 11.32)

That is clear. To Krishna, time as Himself was a real thing.

Bhikkhu Bodhi explained the Buddhist concept writing that the Buddhist text speaks of three kinds of aeons (*kappa* -Sanskrit *kalpa*). These are:

- interim aeon *(antarakappa)*
- incalculable aeon *(asankheyyakappa)*
- great aeon *(mahakappa)*

An **interim aeon** is the period of time required for the life-span of human beings to rise from ten years to the maximum of many thousands of years, and then fall back to ten years.

Twenty such eons equal one **incalculable eon** and four incalculable eons equals one **great aeon**.

He wrote that the length of a great aeon is said by the Buddha to be longer than the time it would take for a man to wear away a mountain of solid granite one yogana (about 7 miles) high and wide by stroking it once every hundred years with a silk cloth.

There is also information about the lifespan of the beings who live in the immaterial spheres, where the lifetime of the gods who attained to the realm of infinite space is 20,000 eons.

It is 40,000 eons for those who attained the sphere of infinite consciousness.

It is 60,000 eons for those who attained the realm of nothingness.

It is 84,000 eons for those who attained the realm of neither-perception-nor-non-perception.

Can it be said then that the Buddha believed in time and actually knew what he presented to be fact?

We may also consider if Buddha learned much of the Vedic information which enumerates the eons. There were a few instances, unknown perhaps to many Buddhists, where in the Pali cannon, Buddha is quoted using information from the Vedic data, especially in relation to stories about certain ancient Indian kings.

Many people who consider themselves to be *ashtanga* yogis or followers of the system of Patanjali, deny the existence of time but Patanjali believed in time. Look at these verses:

अतीतानागतं स्वरूपतोऽस्त्यध्वभेदाद्धर्माणाम्॥१२॥

atīta anāgataṁ svarūpataḥ
asti adhvabhedāt dharmāṇām

atīta – the past; anāgataṁ – the future; svarūpataḥ – true form; asti – there is, it exists; adhvabhedāt – due to different courses or events; dharmāṇām – of the characteristics.

There is a true form of the past and future, which is denoted by the different courses of their characteristics. (Yoga Sutras 4.12)

ते व्यक्तसूक्ष्मा गुणात्मानः ॥१३॥

te vyakta sūkṣmāḥ guṇātmānaḥ

te – they; vyakta – gross; sūkṣmāḥ – subtle; guṇātmānaḥ = guṇā – subtle material nature + ātmānaḥ – of itself.

They are gross or subtle, all depending on their inherent nature. (Yoga Sutras 4.13)

Krishna is interesting because in more than one statement in Bhagavad Gita, he attested himself as Time. Do not let anyone fool you to think that it was symbolic or that Krishna did not mean himself because we would first have to remove all those *ahams* and *asmis* which are pronouns for *I* and Sanskrit verb cases for *am* or *I am* (verb *to be*). In Patanjali also do not let anyone bamboozle you to say he did not mean that time was real because they would have to erase a very important Sanskrit word which is *swarupatah*. So long as you do not know Sanskrit or do not have a standard dictionary these terms can be bleached very conveniently.

Buddha reckoned time and even indicated that even if one goes into the realm of the infinite or the realm of nothingness or the place where one can neither perceive anything or not perceive anything, still one will have to deal with time, even though on those planes time is infinite as compared to our present fatigue with it.

Part 4

Lahiri: Kundalini Bliss Experience

Lahiri requested some breath infusion practices which are not usually discussed in *pranayama* books. One of these is nutrition hormone lift from cells in the body.

This is with a different focus to spinal kundalini rising but it cannot be done successfully unless one did spinal rise for some time successfully. One must also shift one's interest from sensational bliss feelings to non-sensation and very incremental or small bliss burst which is hardly noticeable except to very sensitive minds.

Suppose I place one tablespoon of honey in your mouth, how would that taste?

Now suppose alternately I placed enough honey that would smear the tip of a needle, how would that taste?

In comparison the smear would not register to your sense of taste as having anything to do with honey. And yet, if I were to accumulate millions of such smears it would eventually add up to a tablespoon.

But there is another important way of checking this, which is to consider the flavor.

Suppose I got some honey which the bees made from the nectar of orange blossoms. I then put one tablespoon in your mouth. How would that taste?

You may enjoy both the sweetness and orange flavor.

Suppose I got some other honey which the bees collected from a flavor-neutral nectar-neutral flower?

I put one tablespoon in your mouth.

You would be unresponsive because it would neither be sweet nor flavorful.

This is like when a person feels the rise of kundalini up the spine, while doing *bhastrika pranayama*. It may feel like sex climax experience. It makes the person happy. It is bliss. Kundalini rises quickly and flashes through the head like a bolt of pleasure lightning. Instead of feeling the pleasure in the genitals, it is felt in the spine and head. This serves as a relief from the rigors of yoga and from not having the pleasures of life like an indulgent person who can go to parties, has sex frequently, eats any and everything and enjoys unrestrictedly.

With the rise of kundalini through the spine, there is bliss. According to the force of the rise that bliss may be partial or full. If kundalini hits *brahmrandra* chakra, it will be a full blow out bliss, so that the person experiences sheer spiritual pleasure. This is when the *atma* individual self is lost in an ocean of blissful light but again that self resumes limited consciousness, when the charged kundalini subsides.

In comparison this bliss is subtler and more supernatural then the bliss experienced in sexual climax experience which is the pleasure involved in begetting progeny.

The spiritual bliss, if it occurred because kundalini was infused with sex hormone energy, is to an extent lower than when kundalini hits *brahmrandra*, from a lust-free arousal.

What happens when the yogi has this bliss feeling and there is no contribution from the sex hormone energy?

Is that flavorless bliss like the honey produced from the flavor-neutral flowers?

Can the yogi get enjoyment from that bliss or is he dependent on the sex hormone related bliss?

Lahiri showed how to lift the hormone energy before it reaches the reproduction system of the body, and to pull that into the head just the same and experience the bliss of that. But in comparison to kundalini-up-the-spine bliss, it is not as sensational.

The same process of breath infusion using *kapalabhati/bhastrika pranayama* with the various locks and inner focus is used, but instead of routing the energy through the groin and to *muladhara* chakra and up the spine, it is lifted from the chest-lung area before it falls into the reproductive glands.

Buddha: Shame and Fear

Shame and fear are two qualities which are highlighted by many leaders of spiritual movements.

I was surprised to hear of Buddha appreciation for these aspects in the *"A Comprehensive Manual of the Abhidhamma"* book by *Bhikkhu Bodhi* (page 86).

There he listed the nineteen universal beautiful factors (*sobhanasadharana*) of Buddhism. Shame and fear are the third and fourth in the list.

He wrote that shame has the characteristic of disgust at bodily and verbal misconduct; fear of wrong doing has the characteristic of dread in regards to some misconduct. They both have the function of not doing evil, and are manifested as the shrinking away from evil. Their proximate cause is respect for self and respect for others. Because they protect the world from falling into widespread immorality, these two states are called by the Buddha the guardians of the world.

This is interesting. It comes from a system where some teachers say that there is no self, what to speak of there being other selves.

How about the rating of shame and fear as beautiful factors?

Should shame and fear be wiped off the spiritual map because they ruin self-esteem and cause psychosis?

Should Buddha be laughed out of *nirvana* because he appreciated it?

In contrast, in an unlikely place, in the *Uddhava Gita*, Krishna told *Uddhava* of his appreciation of a certain application of fear:

न ह्य् अङ्गोपक्रमे ध्वसो
गाद् धर्मस्योद्धवाण्व् अपि ।
मया व्यवसितः सम्यङ्
निर्गुणत्वाद् अनाशिषः ॥२४.२०॥

na hy aṅgopakrame dhvaṁso
mad-dharmasyoddhavāṇv api
mayā vyavasitaḥ samyaṅ
nirguṇatvād anāśiṣaḥ (24.20)

na — not; hy = hi — indeed; aṅgopakrame = anga — my dear friend + upakrama — in the effort; dhvaṁso = dhvaṁsaḥ — destruction; mad-dharmasyoddhavāṇv = mat-dharmasu — of my righteous duty + uddhava — Uddhava + anv (anu) — least; api — even; mayā — by me; vyavasitah — is rated; samyaṅ = samyak — perfect; nirguṇatvād = nirguṇa – not being initiated by the mundane influences + tvāt — because of the quality; anāśiṣah — without bad motive.

My dear Uddhava, in the effort of participating in My righteous duty, there is no destruction, not even the least. It is rated by Me as being perfection, because of its quality of not being initiated by the mundane influence, and it is free from bad motive. (Uddhava Gita 24.20)

यो यो मयि परे धर्मः
कल्प्यते निष्फलाय चेत् ।
तद्-आयासो निरर्थः स्याद्

भयादेर् इव सत्तम ॥२४.२१॥

yo yo mayi pare dharmaḥ
kalpyate niṣphalāya cet
tad-āyāso nirarthaḥ syād
bhayāder iva sattama (24.21)

yo yo = yah yah — whatever, any quantity; mayi — to me; pare — the supreme; dharmah — righteous duty; kalpyate — is suitable; nisphalāya — being from the motive for benefits; cet — if; tad = tat — of that; āyāso = āyāsah — the effort; nirarthaḥ — that which has no value; syād = syāt — is; bhayāder = bhaya – fear + ādeḥ — and of such pressures; iva — as; sattama — o best of the realistic people.

O best of the realistic people, whatever is done for Me, the Supreme, is suitable as righteous duty, as it is free from motive for benefits. Even if the effort is prompted by fear and other such pressures, it has value. (Uddhava Gita 24.21)

Buddhism: Four Types of *Kamma*

The Sanskrit is *karma.* It means the social work a person performs. The result is *phalam* or consequence which according to most Eastern traditions is sure to come either in the current life time or in some other.

In Buddhism there is a paradox where some Buddhists propose the idea of no-self and still they speak of consequences of actions for the individual and moral stipulations which are supposed to divert a person from doing social acts which may result in bad consequences in the future.

If I have no self, if I am not a person, why should I be concerned about avoiding bad consequences?

Bhikkhu Bodhi in his *"A Comprehensive Manual of the Abhidhamma"* listed four types of *kamma* by way of function. These are:

- productive *kamma*
- supportive *kamma*
- obstructive *kamma*
- destructive *kamma*

He wrote that *kamma* means action or deed but in Buddha's teaching it meant volitional action. From a technical stand point *kamma* denotes wholesome or unwholesome volition (*cetana*), with volition being the factor responsible for action.

Imagine that!

There is no self. Yet they discuss volition and responsibility. It is mysterious how you could have willpower and responsibility and have no self which is tagged to it. The mystery deepens.

Bodhi then wrote that Buddha declared this:

"It is volition, monks that I call *kamma*, for having willed, one performs an action through body, speech or mind."

Bodhi made an exception. He wrote that all volitional action, except that of a Buddha or an Arahant, constitutes *kamma*. Since they have eradicated ignorance and craving, which are the roots of *kamma.* The buddhas and the arahants do not accumulate *kamma*.

Interestingly, Bodhi adds that nevertheless, even the buddhas and arahants are bound to experience the ripening of their past *kamma* as long as their psychological personality persists, that is, until they pass away.

This suggests that up till the time when their physical bodies die, there is a self even for the buddhas and arahants. Then there will be no self!

This is mind boggling!

Here is the tally.

There is no self in fact but one must face the consequences of wilful actions. Some consequences are wholesome to oneself. Some are not.

If one is a buddha or an arahant, one does not have to deal with the consequences of actions which were made at the time of and after one's enlightenment. Those were not volitional acts which were based on ignorance and craving but up to the time of the demise of the physical body, one must deal with flyback of the volitional acts done before one's enlightenment.

Up to the point of death of the last physical body one would ever have, reactions will find one even though one would have only an illusion-self. But after death there would be no self from this existence to target, no illusion-self that is.

As for the distinction between a buddha and an arahant, a simply way to understand this is to know that a Buddha is one who is enlightened by his own process while an Arahant is enlightened by using the process of a Buddha. It is like there is one Buddha but many arahants. The arahants have to pay respects to the Buddha who owns the franchise and is the founder of the method of liberation.

When a monk is committed, he makes obeisance to three factors one of which is the Buddha, the specific no-self called *Shakyamuni* or *Gautama*. He must respect the teaching of Buddha (the Eightfold Noble Path). He must also honor the sanga or association of monks (which include the arahants like *Sariputta*). But *Gautam* Buddha, as a self or an illusion self, must be distinguished for honor.

Please do not argue with this distinction or feel that it is a letdown, unless you know the history of the Buddha and can quote from the original text, not from spurious information. At the very beginning this distinction was made clear when Buddha converted three ascetics whom he did austerities with. When they wanted to greet him as a fellow ascetic and called him as a friend, he chastised them and said he was the one unique enlightened person who had the right method and that he was not to be addressed as a friend.

How many know that Buddha was frequently addressed as *Bhagavan*. This term really means someone who is recognized as a demigod or as God. It is used frequently in *Bhagavad Gita* and elsewhere for God or incarnation of God. Usually in translations of Sanskrit and Pali text the meaning of this term is not conveyed across cultural and ethnic borders. It may be that many would run from Buddhism if these terms were translated with the full cultural impact.

I suggest that anyone joining Buddhism be told that he would by the process have a good chance if he can do the rigorous mental research required, discover his Arahant nature, not his Buddha nature. To be a Buddha one must have one qualification which is that one must become enlightened without taking help from anyone.

Bodhi explained that the law of karma is self-subsistent in its operation, ensuring that willed deeds produce their effects in accordance with their ethical quality just as surely as seeds bear fruit in accordance with their species. The direct products of karma are the resultant states of consciousness and mental factors that arise when *kamma* finds the right conditions to fructify. *Kamma* also produces a distinct type of matter in the organic bodies of living beings, called materiality originating from *kamma*.

In brief this is how he defines the four types of *kamma*:

Productive *kamma* is wholesome or unwholesome volition which produces resultant mental states and *kamma* born materiality, born at the moment of rebirth-linking and during the course of existence.

Supportive *kamma* is *kamma* which does not gain an opportunity to produce its own result, but which, when some other *kamma* is exercising a productive function, supports it either by enabling it to produce its pleasant or painful results over an extended time without obstruction or by reinforcing the continuum of aggregates produced by another *kamma*.

Obstructive *kamma* is *kamma* which cannot produce its own result but nevertheless obstructs and frustrates some other *kamma*, countering its efficacy, or shortening the duration of its pleasant or painful results.

Destructive *kamma* is wholesome or unwholesome *kamma* which supplants other weaker *kammas*, prevents it from ripening, and produces instead its own result.

He gave examples of each of the karmas. The one for the destructive *kamma* is of someone born as a human being who may, through his productive *kamma*, have been originally destined for a long life-span, but a destructive *kamma* may arise and bring about a premature death.

Remember that even if you are enlightened as an Arahant (not as a Buddha), your karmic reactions from the time before enlightenment would reach you nevertheless and your being totally in the oneness, nothingness or whatever your absolute state would be, hinges on your getting out of that material body at death. At least that is the suggestion here.

Even if one reaches the Arahant stage of enlightenment, the karmic flybacks will pursue one so long as one has a physical body.

Permanent Mergence in Question

Yogeshwarananda was in my subtle head yesterday. He directed the use a mantra and how to meditate at the same time. He asked if I knew anyone who could guarantee that if he merged into the absolute, he would remain there forever and will not ever be from it into being an individual again. He said there were various concepts and beliefs about what that absolute really is but regardless, if there was someone who could guarantee that, he would like to meet the person.

He stated that he entered the absolute many times while he used the last body but, he again came out of it and was himself as an individual living entity. Then he would teach others. Then he would again enter. Then after death he entered but he found himself outside of it again and in an astral dimension.

His idea is that unless a person was the producer of this existence, and is outside of this, the idea of mergence as a permanent feature is worthless, because anyone who found himself in this creation in a human body and who feels he can do this or do that permanently, advocates a gimmick because the person does not have that authority.

If one was in the Absolute prior and then happen to find oneself as an individual being, the question is:

Who or what caused one to partition from the absolute? Whatever person or agency is responsible for that, is the real power not the newly emergent individual self.

If that person or power partitioned one before, it can partition one again at its leisure. There is absolutely nothing one can do to prevent that.

Buddhism: Last Moments before Death

Bhikkhu Bodhi in his *"A Comprehensive Manual of Abhidhamma,"* (page 203) wrote of the ripening of *kamma* or the order in which the effect of *kamma* takes place. The mere mention of order of consequences speaks about the reality of time, because you cannot have a sequence without time monitoring it or being the medium in which incidences occur.

He listed four kinds of manifesting of consequences:

- weighty *kamma*
- death-proximate *kamma*
- habitual *kamma*
- reserve *kamma*

He gave definitions, from which I copy some briefs as follows:

Weighty *kamma* is *kamma* of such powerful moral weight that it cannot be replaced by any other *kamma* as the determinant of rebirth. On the wholesome side, this *kamma* is the attainment of the *jhanas*. On the unwholesome side, it is the five heinous crimes together with a fixed wrong view that denies the basis for morality. The five heinous crimes he listed as:

- parricide
- matricide
- murder of an arahant
- wounding of a buddha
- maliciously creating a schism in the Sanga.

Coming from a spiritual system in which there is no self, this is interesting. It seems that there must be some self, who will be the target of this *kamma*. If there is no self, who can murder whom or wound whom? Why should a person be considered a criminal for creating a schism in the association of Buddhist monks? In one view there is no judgment, no opinion, no prejudice. In another censorship is effective.

To explain this weighty *kamma* further, Boddhi cited the case of a rebel disciple of Buddha who was *Devadatta*, Buddha's cousin. *Bodhi* wrote that this ambitious cousin of Buddha lost his psychic powers and was reborn in hell because he wounded the Buddha and caused a schism in the Sanga.

He also mentioned the case of King *Ajatasattu*, who while listening to Buddha speak the *Samannaphala Sutta*, the *Discourse on the Fruits of Recluseship*, had all the other conditions for reaching stream-entry, but because he killed his father, King *Bimbisara*, he could not attain the path and the fruit.

Consider, who judged whom?

Who sends whom to hell?

Is this happening in the imagination of those monks who wrote the Pali canon and its subsidiary literatures?

Bodhi wrote that **death approximate *kamma*** is a potent *kamma* remembered or done shortly before death, that is, immediately prior to the last *javana* process. If a person of bad character remembers a good deed he has done, or performs a good dead just before dying, he may receive a fortunate rebirth, or conversely, if a good person dwells on an evil deed done earlier, or performs an evil deed just before dying, he may undergo an unhappy rebirth.

This terminal thought adjustment just before passing from a body is expanded in the *Bardo Thodol, Tibetan Book of the Dead*.

In Hinduism, there is a similar idea where in certain sects it is said that if one chants the name of God at the time of death, one will reach God or God's domain. Is this possible? Is this a superstition?

A **habitual *kamma*** is a deed that one habitually performs, either good or bad. In the absence of weighty *kamma* and a potent death-proximate *kamma*, this type of *kamma* generally assumes the rebirth-generative function.

A **reserve *kamma*** is any other deed, not included in the three aforementioned categories, which is potent enough to take on the role of generating rebirth. This type of *kamma* becomes operative when there is no *kamma* of the other three types to exercise this function

To recap this, there are four *kamma*s which may operate in the sequence of circumstances which are fate. These are:

- weighty *kamma* (*garuka*)
- death-proximate *kamma* (*asanna*)
- habitual *kamma* (*acinna*)
- reserve *kamma* (*katatta*)

Any of these happening at the last moments before death would serve as the impetus for the next body. A person would be stuck with that destiny as the son or daughter of this and that man and woman.

Buddhism: Karmic Flyback

Bhikkhu Bodhi in his book *"A Comprehensive Manual of Abhidhamma"* listed four kinds of time when a *kamma* will take effect:

- immediately effective *kamma*
- subsequently effective *kamma*
- indefinitely effective *kamma*
- defunct *kamma*

He elaborated that **immediately effective *kamma*** is *kamma* which, if it is to ripen, must yield its results in the same existence in which it is performed; otherwise, if it does not meet the opportunity to ripen in the same existence, it becomes defunct.

Subsequent effective *kamma* is *kamma* which if it is to ripen, must yield its results in the existence immediately following that in which it is performed; otherwise, it becomes defunct.

Indefinite effective *kamma* is *kamma* which can ripen at any time from the second future existences onwards, whenever it gains an opportunity to produce results. He wrote also of this type that no one not even a Buddha or an Arahant, is exempt from experiencing the results of indefinite effective *kamma*.

Defunct *kamma* does not designate a special class of *kamma* but applies to *kamma* that was due to ripen in either the present existence or the next existence but did not meet the conditions conducive to its maturation. In the case of Arahants, all their accumulated *kamma* from the past which was due to ripen in future lives becomes defunct with their final passing away.

A question arises as to the validity of these Buddhist ideas, especially since some people say that the self has full control of its destiny and does not have to function according to any influence other than the one it creates.

Why is the self or the illusion-self subjected to flyback karmic reaction if it is supreme?

Why even an Arahant or a Buddha would have to deal with any part of any karma, definite or indefinite, at any time after his/her enlightenment?

Buddhism: Four Causes of Death

Bhikkhu Bodhi in his book, *"A Comprehensive Manual of Abhidhamma,"* list four causes of Death. He defined death as the cutting off of the life faculty included within the limits of a single existence (*jivitindriya*).

The four causes are:

- through the expiration of the life-span
- through the expiration of the (productive) *kamma* force
- through the expiration of the life-span and the *kamma* force
- through the expiration of a destructive *kamma*

This is a summary of the definition of each:

Death through the expiration of the life-span is the kind of death that comes about for the beings in those realms of existence where the life-span is bounded by a definite limit. In the human realm too, this should be understood as death in advanced old age due to natural causes. If the productive *kamma* is still not exhausted when death takes place through reaching the maximum age, the kammic force can generate another rebirth on the same plane or on some higher plane, as in the case of the devas, supernatural people.

Death t**hrough the expiration of the (productive) *kamma* force** takes place when the *kamma* generating rebirth expends its force even though the normal life-span is not exhausted and there are otherwise favorable conditions for the prolongation of life.

Death **through the expiration of the life-span and the *kamma* force** is when both the life-span and the kammic force simultaneously come to an end.

Death **through the expiration of a destructive *kamma*** occurs when a powerful *kamma* cuts off the force of the rebirth-generating *kamma* even before the expiration of the life-span.

Bodhi remarked that the first three types of death are known as timely death, the last as untimely death. An oil lamp, for example, he wrote, may be extinguished due to the exhaustion of the wick, the exhaustion of the oil, the simultaneous exhaustion of both or some extraneous cause, like a gust of wind.

This is interesting because it begs the inquiry as to how much control the individual has over his life, but then Buddhism posits that there is, in fact, no self anyway.

Speaking practically however and forgetting for the time being that there is supposed to be no self, an oil lamp has a limited supply of oil and a limit length of wick with limited burning potential. *Bodhi* himself cited a gust of wind which even if there is sufficient oil and wick, the lamp may blow out.

There are factors like the wick, the oil and the wind which could end a person's life. Sometimes the oil finishes before the wick is completely burnt. Sometimes the wick burns at such a fast rate, that it is used before the reservoir of oil is exhausted. And sometimes unfortunately, a gust of wind extinguishes the flame before either the wick or oil is finished.

Stated more precisely, a self (or an illusion-self) is born with a certain potential life span of so many years, as a particular material body being the son or daughter of this and that mother and father. This life span is like the reservoir of oil.

This person (or non-self) also has a purpose which it embodies, for which it will live and function. This is like the length of wick.

If there is no gust of wind, and if the oil is properly refined, and if the wick is set properly in the oil in the container, when the wick is finished, the oil will also be exhausted. This is a natural death. People will say, he/she lived a good life and was blessed by God or fate for a peaceful happy death.

If, however there are no gusts of wind, and the wick is too short and is not of the right length but the oil is sufficient, the purpose of the person will be exhausted before the end of the life because the wick will cease burning even though there will be oil left. Then people will say that he lived his life but was idle, useless and purposeless in the end of his time.

If again there are no gusts of wind and the oil was insufficient so that his body developed terminal diseases early, then he would be unable to fulfill his purpose completely before death. People will say that his life was cut short, that time deprived him of the full opportunity to serve his purpose. He may become dishearten and feel undone at the end of life and may on his death bed, tell people that he wants to live on to fulfill his purpose for achieving this or that objective.

But if something happens and his body dies in youth for instance, long before he would even begin to manifest his purpose and with none of his vital organs being worn down, then people will say that his death was untimely. He was accursed and could not live to fulfilment.

Effects of Association

Association of all kinds, even positive associations, friendly ones with persons who are not serious yogis, is detrimental to spiritual advancement. There are two kinds of associations one can have which are non-yogic. One is downright negative where for instance one is a vegetarian and the other person eats flesh. Or where one's body is healthy and the other person is sickly. Or where one has regular evacuation and the other person is constipated. Or if one does not use herbs, drugs or medications which affect soberness and the other person is addicted to an herb or substance. Or if one is not sexually active and the other person is.

Association is everything in yoga practice. It can make or break an ascetic. This does not mean that one can live without association but it means that the ascetic should not underestimate association. Even minor association with persons who are the least dangerous can bring down a yogi. The main thing is to recognize the effect of the association and work for release from it. As soon as providence provides an exit a yogi should take it and then resume whatever yogic habits were neutralized by the association.

The worse and more blatant influences are the easiest to deal with because they are obvious to the yogi. They will be brought to his attention by someone who will tell him that his situation changed. The subtle and slight influences are the most difficult to detect. These can over time wear away the greatest yogi if he is not vigilant. People, the critics, hardly notice the little deviations which come from friendly yogic associations but these can trash the practice of a yogi over time and eventually wear him away so that he loses advancement and acts as a normal human being.

But there is also a down side to one's practice if one gets positive association from persons who are non-yogic; for instance, if the person likes to do yoga for superficial reasons, or if the person likes to eat vegetarian meals but has no interest in spiritual philosophy or if the person likes to look at yoga videos but cannot understand the value of rising early for meditation.

Recently I was with a person who takes opiate medication. After seeing that person, I noticed that I lost prompt evacuation. When finally, my body evacuated it was strained to do so. It produced dried stools.

Question is:

Did that association influence even my physical body to adopt constipation?

What about moods?

What about the time when I looked at a yoga video with a guy who had no interest in rising early to meditate? The next morning, I slept late and had this reluctance to do yoga all during the day and skipped two sessions. Did that person's habits penetrate my mind?

Maybe I am a beginner and I have not reached the stage where I am like the lotus leaf which is not touched by water?

What do you think?

Buddhism: Wrong View

A contradictory aspect of Buddhism and one which comes up repeatedly unless one is willing to conveniently dismiss it, is the aspect of not having a self. This is because Buddhism has many moral rules and ethical enforcements which were instituted by Buddha and were specific for monks to observe.

Bhikkhu Bodhi in the *"A Manual of Abhidhamma,"* explained wrong view (*micchaditthi*) as one of the unwholesome *kamma*s which operate through the door of speech, and which is a vocal intimation.

He wrote that it becomes a full course of action when it assumes the form of one of the morally nihilistic views which deny the validity of ethics and the retributive consequences of action. He listed three such views which are mentioned often in the *Sutta Pitaka*.

This information is coming from a spiritual process which professes that there is no continuing self, nothing except a stream of ever-changing energy and still there is talk about validity of ethics and retribution.

Bodhi listed the three wrong views as:

- nihilism
- inefficacy of action
- acausality view

He explained these:

Nihilism is the wrong view which denies the survival of the personality in any form after death, thus negating the moral significance of deeds.

The **inefficacy of action** is the wrong view which claims that deeds have no efficacy in producing results and thus invalidates moral distinctions

The ***acausality view*** is the wrong one which states that there is no cause or condition for the defilement and purification of beings, that beings are defiled and purified by chance, fate or necessity

This is problematic, because on one hand Buddhism says that there is no self into perpetuity. But alternately, it denies that there is no self and says that a self survives in some form just to provide a target for giving morality significance.

This suggests that something survives after an incidence for the purpose of tagging results to the correct principal from the original incidence.

Beings must also be purified according to this by deliberate action and not just by random chance. How that could be done without there being a target self is mind-boggling.

The suggestion is that there has to be something residual after a circumstance is enacted, so that returns from that incidence can target the original factors or persons involved. It is like the shadow-self or illusion-self cannot get away from the liabilities of actions which are performed in the impermanent world.

Buddhism denies the permanency and even existence of a self but it simultaneously says that there has to be a self for the purpose of serving as a target of moral or immoral kammic flybacks as Buddha defined it.

This reminds me of Schrodinger's cat. The poor thing: it was at the complete mercy of chance. It existed in a state of limbo with its fate suspended until someone would open the box, when it would either be killed or would have its life fully activated. But until the box was open, it was considered to be neither dead nor alive.

The poor self, it neither exists nor does not exists, but it does exist until it becomes fully enlightened because until them, it must serve as the target of good or bad consequences.

It is like Buddha stuck a bargain with fate that he would supply a self but only for unenlightened monks, and only in so far as fate needed a target for rewarding morally approved behaviors and for punishing morally disapproved ones. Buddhism distinguishes itself from the other nihilistic non-self philosophies which existed in the time of Buddha and also the theistic self-asserting philosophies as well.

Lahiri / Not Having Disciples

Today, Lahiri explained that a kriya student should not have disciples. During the breath infusion practice and the meditation which followed, he entered my subtle head, During the meditation, he said this:

> *There is no need to make disciples. Students should stop the quest for disciples. They should be students, loyal and perfect to the satGuru. There*

is no need to have so many gurus running here or there, giving partial methods and incompletely instructions.

Suppose there is a market vendor who year after year, brings to the market the very best mangoes, choice mangoes which have the best color, shape and taste, what is the need for ten other vendors with inferior fruits? It is best that we support that guru who has the best process for kriya yoga. That person is of course, Babaji. But someone may state that if this is a fact, why is Lahiri a teacher?

The answer is that I teach under the auspices of Babaji. I do not have an independent concern for anyone. Outside of Babaji's interest in others, I care for no one. Love comes from above, where Babaji has interest in someone. Out of his concern, I have an interest under his direction,

It is like the old way of marriage, where the son gets married to a girl which his parents selected. He does not find a girl and then say," I love her. I will marry her". The girl is loved by the parents and then the son out of his parent's interest, takes the girl as wife.

When a disciple is commissioned by a guru to teach, that disciple should not love those new disciples more than he loves the teacher. If he breaches with the teacher by having more interest in the new disciples, his course will be upset.

Becoming famous on earth as a great kriya master because of having many disciples is no indication of the relationship with the yogaGuru. People think that if a kriya student is successful as a guru, his spiritual master blessed him but that is necessarily the case.

A teacher can thrive from the energy he receives from students even if he breached the connection from his guru. Some teachers become psychologically-obese with the energy they receive from their doting students, but that is no indication of spiritual advancement.

Why should I be concerned with others? Suppose you are wounded in battle. A sword was pushed through your stomach. Then you notice that another warrior is wounded in the same way. What can you do to assist? How is it that he is your concern? You cannot move. You are in pain. He cannot move his body. He is in pain.

What should you do? Should you play physician and pretend that you can fix him. To help you must first help yourself but you cannot if the wound is fatal.

Thus, a kriya student is like the wounded warrior who lays on the battlefield beside other wounded people, with each unable to help the other.

Why make disciples if you have a worthy and able guru? Why not let that guru help others? If you find someone take him to that guru. Of course, if he tells you to give a treatment, give it on his behalf. That is all you do. You do not become a pretend physician.

However, the essential reason why I recommend that a student should not have disciples is for the benefit of the student. If you have disciples it will distract from self-purification. As you become more and more occupied helping others, you will hear less and less from the guru. Eventually you will be declared as a lineage guru. You will become obsessed with helping others. Your footing in spiritual life will be lost. Your guru will forget you. You will digress. Foolish students cannot see the digression. They will encourage you to be their guru as you become more and more occupied teaching, instructing and blessing. That will ruin you.

Buddhism: Nutriments

From the *Abhidhamma* (page 275), *Bhikkhu Bodhi* listed four nutriments. The Pali word is *ahara* which is derived from the Sanskrit, which is the same and which has the common meaning of food. The technical meaning in the Sanskrit is consumption or experience, anything which can be sensually apprehended.

You may have heard the terms *pratyāhāra* from the Patanjali *ashtanga* yoga system where that is the fifth stage of the eighth part discipline which Patanjali defined as yoga.

Pratyāhāra has the word *āhāra* with the prefix *praty (prati)* which means against or in opposition, so that *pratyāhāra* means that which is against consumption, against experiencing, against sensual acquirement.

Going back to the Buddhist meanings for these terms and taking care not to mix them and say that they are one and the same as in the *Yoga Sutras*, *Bodhi* wrote that there are four nutriments:

- edible food
- contact
- mental volition
- consciousness

He wrote that the word nutriment (*āhāra*) means that which sustains by acting as a strong supporting condition. According to the *Suttanta* method of explanation, **edible food** as nutriment sustains the physical body; **contact** sustains feeling; **mental volition** sustains rebirth in the three realms of existence, because volition is *kamma*, and *kamma* generates rebirth, and **consciousness** sustains the compound of mind and body.

This indicates that we take nourishment on the physical and psychological planes. Food on the physical side, contact on the emotional level, mental volition on the psychologically plane and consciousness as governing both levels and supervising the intercourse we have with anything sensually.

Even though Buddhism denies that there is a self, regulation of this contact is vital for controlling the feedback between the self and the environments. There has to be something there if we speak about rebirth because the question is:

Rebirth of what?

Even if you say that contact is always between energies and not between one self and another or between one self and an environment, still one should explain who observes the contact. Who communicates about the observation?

But Patanjali said that to speak of the contact of minds only without mentioning an observer is absurd.

Naad / Secret Companion

A yogi should take naad as a most sincere companion who removes all tendencies for loneliness and isolation. For yoga, isolation is a necessity, but one can do it with naad as one's secret companion, one's secret lover even.

Sneak inside the subtle head with naad waiting there for you. Nobody will know that you are not alone, that you have a lover secretly waiting. Everyone will think that you are a serious yogi, a meditator, a buddha. Naad will never come with you to the outside world. It will never tell anyone what you do in the privacy of the mind.

This is a lover whom you can resume after a big break up, after not paying attention for some time, after isolating yourself by abandoning naad meditation and then beginning it all over again, and getting yourself back into the confidence of naad resonance.

You were battered by your mind with its conventional thoughts and images. You left meditation aside because you were busy or because you had pressing non-yogic concerns. You successfully cheated your friends and followers by telling them that you meditate daily when the fact was that you ceased for a time and worried about this and that, hashing this and that in the mind?

Better hurry before your friends and disciples realize that you are a fake. Secretly go within. Listen to naad. Get close with naad so there is no space between you and the resonance.

Buddhism: Suffering is Real?

Buddhism has come to be known as a system of philosophy, and even as a religion to some, which is concerned primarily with compassion for all beings. However, when studying the life of Buddha and his teaching from the original sources in the Pali cannon, I find no evidence to support this.

Buddhism concerns the remove of suffering for the particular person who takes up the process, not for the whole world. The removal of personal suffering, my own, your own, seems to be more of the basis rather than concern for others.

In *"A Comprehensive Manual of Abhidhamma"* (page 288), *Bhikkhu Bodhi* wrote of the Four Noble Truths, which he listed as:

- Noble Truth of suffering
- Noble Truth of the Origin of Suffering
- Noble Truth of the Cessation of Suffering
- Noble Truth of the Path Leading to the Cessation of suffering

This pertains to the individual monk who took instructions from Buddha. The idea that Buddha noticed suffering in the world and took to renunciation to settle that, is questionable because I have found no evidence for that. He wanted to relieve himself of suffering. He did notice the suffering of others but his concern was his anguish. He did not set up institutions or *dharmashals* to help people who suffered. He was no Jesus Christ, raising the dead, healing the sick, making bread and fish for the starving.

I have not found one single instance where Buddha discussed with a monk about being compassionate for the whole world and about saving the world and or being liberated until the whole world was rescued. Other Buddhist teachers after Gautam introduced those ideas as totally different developments.

Some people today are saying that suffering is not real, that it is imagined by us and then we are traumatized by visualization of it, but Buddha did not say that. At least up to now I am unable to find any of the original literatures which show that he did.

This is interesting from the perspective of there not being a self in existence, as to what suffers and as to what or who inflicts suffering on whom. To Buddha no doubt, suffering was real. Here is a summary of the Four Noble Truths which Buddha declared. Remember that these are supposed to be Truths, and not just any truth but Noble ones which are declared for this system of austerity which *Gautam* introduced.

This is from what *Bhikkhu Bodhi* summarized:

The Four Noble Truths are the fundamental teaching of the Buddha, discovered by him on the night of his enlightenment and expounded by him repeatedly during his long ministry. He wrote that they are real, unalterable, undeceptive truths about existence.

The **Noble Truth of Suffering** is twelvefold as

- birth
- aging
- death
- sorrow
- lamentation
- pain
- grief
- despair
- association with the unpleasant
- separation from the pleasant
- not to get what one wants
- five aggregates of clinging

This noble truth of suffering, he wrote, comprises all phenomena of the three mundane planes of existence except craving.

Essentially this means that in Buddhism there is only suffering and craving and nothing else on what they figure to be the three mundane planes of existence.

Bhikkhu explained the **Noble Truth of the Origin of Suffering** as a single factor, namely craving, which is identical with the *cetasika* of greed *(lobha)*. Craving, he wrote, has three aspects:

- craving for sensual pleasures
- craving for continued existence
- craving for annihilation

One is not supposed to be involved in sensual pleasures. One is not supposed to want to continue as an existence. One is not supposed to want to be annihilated as an existence either.

Bhikkhu explained the **Noble Truth of the Cessation of Suffering** as being singlefold: It is nibbana, which is to be realized by the eradication of craving.

There is not a word about oneness, not even in the Pali language.

Buddhism: Dependent Arising/Ignorance

In the "Comprehensive *Manual of Abhidhamma*," *Bhikkhu Bodhi* explained the Buddha's analysis of dependent arising. He listed the basic formula as:

- dependent on ignorance arises kammic formations
- dependent on kammic formations arises consciousness
- dependent on consciousness arises mind-and-matter
- dependent on the six sense bases arises contact
- dependent on contact arises feeling
- dependent on feeling arises craving
- dependent on craving arises clinging
- dependent on clinging arises existence
- dependent on existence arises birth
- dependent on birth arises decay-and-death, sorrow, lamentation, pain, grief, and despair

Bodhi wrote that thus arises the whole mass of suffering.

Taking this at face value, any type of despair (depression/loss of hope), grief, pain, lamentation, sorrow, decay-and-death experience originated ultimately in ignorance, which as the source, developed into kammic formation, which in turn converted into consciousness, from which came mind-and-matter, which produced the six sense bases, which produced feeling, which produced craving, which produced clinging, which produced existence, which produced birth, which yielded despair/suffering and its variations.

However, it is not that simple. It is not good to substitute meanings for these terms. One should not assume that Buddha's meanings are the same as one figured. More than likely they are not. Being too eager to come to an agreement, to say that what one knows is what Buddha knew, serves the purpose of boosting one's enlightenment credentials, convincing oneself and the world that one is an equivalent buddha.

On page 295, *Bodhi* wrote that dependent arising is essentially an account of the causal structures of the round of existence, disclosing conditions that sustain the wheel of birth and death and make it revolve from one existence to another. He wrote that no single cause can produce an effect, nor does only one effect arise from a single cause. Rather, there is always a collection of conditions giving rise to a collection of effects. When in the familiar formula, one state is declared to be the condition for another, this is said in order to single out the chief condition among the collection of conditions and relate it to the most important effect among a collection of effects.

At this point, if you feel you understand this; if you think that you know all of it, and that you are in agreement with Buddha, or that you can simplify this and make it easy for everyone to understand, without having to go through so much intellectual analysis as Buddha did, and as he required of his monks, then what it the original cause? How would you define that origin which is given as ignorance?

Think about it honestly. Does your definition match his?

Bodhi wrote that according to the *Suttanta*, ignorance is non-knowledge of the Four Noble Truths and according to the *Abhidhamma*, it is non-knowledge of eight things: Four Noble Truths, the pre-natal past, the post-mortem future, the past and the future together and dependent arising.

Is that how you define it?

You agree with this definition of ignorance? You believe that future is real and that past is real. You know your pre-natal past? You know what your post mortem future will be?

Buddhism: Two Types of Meditation

Bhikkhu Bodhi in *"A Comprehensive Manual of Abhidhamma,"* list two methods of Buddhist meditation:

- calm *(samatha)*
- insight *(vipassana)*

Vipassana is a word which is used randomly with many groups claiming to give *vipassana* retreats and workshops. It may be of interest that *vipassana* is Pali from the Sanskrit original of *vipaśyanā (विपश्यना.*

The common meaning of *paśyanā* is seeing and when the prefix *vi* is added it means insight perception or integration.

However, it is not a good idea to run with root meanings of Sanskrit derived words. It is best to check the meaning used by the writer.

Leaving aside the common meaning, *Bhikkhu* gave this clarification as follows:

He wrote that in Buddhism two approaches to meditation development are recognized, calm and insight. Of the two, the development of insight is unique to the Buddha's teachings and is intended to generate direct personal realization of the truths discovered and enunciated by the Buddha. The development of calm is also found in non-Buddhist schools of meditation. However, in the Buddha's teaching calming meditation is taught because the serenity and concentration which it engenders provide a firm foundation for the practice of insight meditation.

He wrote that technically *samatha* or calm meditation is defined as the one-pointedness of mind in the eight meditative attainments -- the four fine material sphere *jhanas* of the *Suttanta* system and the four immaterial sphere *jhanas*. These attainments are called calm because, owing to the one-pointedness of mind, the wavering or trepidation of the mind is subdued and brought to an end.

Bhikkhu gave clarification about what Buddha intended *vipassana* to be:

The word *vipassana* rendered "insight" is explained as seeing in diverse ways. Insight is the direct meditative perception of phenomena in terms of three characteristics -- impermanence, suffering and non-self. It is a function of the *cetasika* of wisdom (*panna*) directed towards uncovering the true nature of things.

He gave the Buddhist text named, *"Visuddhimagga,"* as the main reference to get the details for this.

I would state:

If *vipassana* is the direct insight into impermanence, suffering and non-self, then there must be hundreds of different uses of the terms *vipassana* which have nothing to do with what Buddha intended.

Apart from this the statement of *Bhikkhu* that the development of insight is unique to the Buddha's teachings, is inaccurate because the yoga system in the time of Buddha, before his time and after his time, independently has insight meditation.

I think what is unique about Buddha's *vipassana* or insight meditation is the three objectives, not the quest of insight itself. Other systems have different quests and use insight as well. Buddha uses insight into the specific three aspects which Bhikkhu listed as

- impermanence,
- suffering
- non-self

For instance, there is much talk about insight *(buddhi, jnana, vijnana, jnana-dipa, jnana-chakshu)* in the *Bhagavad Gita* for example but while Buddha's application is to non-self, the *Bhagavad Gita* is to self or assertion of an eternal self which reincarnates.

Impermanence is tackled in the *Bhagavad Gita*. It is contrasted with a spiritual environment which has permanence.

Suffering is tackled in *Bhagavad Gita* too. In this respect the two systems are similar because Krishna like Buddha spoke of suffering and enjoying as being basically the same energy. But Krishna piloted Arjuna to a spiritual state of indifference and to attaining perpetual happiness or bliss, something which Buddha did not highlight.

Buddhism: Recollection of gods?

There is something very strange about a discipline which is portrayed by some as having no ideas about deities and God, where the founder of the system admitted many times to seeing, hearing and discoursing with both negative deities and positive ones.

However, as the saying goes, the devil is in the details. If you are not reading the fine print, your view of Buddhism may be contrary to the ideas of its founder. In the "*Comprehensive Manual of Abhidhamma, Bhikkhu Bodhi* wrote (page 333) about the ten recollections which he listed as:

- recollection of Buddha
- recollection of *Dhamma*
- recollection of *Sangha*
- recollection of morality
- recollection of generosity
- recollection of the *devas*
- recollection of peace
- recollection of death
- recollection of mindfulness occupied with the body
- recollection of mindfulness of breathing

Yes, that is the list, and it does include Buddha specifically.

Why?

Only heaven knows. Why should I remember him because after all I am supposed to focus on my buddha nature? Once at a Buddhist temple in South Korea, a monk who was resident dismissed Buddha and the Buddha idol installed, as being of little value in comparison his Buddha nature.

Perhaps he forgot his daily prayers, and his vow which has as its first acclaim Gautam Buddha.

And what does the word *deva* mean. Before I gave my meaning; let us see what *Bhikkhu* an authorized commentator, wrote:

The recollection of the *devas* is practiced by mindfully considering: "The deities are born in such exalted states on account of their faith, morality, learning, generosity, wisdom. I too possess these same qualities." This meditation subject is a term for mindfulness with the special qualities of one's own faith, etc., as its object and with the *devas* standing as a witness.

At the end of the book, in his glossary he gives the meaning of *deva* as god.

In respect to the recollection of breathing, he wrote the following:

Mindfulness of breathing is attentiveness to the touch sensation of the in-breath and out-breath in the vicinity of the nostrils or upper lip, wherever the air is felt striking as one breathes in and out.

This is obviously different to the *pranayama* practices of Indian yogis, even though their system does include similar practices.

Buddhism: Supernormal Powers

There is no question that Buddha had and used siddhis. He described them as having developed and used during the austerities he performed before enlightenment. However, in his teachings there is what is termed as *jhanas*, which *Bhikkhu Bodhi* in *"A Comprehensive Manual of Abhidhamma,"* defines as meditative absorptions.

Bhikkhu wrote that having emerged from the fifth *jhana* taken as a basis for direct knowledge, one enters into the fifth fine-material-sphere *jhana* occurring by way of direct knowledge with respect to such objects as visible forms, etc.

He then defined the direct knowledges as

- supernormal powers
- divine ear
- knowledge of others' minds
- recollection of past lives
- divine eye

The details of these are as follows:

Supernormal powers include the ability to display multiple forms of one's body, to appear and vanish at will, to pass through walls unhindered, to dive in and out of the earth, to walk on water, to travel through the air, to touch and stroke the sun and moon, to exercise mastery over the body as far as the Brahma world.

The **divine ear** enables one to hear subtle and coarse sounds, both far and near.

The **knowledge of others' mind** is the ability to read the thoughts of others and to know directly their states of mind

The **recollection of past lives** is the ability to know one's past births and discover various details about those births.

The **divine eye** is the capacity for clairvoyance, which enables one to see heavenly or earthly events, both far and near. Included in the divine eye is the knowledge of passing away and rebirth of beings, that is, direct perception of how beings pass away and re-arise in accordance with their karma.

Bhikkhu added that these kinds of direct knowledge are all mundane and are dependent on mastery over the fifth *jhana*. He said the texts list a sixth direct knowledge which is the destruction of taints which is supramundane and arises through insight.

Of interest is beings passing away and then re-arising in accordance with their *kamma*. At least if there is no self, here is admittance that there is a being, which has the potential to arise again in a new physical life.

Spiritual Practice / Lack of Progress

Even though I have not filed a practice report for some time, you can rest assured that progress is made. I keep contact with yogaGurus. It is a good idea that every yogi file reports of practice, irrespective of whether I file or not.

Reasons for my not filing are as follows:

- indistinct progress
- being in super-subtle dimensions which are hard to visualize
- Doing new kriyas which are irrelevant at lower stages and which are useless to persons whose practice have not gone into the neutral zone.

Indistinct progress means that progress is made but it is in a terrain where one can hardly distinguish what happens. That would be like if you walk in the Sahara Dessert. There are no landmarks, no trees, nothing. To say that you make progress makes no sense. One cannot give a start location and a destination. There is no reference which anyone would use as a marker from where one began.

How does one know that one makes progress?

There are two methods of knowing this; one is that one has super-subtle senses which do not exist in the earth body and which cannot report in a way which makes sense to an intellect which is reference to the earth body. There is a special difficulty teaching this. Most students want to hear what makes sense to their mundane point of reference. They are annoyed when they are told not to use that as a reference. They get quarrelsome, disrespectful and offensive.

The other method of knowing is the advice given by a yogaGuru who is on the super-subtle level or who comes to that level with instructions. This is the sure way of knowing the progress is made.

We may understand this by studying modern aircraft where a large jet can land even in fog, even when there is no visibility. The pilot uses instruments which tell him where the runway is located. some of these landings are smoother than the ones made in broad daylight when the pilot can see the runway clearly.

When a yogi is in **super-subtle dimensions** which are hard to verbalize, when he returns to the earth plane, he may struggle to explain what occured. He may know what happened but his vocabulary may be inadequate. It does happen however that as he repeatedly goes back to the super-subtle locales, he develops clarity.

When a yogi does **new kriyas which are irrelevant at lower stages** and which are useless to persons whose practice has not gone into the neutral zone, that yogi may never divulge what happened. There are two reasons for this:

- Fear of envy of neophyte yogis
- Fear of reaction from those sincere neophyte yogis who may become discouraged hearing that their development is the beginning stage of yoga.

Some neophyte yogis become envious of an advanced one when those neophytes hear of the progress made by the advanced ascetic. This envy is released into the atmosphere where it releases a discouraging influence.

If a Princess wears a diamond ring, people will observe it. If she does not wear a diamond ring, no one will know that she has one in her pocket. Even for advanced yogis, modesty is relevant. It means that one has an item of value but one is discretionary and does not display it.

Modesty in advanced yoga, unlike modesty in morality, has nothing to do with sexuality. It has everything to do with not letting others know what takes place in meditation. I publish advanced kriyas. Hence, I am not a modest yogi. I am excused because I have powerful yogaGurus sponsoring me.

Suppose an attractive actress with revealing clothing walked through the worse part of city but suppose she had armed bodyguards, no one will interfere with her. She is protected. Her immodesty will not result in the loss of dignity. It is a similar situation with my immodesty in terms of publishing confidential procedures.

If students hear of one's progress and if they cannot attain it or do not understand the basis for it or cannot reach the level where one practices, there is the likelihood that envy will arise or resentment or discouragement. One will have to counteract that energy or find a way to have the universe absorb it without having it stunt the progress.

The Body / Most Amazing

One amazing event is that when one uses an infant, a teenaged or a young adult body one does not realize that at every step the body is like the one the parent has. One has no understanding that one's body will age in nearly or exactly the same way as the parent body. One feels that one's body is of a different type, is youthful.

Why does this occur even in the case of persons who do yoga and meditation, where there is a pretense that one has a different body because one does yoga or because one is a vegetarian and the parent is a flesh eater, or because the parent's body is diseased and one's is healthy?

Usually at sixteen one does not realize that one will have grey hairs, that the head will be bald or scanty. One has no understanding that the teeth will develop defects and one may use dentures or have dental surgery. One feels that one can eat any and everything and nothing will happen to the body. It will remain healthy for all time.

One may if one can afford, acquire a savings or financial scheme which when projected would cause one to have a large sum of money in the elderly years but one has no idea of what the condition of the body will be during those years. Instead, one plans as if one will be using a youthful body at sixth-five years of age, as if one can enjoy life in exactly the same way one did during the young adult years. Even for spiritual seekers who speak about liberation, the extent of this ignorance is marvelous.

Buddhism: Purification of View

Bhikkhu Bodhi in his *"A Comprehensive Manual of Abhidhamma,"* page 349, mentions the Buddhist process of *Purification of View*.

He defined this as the discernment of mind and matter with respect to their characteristics, functions, manifestations and proximate causes.

He wrote that purification of view is so called because it helps to purify a wrong view of a permanent self. This purification is arrived at in the course of meditation by discerning the personality as a compound of mental and material factors which occur interdependently, without any controlling self behind them. This state is also called the analytical knowledge of mind-and-matter because the mental and material phenomena are distinguished by way of their characteristics.

Please read the above properly because it denies any definite personality, any definite you, and states that you are a compound of mental and material factors which occur interdependently without yourself controlling the formation.

Evacuation and Yoga Practice

For breath infusion and meditation, it is required for a student to be attentive to evacuation; to be sure that it is regular each day. Any skips and delays should be noted and steps taken to regularize the process. Not a day should go by where the student does not check evacuation to be sure that it is prompt.

Once one notices a change, one should figure why it occurred. If one cannot figure that at the spur of the moment, at least within two or three days for the most, one should know why the system slowed.

There are many reasons why regularity may be affected. Some are:

- travel
- sitting too long in automobiles
- change of diet
- lack of sufficient liquids in food
- dehydration due to heat or due to being in a super dry climate
- working more than usual

- walking or running for long distances
- preoccupation with a new lifestyle
- association with persons who are constipated
- spontaneous lifeForce adjustments
- using sleeping medications
- using pain killers
- using marijuana
- using opium or any of its derivatives
- using caffeine
- elderly years of the body which cause routine deterioration of its functions
- thinking of doing things which one does not usually do

These are some reasons. In any case the student should track to know what caused evacuation to slow. Recently I travelled. During the trip the vehicle ceased working. I spend about one entire day sitting at a mechanic shop waiting for repairs to be done. My schedule for eating went haywire. The weather was hot. I was dehydrated even though I drank water. The result was a full day's delay for evacuation, meaning that if evacuation was due in 24 hours after eating a main meal, it did not occur. Instead, it began in about 48 hours.

After this because I resumed the regular diet, the system resumed its regularity.

As soon as the lifeForce finds that it has to do something besides the routine, it ceases certain functions and focuses on the new task. This could mean that it ceases processing food waste which means that it will give an instruction to the peristalsis muscles to cease operation which means that there will be no urge to evacuate. Even if one tries to evacuate nothing will happen. The waste will not reach the rectum. It will be stalled like railway cars which have no engine attached to them.

One should understand that the lifeForce may cease peristalsis movements once every two weeks or so. When it does this, it will induce drowsiness. Its idea is to cause the person to sleep so that it can repair parts of the large colon and rectum. Thus, if the person rests during the day when that drowsiness occurs, the lifeForce will do the repair and will quickly move the food waste to the rectum, so that as soon as the person arises from the rest, he/she will feel the urge and will find that to be a surprisingly easy flush.

Learning how to relate to the lifeForce of the body is important. Otherwise, one will neglect to assist it, which will be to one's detriment.

Here are some details about the causes which I listed:

Travel causes the lifeForce to focus on the movement of the body or vehicle in which the body is positioned. This shift in focus may cause the peristalsis movements of the large intestines to grind to a halt, which means that no food waste will be transported to the rectum. The system will, however, continue extracting food nutrients from the food waste. This will cause the waste to become dryer which will cause a slower transport once the system is triggered later. This means that the evaluation will be delayed. There may be difficulty expelling the waste once the material reaches the rectum.

Sitting too long in automobiles, does affect the peristalsis muscles so that they become confused and do not know what to do. This is because of the vibration of the vehicle's movement as well as the engine vibration which moves through all materials in the vehicle. Persons who drive vehicles for a living, for instance trunk drivers, package deliverers and taxis drivers, are prone to constipation.

Change of diet can cause evacuation for numerous reasons. If for instance one used a drier food or a food which gums in the stomach and intestines, one may become constipated. Some foods become hard compacted as they pass through the intestines, these foods are liable to cause constipation because it is more difficult for the system to transport these through the long winding intestines. Foods which are sticky to the intestinal walls are transported slowly and may cause lumps, resulting in constipation.

Lack of sufficient liquids in food means that the food is dryish when it enters the stomach. If it is too dry, if it is like chips for instance, it will absorb moisture from the intestines. These foods will swell with whatever moisture is absorbed. These will then be transported with difficult through the intestines and may cause constipation. If a food has insufficient liquid, it will become dryer by the time it reaches the large colon. Such dryness is conducive to constipation.

Dehydration due to heat or due to being in a super dry climate will cause constipation because the system will extract whatever moisture it finds in the food waste. As the waste moves through the intestines, it will become dryer and dryer which means that its transport will take place with difficult and will be slower. Evacuation will then occur after three or four days or more even.

Working more than usual is likely to cause a delay in evacuation. This is because the lifeForce can only do some much in twenty-four hours of one day. It has limited time expenditure for doing chores in maintaining the body. If a man works say for six hours per day and his evacuation is regular in a certain way, if he increases these hours, to say, eight hours per day, it means that whatever other maintenance tasks for the body the lifeForce performs, will be lacking two hours of time for completion. Hence if a person increases the number of hours, it may disrupt the evacuation schedule.

Walking or running for long distances may affect the rate of evacuation because even though some walking or running, may aid in evacuation, much of it may have the reverse effect because of sweating and increase absorption of moisture from the food waste in the colon. The action of waking and running, by itself with the thighs moving against each other may cause food waste in the colon to become compacted which may result in evacuation delays.

Preoccupation with a new lifestyle may cause constipation if that lifestyle in some way or the other causes the lifeForce to be distracted from its duty of promptly removing food waste.

Association with persons who are constipated may cause one to become constipated because of the adoption of their lifestyle.

Spontaneous lifeForce adjustments occur for one reason or the other depending on what the lifeForce is urged to do. A yogi should note how the lifeForce executes its duty, and should as far as possible, assist to maintain proper health in the body.

Using sleeping medication, pain killers, marijuana, opium or any of its derivatives, or caffeine may cause delay in evacuation or even permanent damage to the peristalsis muscles because the chemicals in these substances may permanently alter the muscles' response.

Elderly years of the body which cause routine deterioration of its functions will cause constipation. As the body ages it naturally experiences deterioration of functions.

Thinking of doing things which one does not usually do, could cause delay in evacuation because the lifeForce may become so distracted, as to not give the commands for the peristalsis movements, which transport food waste. Thus, these movements may not occur, resulting in waste not reaching the rectum.

Part 5

Buddhism: Insight Knowledge

Bhikkhu Bodhi in his *"A Comprehensive Manual of Abhidhamma,"* listed the nine insight knowledges:

- knowledge of rise and fall
- knowledge of dissolution
- knowledge of the fearful
- knowledge of danger
- knowledge of disenchantment
- knowledge of desire for deliverance
- knowledge of reflective contemplation
- knowledge of equanimity towards formations
- knowledge of conformity

Of interest is his description of the knowledge of the fearful where he wrote that as the meditator contemplates the dissolution of formation in all three periods of time, he recognizes that all such dissolving things in all realms of existence are necessarily fearful.

This brings to fore the original motivation of Buddha for wanting to reach the stage of enlightenment where he was spooked by conventional trauma and decided to perform austerities to know the whys and wherefores of suffering.

Who else approaches spiritual life with this mentality?

Most human beings are accustomed to the trauma of sickness, old age and death and even that of seeing people like monks who moved aside from society, who will not raise a family, who exhibit indifference to the social development.

Krishna's Mixed-Up Instruction?

Chapter three of Bhagavad Gita begins with a challenge to Krishna. In chapter two Krishna explained his idea of the eternal soul using bodies and being capable of acting in the physical world with the backdrop of knowledge and realization that the body is temporary but the coreSelf is eternal. Arjuna heard Krishna's ideas which seem to be contradictory. To Arjuna, it seemed that a person could be involved in the world or be indifference to it but one could not be involved and indifferent simultaneously.

Arjuna boldly challenged Krishna.

अर्जुन उवाच
ज्यायसी चेत्कर्मणस्ते
मता बुद्धिर्जनार्दन ।
तत्किं कर्मणि घोरे मां
नियोजयसि केशव ॥३.१॥

arjuna uvāca
jyāyasī cetkarmaṇaste
matā buddhirjanārdana
tatkiṁ karmaṇi ghore māṁ
niyojayasi keśava (3.1)

arjuna — Arjuna; uvāca — contested; jyāyasī — is better; cet = ced — if; karmaṇaḥ — than physical action; te — your; matā — idea; buddhirjanārdana = buddhiḥ — mental action + janārdana — motivator of men; tatkiṁ = tat (tad) — them + kiṁ — why; karmaṇi — in action; ghore — in horrible; māṁ — me; niyojayasi — you urge; keśava — handsome-haired one

Arjuna contested: O motivator of men, if it is Your idea that the mental approach is better than the physically-active one, then why do You urge me to commit horrible action, O handsome-haired One? (Bhagavad Gita 3.1)

व्यामिश्रेणैव वाक्येन
बुद्धिं मोहयसीव मे ।
तदेकं वद निश्चित्य
येन श्रेयोऽहमाप्नुयाम् ॥३.२॥

vyāmiśreṇaiva vākyena
buddhiṁ mohayasīva me
tadekaṁ vada niścitya
yena śreyo'hamāpnuyām (3.2)

vyāmiśreṇaiva = vyāmiśreṇa — with this two-way + iva — like this; vākyena — with a proposal; buddhiṁ — intelligence; mohayasīva = mohayasi — you baffle + iva — like this; me — of me; tad — this; ekaṁ

— one; vada — tell; niścitya — surely; yena — by which; śreyo = śreyaḥ — the best; 'ham = aham — I; āpnuyām — I should get

You baffle my intelligence with this two-way proposal. Mention one priority, by which I would surely get the best result. (Bhagavad Gita 3.2)

As far as Arjuna was concerned, Krishna contradicted himself by proposing a psychological treatment and then saying that Arjuna should commit physically horrible acts like killing and wounding (*karmani ghore*) people on a battlefield. For simplicity's sake, Arjuna asked for either method. He would mentally resolve the problems with the Kurus or use his weapons in warfare.

Buddhism / Categories of Followers

In Buddhism there are categories of followers with the Buddha, *Guutam Shakyamuni*, being the unique unexcelled accomplished one, the supreme teacher of the process he pioneered. I went through many authorized literatures and never found Buddha being referred to as a personality or self, except indirectly.

Why is this?

Only heaven knows but I surmise that it may be because of the no-self, *anatta* declaration in Buddhism. For that Buddha has to be anything but a self, hence he is addressed frequently as the fully-accomplished one, the unique one but never as the fully-accomplished personality. The Sanskrit term *purusha* which is the match for the English word person is conspicuous by its absence in the Buddhist literature.

In the *"A Comprehensive Manual of Abhidhamma," Bhikkhu Bodhi* explained the analysis of individuals (page 358), giving these four:

- stream-enterer
- once-returner
- non-returner
- arahant

In brief, the **stream-enterer** is a person who is in the Buddhist Sanga and who by a swipe of fate is destined to become liberated no matter what. This person is condemned, so to speak, to be liberated. He cannot turn back from the course of spiritual realization which was founded by Buddha. Poor chap, he is fated for enlightenment. He cannot turn back even if he wanted to.

Then there is the **once-returner**. This fellow will take one more body somewhere and will not take any other body besides that. He is fated for enlightenment but he will take only one other body. He will be enlightened either in that last life or somewhere else in existence.

Then there is a **non-returner**. This yogi is in the course of his past life. He is fated for enlightenment either during that life or soon after in another existential situation.

Then there is the **Arahant**, who is the person who is enlightened while using the current body. This is similar to the yogi terminology of *jivanmukta* which is supposed to be the person who is liberated while using the physical form even before that body dies.

Bodhi listed three types of stream-enterers:

- One who will be reborn **seven times** at the most in the human or celestial world.
- One who takes birth in good families **two or three times** before attaining Arhantship
- One who will be reborn only **once more** before attaining the goal

In describing the stream enterer, Boddhi wrote that this one entered the stream that leads irreversibly to Nibbana, that is, the Noble Eightfold Path. He wrote that a stream enterer cut the courses three fetters -- personality view, doubt and adherence to rules and rituals; he has unshakable confidence in the Buddha, Dhamma and Sanga; and he is free from the prospect of rebirth in any of the woeful realms

Wait a minute, before we misunderstand this and feel that Buddhism has no restriction, let us note that the stream enterer cut personality view, doubts and adherence to rituals, but we need to understand that he does so up to the point of having to follow whatever Buddha established as rules for monks, as well as rule of the dhamma or doctrine and belief system of Buddha, and rules for how to associate with other monks and with lay people. This is not a free for all even though it was freedom from the Vedic rituals which were current in the area where Buddha practiced.

This individual, the stream enterer, cannot again become materialistic, his freedom of choice is done, he must stay on the course and become liberated for seven births for the most. Poor fellow, he can enjoy himself no longer. His fate is sealed.

The second type of individual, the once-returner, eliminated the grosser forms of lust, hate and delusion. Thus, although attenuated forms of these defilements can still arise in him, they do not occur often. Their obsessive force is weak. Good fellow, he will never have to say that Christian prayer about lead us not into temptation and deliver us from evil. He does not have the psychological mechanisms in his nature which will pull him obsessively to lust, hate or delusion.

For him there is no more sexing, craving, cursing, abusing or becoming disenchanted and mistaken about anything. Fate freed him. Except for some slight involvements with trauma, he is free.

Bodhi, quoting from a Buddhist text called the *Puggalapassatti*, list five kinds of once-returners:

- One who attains the status of once-returning in the human world, then takes rebirth in the human world, and attains final Nibbana here.
- One who attains the status of once-returning in the human world, then takes rebirth in a heavenly world and attains final *Nibbana* there.
- One who attains the status of once-returning in the heavenly world, then takes rebirth in a heavenly world and attains final *Nibbana* there.
- One who attains the status of once-returning in the heavenly world, then takes rebirth in a human world and attains final *Nibbana* there.
- One who attains the status of once-returning in the human world, then takes rebirth in a heavenly world and passes the full lifespan there and then takes rebirth again in the human world, where he attains final nibbana.

This is interesting because it means that the course of persons who must take one more birth before becoming enlightened is variant. One may have to assume another physical body or one may have to get a celestial or heavenly body. Because of the idea of no-self in Buddhism, the question as to who is the subject of this activity, remains. However, we may overlook that issue for the moment, just as the Buddhist authorities frequently do.

The next category is the non-returner. *Bodhi* states that this involves totally abandoning sensual lust and ill will, which is for those who become non-returners. They do not return to this (sensuous) plane.

Thus, this means that the return bit is in reference to this sensual plane. It is not left open for me or you to define. It is specific to not returning to this sensuous plane.

The achievements of the non-returner are listed:

- Full eradication of sensual lust and ill will which are the fetters which bind to the sensuous world
- Eradication of the taints of sensual desire and unwholesome *cetasikas*, hatred and worry, as well as all greed taking a sensuous object.

Bodhi wrote that this person will be spontaneously reborn in a fine-material realm and there attain final nibbana. It should be noted that while only non-returners are reborn in the Pure Abodes, there is no fixed determination that all non-returners are reborn there. He list five types of non-returners:

- One who was reborn spontaneously in a higher world, and who generates the final path before he reached the midpoint of the lifespan.
- One who generates the final path after passing the midpoint of the lifespan, even when on the verge of death.
- One who attains the final path without exertion.
- One who attains the final path with exertion.
- One who passes from one higher realm to another until he reaches the *akannittha* realm, the Highest Pure Abode, and there attains the final path.

It is interesting that there are pure abodes, higher realms which are more than just the imagination of the said monk. Heavens in Buddhism?

Boddhi explained the *Arahant* individuals whom he wrote of as having total abandonment of defilements. An Arahant is a destroyer of taints, a supreme recipient of offerings in the world. With the attainment of *Arhantship*, even the five higher fetters are eradicated. These are

- desire for fine-material existence
- desire for immaterial existence
- desire for conceit
- desire for restlessness
- desire for ignorance

There is also the eradication of the remaining unwholesome *cetasikas* left unabandoned by the earlier paths: delusion, shamelessness, fearlessness of wrongdoing, restlessness, conceit, sloth and torpor.

Buddhism: The Beginning of These Lives

It appears from the Buddhist texts that Buddha did not ascertain a beginning point for any being. I cannot say for any self or person because the notion of self or person is vague or totally absent in Buddhism but being is mentioned frequently. *Bhikkhu Bodhi* in the book *"In the Buddha's Words,"* (page 37) states that once Buddha explained to some monks that this *samsara* is without discoverable beginning. A first point is not discerned of beings roaming and wandering on hindered by ignorance and fettered by craving.

Buddha said this,

> *Suppose, monks, a man reduce this great earth to balls of clay the size of jujube kernels and put them down saying (for each one): "this is my father, this is my father's father." The sequence of that man's fathers and grandfathers would not come to an end, yet this great earth would be used up and exhausted. For what reason? Because monks, this* samsara

is without discoverable beginning. A first point is not discerned of beings roaming and wandering on hindered by ignorance and fettered by craving. For such a long time, monks, you have experienced suffering, anguish and disaster, and swelled the cemetery. It is enough to become disenchanted with all formation, enough to become dispassionate towards them, enough to be liberated from them."

With no-self, and with a being according to Buddha there was perpetual suffering and anguish in the past and one should adopt his process to get out of it. Births before this current one, are infinite from the analogy of the jujube kernels. Taking the situation as it stands one can follow the reasoning of Buddha if one either knows for sure that there were these trillions of births before and one suffered and had anguish in these or if one does not know for sure but believes that Buddha has the correct infallible insight into this.

Special Note / Samsara

On page 2, Boddhi wrote that this is a world in which sentient beings are propelled forward by their own ignorance and craving, from one life to the next, wandering blindly through the cycle of rebirths called *samsara*.

Rescue One's Individual Energy

On the morning of August 6th 2014, during breath infusion practice there were two yogaGurus present but each was in a different dimension so that it was as if each was present alone. In the astral existence there are trillions of dimensions and sub-dimensions, so that one person may be standing exactly where another person is located or may be near to where that other person is situated, and still, they are worlds apart dimensionally.

There is also the space created by the level of existence of each individual where one person may be existentially at a distance from another person and be located in exactly the same place. We may consider this in terms of rich and poor, where two persons living in the same city may have different means of income, where one person can purchase whatever is desired while the other can barely buy what is needed for even basic subsistence. They are located in the same city, and may even be located in the same building and yet their situations show a glaring disparity.

Yogeshwarananda was the one who spoke during the breath infusion, Lahiri said nothing but looked on, checking to see how I complied with his instruction about causing the subtle body to be divested of its heavy astral energy which was in the thighs, legs and feet.

I had some luck with the practice and still have much to complete but overall, he was pleased with the endeavor even though I exceeded the time he assigned for it to be completed.

Yogeshwarananda made these comments:

This is a conglomerate, a joint venture. This creation is so. No one is free to say that he/she has his/her energy invested separately. It is a mix at every stage. One cannot get a body without being in a conglomerate with the parents and relatives. There are political factors which are involved in any birth anywhere, even in the most primitive societies with their elders and shamans. Even in the animal kingdom if one takes a body, one will be obligated to this or that animal parent, and this or that environmental condition.

Since there is no way to become totally isolated, the alternative is to try to rescue one's individual energy if one can isolate it. Can you elevate your mother and father? Can you elevate your clan? Suppose you elevated your parents, what would that mean, because they are hooked into a conglomerate of their ancestors and friends? If you elevate one of them, say the mother or the father and you shift her or him you will find others attached. How many can you upgrade and being that they are related, when will the connections be broken.

If everyone is hooked to someone else endlessly, then if you try to rescue one you will find that as you lift that one, another one is linked to that one. When will you stop uplifting the linked personalities?

The student should leave everything as it is in this creation. He/She should work for his/her deliverance and slip out of the connections out of the conglomerate.

What percentage of you is you?

Calculate that!

Extract that you-percentage. Work for that. Leave the rest of you in the mix. It is not you. It is the investment of others which somehow is mixed with you.

Lahiri: Uplift of Nutritional Energy

The diagram below is a new configuration which is being formed in my subtle body. This is part of an experiment which I do under direction of Lahiri concerning the development of a *yogaSiddha* body before leaving the physical one, so that the subtle body configuration is changed to make it suitable for association with *siddhas* in the world hereafter in one of the zones called *Siddhaloka*

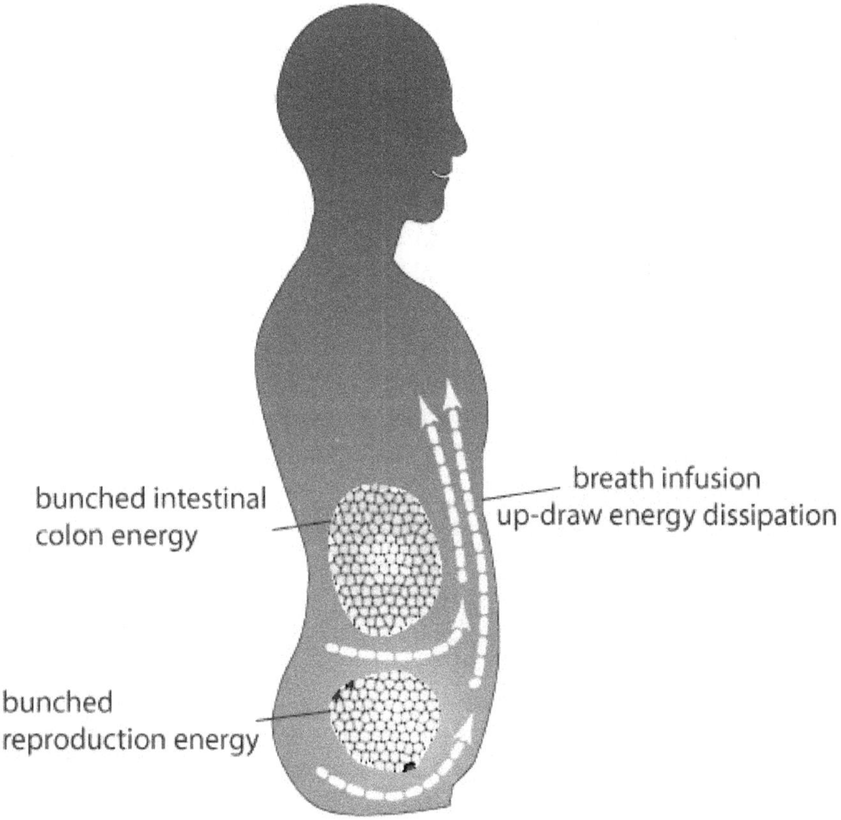

This configuration may occur in the psyche of a yogi after the kundalini was demolished from the *sushumna nadi* central passage and relocated into the brain. There must also be a bid for celibacy to the extent of abandoning the interest that the yogi has for sex excitement in terms of the coreSelf in relation to its adjuncts. It is only relevant for the energy of the coreSelf and does not apply to the energy of ancestors or their ownership of parts of the energy of the physical and subtle body of the yogi.

Whatever is owned by others, is owned by them and cannot be controlled by the yogi. Hence, with help from superior souls, he/she must learn how to extract only his/her energy and deal with that, leaving the rest to the command of the other shareholders. Lahiri was concerned with the uplift of the nutritional energy as compared to the traditional means which is the uplift of the sex hormone energy *(reta/rajas).*

He is interested in the development which is *urdhvapoṣaṇa*, where *poṣaṇa* is nutrition energy. Lahiri's idea is that one should not bother with anything which is an after-effect or a sub-production but should instead target the original energy which accumulates in the psyche, leaving aside the after-effect productions like sexual energy for instance and any other hormonal energy which is generated.

In the diagram, one should observe the two masses of pixelated compressed infused energy which has the infused air compressed into it. These are the intestinal mass energy and the reproduction energy which is usually misidentified as sex energy. Its purpose from the perspective of nature which is the real controlling force, is reproduction but its use by the entities is generally termed as sexual pleasure because of the perspective assumed by the souls when they are involved in its usage.

Soldiers, who are on the front line, interpret that they are going to kill the enemy but the commanders who sent them to fight regard them as tools of fate. This is due to varying perspectives regarding the same phenomena.

The breath up-draw energy distribution lines are four in this case. (See previous diagram.) These show the direction of the flow of energy where no traditional spinal kundalini is involved. With each of the breath infusions instead of the energy going down to *muladhara* chakra, the energy causes dissipation of the hormonal force and pulls that vaporized energy upward through the trunk of the subtle body through the neck into the brain.

Mulabandha **Base Chakra Lock**

Every teacher advises according to his/her training and experience, which means that advisories will vary. The same practice used by one teacher may be used by another for a different reason and for a different result even. Some teachers because of a particular experience may give strict instructions which apply because of some specific problem that teacher had while practicing.

In my practice everything is focused for results in the subtle body. The idea is to target the subtle body, using the physical one to get into the subtle and to be more aware of what happens on the psychic side.

I do not and did not in the past practice *mulabandha* continuously at all times, but there was a period of practice about forty years ago when I applied *mulabandha* through the day as much I could remember to apply it. There was a period when I contracted and then released, contracted and then released that lock continually anytime I remembered it. This lock is *ashwini mudra*.

I experienced that when I did breath-infusion using *kapalabhati/bhastrika pranayama*, when energy was surcharged near the base chakra, there would be a heat force there. It vented itself through the bottom of the trunk, at the anus. In the subtle body simultaneously, there would be a microscopic hole, through which energy would escape outwards. This was when I did breath-infusion, and energy would accumulate in the bottom of the trunk. To stop the energy from escaping, as soon I would stop a series of rapid breaths, I would apply *ashwini mudra,* thus restricting, the energy from escaping through that tiny hole.

As a rule, as soon as I finish a series of rapid breaths, I applied the base chakra lock, sex organ lock, navel lock and chin locks almost simultaneously. This prevented any accumulated energy from escaping through those chakras or their zones, resulting in kundalini being force up the spine into the brain.

However, while doing a series of breaths I do not apply *ashwini mudra* until I cease the breathing on an inhale. Then I immediately apply that lock with the other ones mentioned. I focus in the subtle body to observe and direct the infused energy and the kundalini or the combination of the two if they are combined already.

Because of doing these practices for years, I find now that I no longer have to apply the base lock, because it is sealed at the bottom. Energy no longer leaks through it, even when the lock is not applied. The energy stays in the psyche and makes no attempt to course outwards through a chakra except through the third eye or crown chakras. Sometimes after a session of rapid breaths, when I check I find that the infused energy in combination with kundalini stays put in the psyche or courses upwards through the spine into the head. It makes no attempted to travel through the tiny hole at *muladhar* chakra. The hole appears to have vanished. There is no need to apply the locks but as a matter of course and because of habit I usually apply it anyway. I also apply locks to compress the accumulated pranic energy in on itself until it implodes in the subtle body.

Here are verses from the *Kundalini Hatha yoga Pradipika* about that lock.

अथ मूल - बन्धः

पार्ष्णिभागेन सम्पीड्य योनिमाकुनछयेद्गुदम् |

अपानमूर्ध्वमाकृष्य मूल - बन्धो|अभिधीयते || ६१ ||

atha mūla–bandhaḥ

pārṣṇi bhāgena sampīḍya yonimākuñchayedgudam |

apānamūrdhvamākṝṣya mūla–bandho|abhidhīyate || 61 ||

atha – now to be explained, mūla – anus–coccyx complex, bandhaḥ = physio–psychic compression, pārṣṇi – heel, bhāgena – region, sampīḍya – compressing, yonim – vaginal passage, ākuñchayed = ākuñchayet = should contract, gudam – rectum, apanam – negatively charged breath energy, ūrdhvam – upward, ākṝṣya – upward coursed, mūla = anus–coccyx, bandho = bandhaḥ = physio–psychic compression, abhidhīyate – called

Now the mulabandha physio-psychic compression of the anus-coccyx complex is explained:

Pressing the heel against the vaginal or potential vaginal passage, the yogi should contract the rectum. This causes the negatively charged breath energy to course upward. It is called the *mulabandha* anus-coccyx physio-psychic compression. (Kundalini Hatha Yoga Pradipika 3.61)

अधो - गतिमपानं वा ऊर्ध्वगं कुरुते बलात् ।

आकुञ्चनेन तं पराहुर्मूल - बन्धं हि योगिनः ॥ ६२ ॥

adho–gatimapānaṁ vā ūrdhvagaṁ kurute balāt ।

ā kuñcanena taṁ prāhurmūla–bandhaṁ hi yoginaḥ ।। 62 ।।

adho = adha = downward, gatim – coursing, apānaṁ – negatively charge breath energy, vā – indeed, ūrdhvagaṁ – going upward, kurute – should go, balāt – due to being forced, ākuñcanena – by contraction, taṁ – that, prāhur = prāhuḥ = said, mūla = anus–coccyx complex, bandhaṁ = physio–psychic compression, hi – indeed, yoginaḥ – yogis

The downward coursing negatively charged breath energy should go upwards by forceful contraction. The yogis call that procedure the anus-coccyx physio-psychic compression. (Kundalini Hatha Yoga Pradipika 3.62)

गुदं पाष्ण्या तु सम्पीड्य वायुमाकुञ्चयेद्बलात् ।

वारं वारं यथा चोर्ध्वं समायाति समीरणः ॥ ६३ ॥

gudaṁ pārṣṇyā tu sampīḍya vāyumākuñcayedbalāt ।

vāraṁ vāraṁ yathā cordhvaṁ samāyāti samīraṇaḥ ।। 63 ।।

gudaṁ – rectum, pārṣṇyā – with the heel, tu – indeed, sampīḍya – pressing, compressing, vāyum – infused air, ākuñcayed = ākuñcayet = should contract, balāt – due to force, vāraṁ vāraṁ = repeatedly, yathā – accordingly, cordhvaṁ = ca (and) + urdhvam (upward), samāyāti – goes, samīraṇaḥ – breath energy

Indeed, by pressing the rectum with the heel, the infused air should be forcibly contracted. Doing this repeatedly the breath energy will go upward. (Kundalini Hatha Yoga Pradipika 3.63)

प्राणापानौ नाद - बिन्दू मूल - बन्धेन चैकताम् ।
गत्वा योगस्य संसिद्धिं यच्छतो नात्र संशयः ॥ ६४ ॥

prāṇāpānau nāda–bindū mūla–bandhena caikatām ।
gatvā yogasya saṁsiddhiṁ yacchato nātra saṁśayaḥ ।। 64 ।।

prāṇāpānau – positively and negatively charged subtle force, nāda – naad supernatural sound resonance, bindū – causal node sources, mūla = anus–coccyx complex, bandhena = physio–psychic compression, caikatām = ca (and) + ekatām (one, unity), gatvā – gives way, causes, yogasya – of yoga, saṁsiddhiṁ – full perfection, yacchato = yacchataḥ = yields, nātra = not here, saṁśayaḥ – doubt

When positively and negatively charged subtle forces, as well as the naad supernatural sound resonance and the causal node sources are united by the application of the physio-psychic compression of the anus-coccyx complex, then that yields full perfection of yoga. Of this there is no doubt. (Kundalini Hatha Yoga Pradipika 3.64)

Buddha: View of Time

So far in going through the Buddhist canons especially the parts about what Buddha said and done, I found no evidence that he denied the reality of time. I found no statement where he declared time as an illusion or that the past and future times are unreal.

In *Bhikkhu Bodhi's "In the Buddha's Words,"* page 38, in a conversation with a monk who asked Buddha to explain an eon, Buddha replied:

"An eon is long, monk. It is not easy to count it, to say it is so many years, or so many hundreds of years, or so many thousands of years, or so many hundreds of thousands of years."

The monk then asked for a simile.

Buddha replied that suppose there was a great stone mountain a yojana long, a yojana wide and a yojana high, without holes or crevices, one solid mass of rock. At the end of every hundred years a man would stoke it once with a piece of fine cloth. That great stone mountain may by this effort be worn away and eliminated but the eon would still have not come to an end. So long is an eon monk. And of eons of such length, we have wandered through so many eons, so many hundreds of eons, so many thousands of eons, so many hundreds of thousands of eons. For what reason? Because, monk, this *samsara* is without discoverable beginning. It is enough to be liberated from them."

In the glossary, a *yojana* is given to be approximately six miles.

What is interesting in this is the Buddha's direct admission of selves which he termed as we having wandered for hundreds of thousands of years.

It would be interesting how one would negotiate one's way around the reality of a self with his statement.

Failure to define a self does not in any way mean there is no self, because there has to be something which observed the wandering in the eons, as Buddha observed.

Denying the social self, the person from one birth, does not in any way prove that there is no permanent unalterable core around which such a social self is formulated in one life and then in another. It only questions the validity of the social self as being a temporary composite but there must be some unit reality upon which that social self is formulated in each of the many hundreds of thousands of lives.

For that core, it is enough for it to be done with the transmigrations and to shed the temporary masks which it uses as a social person function in each particular time and place of each particular birth in each particular temporary physical or psychic locale.

Gayatri Mantra Bestowal

Recently I was given a sun-ball by the sun deity of the current sun planet which sustains this earthly place and its inhabitants.

When the sun ball first entered the top of the subtle head, it went downward through the neck, then through the trunk and then it split into two orbs and went through the thighs, legs and into the ankles, where each glowed. These remained there for two days.

After that some sun energy was pelted against the right side of the subtle head. It fractured that right side into fragment-pixels which fell away. The fracturing produced no sensation. It was as if there was a bodiless formless condition on that side of the subtle head.

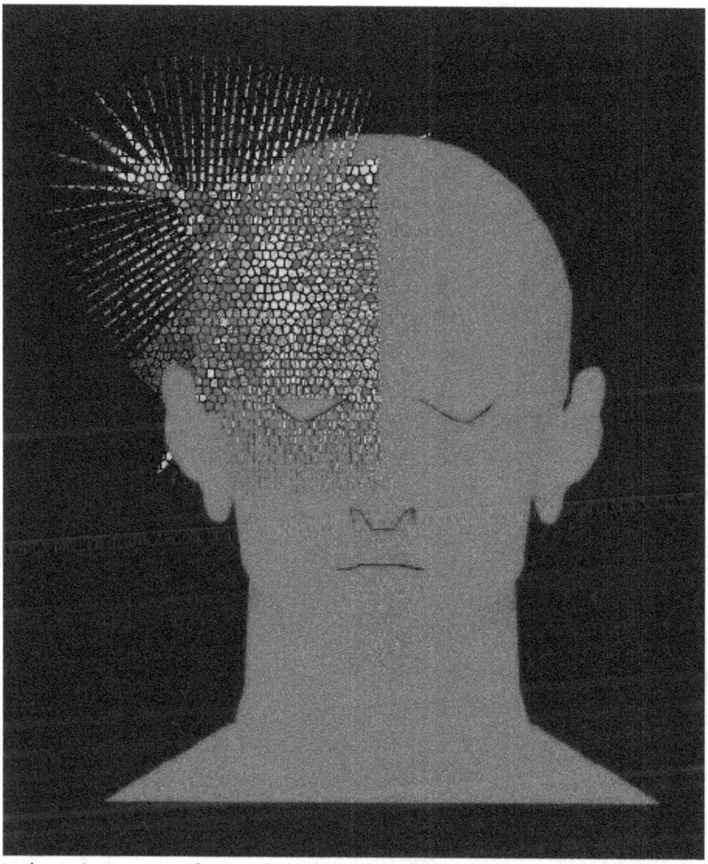

When it is complete, this disintegration of the subtle body, causes the ascetic to move beyond the Swarga heavenly world, and move up beyond Siddhaloka to enter the Satyaloka and such places where one uses a supernatural body which is higher than the subtle body which we current endure in astral projections and lucid dreams.

Some yogis after the completion of this fragmentation, or break-up of their subtle forms, enter what is called the bodiless state. Some stay there for a time, for millions of years while others go to even higher zones.

At some stage, a student must take assistance from the sun deity. This is why the original and most frequently used *gayatri* mantra is the glorification and recognition of the assistance rendered to the ascetic by *Savitur*, the sun-god. The fact remains that the physical and subtle bodies which we currently use, are sustained by energy from the sun. There is no way for such bodies to exist in sentiency without that energy. The sun deity is the lord of this situation, the functional and immediate existential godFather.

There are many persons who recite the *Savitur gayatri* mantra but it is ineffective for them because either they did not get it from the right agent or they were not directly inspired by the sun-god. As the story goes, *Yajnavalkya* got in a quarrel with his guru *Vaishampayana* (Vai-shum-pai-a-nuh). When the guru told the student to return the teachings of the *Yajur Veda* forthwith, the student, *Yajnavalkya,* vomited the techniques and information. It was then eaten by some other disciples, who for the filthy task of eating vomit, assumed the form of birds (*tittiri*) and subsequently composed it as the *Taittiriya* Upanishad.

Yajnavalka for his part, being condemned by his spiritual teacher, went to perform austerities. He was so proficient, that the sun-god noticed. This deity directly instructed *Savitur gayatri* mantra and other Vedic sounds and information to *Yajnavalkya.*

Unless one is connected to *Yajnavalka* or to the sun god or to their agent, one cannot use the mantra effectively. But there is another important thing to consider which is that one should not request the mantra from a guru or deity. This is because if one is fated to get the mantra, it will be inspired into one's mind or one will be introduced to it and its usage by the deity or yogaGuru. There is no need to request this mantra. One should not get the idea that one should use this mantra.

It is not true that gurus own mantras, unless those mantras pertain to their names and vibrations only. Mantras of deities are not owned by a guru. He is not authorized by a deity to divulge the mantra to anyone merely because that person is follower or faithful attendant. The deity must himself/herself want to bestow the mantra for it to be effective. In other words, the desire to give the mantra should be that of the deity not that of the guru. The student should not request a mantra or pester the guru to get one from him. If the deity wants to give the mantra even if the guru does not transmit it to the student, the deity will himself give it just as in the case of *Yajnavalka* who was rejected by his guru and was told to return all training. Still, he was blessed by the deity.

A guru is not the indispensable aspect in giving mantras. It is the deity who is the feature. If a guru is unwilling to give it, then if the deity wants the disciple to have it, the deity will send another agent or will render it directly into the mind of the disciple.

One cannot from this end of existence puncture one's way into the realm of any substantial deity like the sun-god. One has to be invited into their realms. They cannot invite one by coming under one's influence or desire. It simply does not manifest like that.

If one got the gayatri mantra from someone and it is not effective to link one with the sun deity, that means that the person who awarded the mantra was not properly connected with the deity. And in fact, no guru can give the mantra effectively if he is not inspired to do so.

Ego of Gautam Buddha?

The most interesting thing about Buddhism is the fact that, one is told that one has all possibilities, that one has the Buddha nature and that one should focus only on that. Alternately, one is required to honor and even kowtow to Buddha. Sometimes the Buddhist authorities downplay the obeisance which is require but when one reads the Pali cannon literature about what actually took place during the life of Buddha, one finds that it is unavoidable and was in fact a mandatory requirement for every monk to recognize Buddha uniqueness.

In *Bhikkhu Bodhi's* book, "*In the Buddha's Words*," there is mention of a conversation given to the monks where Buddha described his uniqueness:

He said this.

There is one person who arises in the world for the welfare of the multitude, for the happiness of the multitude, out of compassion for the world, for the good, welfare and happiness of the devas and humans. Who is that one person? It is the Tathagata (Tut-haa-guh-tuh), the Arahant, the Perfectly Enlightened One. This is that one person.

Monks, there is one person arising in the world who is unique, without a peer, without counterpart, incomparable, unequalled, matchless, unrivaled, the best of humans. Who is that one person? It is the Tathagata, the Arahant, the Perfectly Enlightened One. This is that one person.

Monks, the manifestation of one person is the manifestation of great vision, of great light, of great radiance; it is the manifestation of the six things unsurpassed, the realization of the four analytical knowledges; the penetration of the various elements; of the diversity of the elements; it is the realization of the fruit of knowledge and liberation; the realization of the fruits of stream-entry, once-returning, nonreturning, and arahantship. Who is that one person? It is the Tathagata, the Arahant, the Perfectly Enlightened One. This is that one person.

How is this to be accepted, this uniqueness of this individual who many of his followers say taught about no-self (anatta), who, they say should not be distinguished, who is like everyone else, who supposedly did not sort himself from others? Why did he make these statements even after the enlightenment? Was this his ego? Is it a fact that he is unique?

Did he slip from enlightenment when he made these statements?

Only one person? What does that mean?

- He has no equal anywhere!
- He is without peer!

- He is without counterpart!
- He is incomparable!
- He is unequalled!
- He is matchless!
- He is unrivaled!
- He is the best of humans.

That is what he said but others are saying,

"No, he is like every one of us. We are like him. There is nothing special about him."

"Neither of us have real selves, neither us nor him."

Intricacies of Celibacy

In terms of celibacy, it is mostly a farce. This is because of the outlay of nature when it creates these bodies which are done with the help of the kundalini. Since the kundalini has its own plan and nature also has her plan, the desire and wishes of the tiny coreSelf are more or less wishes only and is not actuality.

Does this mean that the self should do nothing about it or that the self should accept whatever the individual kundalini or nature arranges? The answer to this is an obvious no.

The reason being that in all cases, one is not allowed to ignore the kundalini or nature's plan. In some cases, even when one can do absolutely nothing about it, one is still motivated impulsively to resist or to comply with nature no matter what.

A man who is thrown from a ship in the middle of the Pacific is bound to splash around even if he knows that he is not a swimmer and that he will perish in any case.

A boy, who has chiggers in his pores, is bound to scratch the area even if it is explained scientifically that his finger nails cannot remove the tiny insects and that by scratching, he would irritate his skin further.

In the celibacy effort there are many aspects, so that if one objective is not achieved, the whole effort is spoilt because of that missing accomplishment. Still the ascetic should strive to master whatever portions of the practice he may achieve.

Even though there is no possibility of permanently removing the bacteria, people scrub the teeth each morning. After the scrub, the mouth will always be re-infested.

In a physical body, celibacy is rooted in the nutritional feature of the body. Without food, there can be no sexual expression. It hinges on the food eaten and how the particular body of a student processes those nutrients.

Have you ever seen a family walking, where one member is obese, and the others have non-obese forms? Even though they share food equally and even though each eats to its heart's content, still one member is obese. That person's system processes the same food differently.

How does my body process food?

How much of the nutrients which my body takes from the intestines are dedicated to the manufacture of sex hormones?

If I were to starve my body, would it still hoard a greater percentage of nutrients for sex hormone manufacturing?

If I were to be locked in a prison with no means of sexual expression, with even my hands handcuffed behind my back, would my body still hoard most of the nutrition energy for sex expression?

Besides the status I would derive and the pride I may have, what then is the use of being celibate if the body will continue hoarding nutrients primarily for sexual expression?

This concerns the ways and means of the inner attitude of the psyche and not the external display of celibacy or the lack of it.

Subtle body/ Memory/ Science

The perpetuity of the subtle body is infinite in relation to the physical one but it is finite in relation to the coreSelf or *atma*. For the time being while the core is aware of this physical environment (manifest *prakriti*) the core has no choice but to use the subtle body and on occasion the physical one. The value of the subtle form is that unless the core has such a body, it cannot access either the subtle astral world or the physical reality.

The system which transmigrates is the subtle body. It requires a physical form for completion. It generates a physical body anytime nature provides materials and conditions in which such a body can be manufactured. If we remove the subtle body, transmigration through physical forms is over.

Even though the subtle body is perpetual in reference to the short-lived physical form, still that perpetuity is not realized by the coreSelf usually. This is because the core does not have a direct memory. This lack of memory is a problem which was addressed in *Bhagavad Gita* where when Arjuna challenged Krishna for stating that he, Krishna, taught *Vivaswan* and others from a remote time. Krishna replied that he, Krishna, could remember but Arjuna could not. The idea is that Arjuna even as a self does not have memory of the long-lost past.

The self is absolutely perpetual. The subtle body is perpetual in a relative sense but since the memory of the self is reliant on the type of body, he/she uses, that perpetuity may not be realized unless the self is infallible like Krishna.

The coreSelf as it is, does not have access to a deathless mind which is full of memories, talent and information. If it did, it would resume such memories when it takes another body. The fact is that when it takes another form, we find that it does not have the memory from its past lives, even from the most recent one.

If anything, it has instincts from the past lives but that is not coherent memory. That is urges and predispositions. In the Sanskrit literature we are confronted with a psyche or subtle body which has components. How so?

Let us check these Sanskrit words and their meanings:

- atma
- ahankara
- buddhi
- indriyas
- smriti
- kundalini

If these are psychic components, we are in a fix as to how to study their relationships. For instance, in regards to memory, Western psychology confronted us with the idea of unconscious, subconscious and conscious. Does this relate to types of memories as well?

It may be possible to use an electronic machine to scan the mind for events from the past. The reason for this is that people of the past who did not take other physical bodies and who lived in the astral world, are currently there thinking and feeling. These incidences occur within the medium of space-time. They use light and radio frequencies. If a machine can coherently detect those vibrations, it may be possible for it to relate the information in a useful way.

In the *Puranas* there are stories, where we read of persons, even criminal yogis like *Madhu* and *Kaitabha*, who survived the dissolution of the cosmos which resulted from the assumption of slumber of the mind of the Brahma deity, where *Madhu* and *Kaitabha* were in the process of taking that deities' mental contents, his cosmic creative skills.

If a yogi, even a criminal one, can steal the contents of someone's mind, even of a deity, then why should we doubt that one day, digital devices may correctly render thoughts and memories.

Shankaracharya made sexual use of the bodies of some wives of a recently deceased prince when *Shankara* was challenged about carnal knowledge and need the information to defeat *Mandana Misra*. In that case he left his body and assumed the body of the recently deceased prince and experienced sexual pleasure through that prince's form. Then *Shankara* resumed his body and transfered the memory into his physical form. Of course, he is not an ordinary person, but it shows some of the possibilities.

Astral Body Situation

For those persons who fulfilled the purpose of taking a specific body, the life purpose ends with the death of the form. For others, the remnant of the purpose remains in the subtle body, and moves with it, in it, to the hereafter. This purpose energy is then reformulated and is put into the purpose for the next body which that person would be, as the son or daughter of parents.

There is a story from the *Puranas* which may illustrate this. That is the one about *Bharat* the son of *Rishabha*. *Bharat* was a yogi but when he passed from his body, he was drawn into a deer body and assumed life as a deer calf. He nibbled at the palm leaf manuscripts of the forest ascetics. This shows that because he did not complete his purpose as a yogi in the past birth as a human being, that purpose was repackaged in the subtle body, so that when he took the new physical body as a deer calf, he tried to fulfil that yoga purpose through his interest in yogic books which in that deer body he could not read but could only nibble.

The purpose energy is exhausted if the person fulfills the purpose or is frustrated in trying to fulfil it and decides to abandon it for one reason or the other. Otherwise, it remains in the subtle body. Usually, it goes into the subconscious part of the mind and resurfaces as soon as there is an opportunity for expressing it.

Talented people irrespective of age carry their skills or potential skill energy with them when they depart from the physical world. These abilities remain in the subtle body in suspension (*samskaras*) until there is a time and place, where nature will provide opportunity to accommodate them.

Suppose I am killed but I had a desire to be a great scientist. Suppose that soon after the earth was rendered hostile to human bodies. This earth becomes uninhabited, meaning that I could not get a physical body. Then unless I can find another earth environment with opportunities, I would still have the desire in my subtle body but it would go into suspension until nature again provided a suitable environment, even if it did so millions of years hence or even if it does so in some other universe which it would create. As soon as it makes that place available, I would again strive to be a great scientist.

According to the *Bhagavad Gita* and information elsewhere in the *Puranas*, there is another world which affords the continuity of personality. That place already exists. This physical place is differently constituted and cannot be made to be other than what it is. The suggestion is that those who want permanence, who do not want to use temporary bodies, who do not want to be parted from loved ones, they should strive to go to the other place, the divine world.

Lord Krishna gave information about that other place.

भूतग्रामः स एवायं
भूत्वा भूत्वा प्रलीयते ।
रात्र्यागमेऽवशः पार्थ
प्रभवत्यहरागमे ॥८.१९॥

bhūtagrāmaḥ sa evāyaṁ
bhūtvā bhūtvā pralīyate
rātryāgame'vaśaḥ pārtha
prabhavatyaharāgame

bhūtagrāmaḥ — multitude of beings; sa = saḥ — this; evāyam = eva — indeed + ayam — this; bhūtvā bhūtvā — repeatedly manifesting; pralīyate — is shifted out of visibility; rātryāgame — at the arrival of Brahma's night; 'vaśaḥ = avaśaḥ — happening naturally; pārtha — O son of Pṛthā; prabhavaty = prabhavati — it comes into existence; aharāgame — on the onset of Brahma's day

O son of Pṛthā, this multitude of beings which is repeatedly manifested, is naturally shifted out of visibility at the arrival of each of Brahmā's nights. It again comes into existence at the onset of Brahmā's day. (Bhagavad Gita 8.19)

परस्तस्मात्तु भावोऽन्यो
ऽव्यक्तोऽव्यक्तात्सनातनः ।
यः स सर्वेषु भूतेषु
नश्यत्सु न विनश्यति ॥८.२०॥

parastasmāttu bhāvo'nyo
'vyakto'vyaktātsanātanaḥ
yaḥ sa sarveṣu bhūteṣu
naśyatsu na vinaśyati

paraḥ — high; tasmāt — than this; tu — but; bhāvo = bhāvaḥ — existence; 'nyo = anyaḥ — another; 'vyakto = avyaktaḥ — invisible; 'vyaktāt = avyaktāt — than the unmanifest state of the dissolvable creation; sanātanaḥ — primeval; yaḥ = which; sa = saḥ — it; sarveṣu —

in all; bhūteṣu — in creation; naśyatsu — in the disintegration; na — not; vinaśyati — is disintegrated

But higher than this, there is another invisible existence, which is higher than the primeval unmanifested states of this dissolvable creation. When all these creatures are disintegrated, that is not affected. (Bhagavad Gita 8.20)

अव्यक्तोऽक्षर इत्युक्तस्
तमाहुः परमां गतिम् ।
यं प्राप्य न निवर्तन्ते
तद्धाम परमं मम ॥८.२१॥

avyakto'kṣara ityuktas
tamāhuḥ paramāṁ gatim
yaṁ prāpya na nivartante
taddhāma paramaṁ mama

avyakto = avyaktaḥ — invisible world; 'kṣara = akṣara — unalterable; ity = iti — thus; uktaḥ — is declared; tam — it; āhuḥ — authorities say; paramām — supreme; gatim — objective; yam — which; prāpya — attaining; na — not; nivartante — return here; tad — that; dhāma — residence; paramam — supreme; mama — My

That invisible world is unalterable, so it is declared. The authorities say that it is the supreme objective. Attaining that, they do not return here. That place is My supreme residence. (Bhagavad Gita 8.21)

Buddha's Magic Birth

One aspect about Buddha which is wonderful (*adbhuta*) is his magical birth. It was described by him to *Ananda*, one of his closest disciples and personal servant. This is worthy of note because this concerns a person who is supposed to be anybody, who is not supposed to be someone special, not supposed to be a divinity from day one, just supposed to be anybody who became enlightened just like anyone else.

In the book, *"In the Buddha's Word," Bhikkhu Bodhi* wrote about this on the basis of the records which became known as the Pali cannons, which are the most authentic reports about what Buddha did and said during his lifespan. On page 52, *Ananda* said to some monks,

"I heard and learned this from the Blessed One's own lips: 'When the *Bodhisatta* passed away from the *Tushita* heaven and descended into his mother's womb, an immeasurable great radiance surpassing the divine majesty of the devas appeared in the world with its devas, *Mara*, and Brahma, in this population with its ascetics and brahmins, with its *devas* and human beings. And even in those abysmal world intervals of vacancy, gloom, and utter darkness, where the moon and the sun, as powerful as they are, cannot make their lights prevail, there too an immeasurable great radiance surpassing the divine majesty of the *devas* appeared. And then this ten-thousand-fold system shook, quaked and trembled, and again an immeasurable great radiance surpassing the divine majesty of the *devas* appeared in the world."

Ananda continued the description stating that when Buddha as a *Bodhisatta* descended into his mother's womb, she became intrinsically virtuous, refraining from killing living beings from taking what is not given, from sexual misconduct, from false speech, and from wines, liquors and intoxicants, the basis of negligence. His mother gave birth standing up as compared to other women who usually gave birth while lying down. He was carried in the womb for ten months not nine.

When Buddha first came from the womb, five *devas* received him, then human beings, and he did not touch the earth. His body at birth was unsullied, unsmeared by water, humors, blood, or any kind of impurity, clean and unsullied. As soon as he was born, he stood firmly with his feet on the ground and took seven steps facing north, and with a white parasol held over him, he surveyed each quarter and utter the words of the leader of the herd.

He said:" I am the highest in the world; I am the best in the world; I am the foremost in the world. This is my last birth, now there is no renewed existence for me."

Being that Buddha told *Ananda* about this personally, what conclusion should be drawn about this?

Breasts Shaped like Mangoes

Today in mediation after breath infusion, I had an energy surge from the sun-deity. This was a surge of sun energy into the subtler body. Subtle energy from the sun is not the same as heat which the physical body feels from the sun.

In this surge some unresolved issues and things which I carried in my psyche were removed. These were removed not destroyed, so that they were taken out like if one takes a box out of room and relocates it into another building. I do not know where the stuff was relocated but it was removed.

Sometimes there is a mission change for a yogi, where he was assigned one mission, then suddenly that energy is absent from his psyche and some other mission is installed. A yogi may appear to change from time to time because of the content mission of the subtle body.

One may carry energies in the psyche which belong to others, either to ordinary spirits or to deities even. From time to time these energies may be shuffled or changed either by contact with other ordinary entities or by movements of deities. One may or may not be aware of the adjustment. It depends on psychic and mystic sensitivity. We heard of educated people who all of a sudden became crazy and did things which made no sense. In their case there was an energy shift in the psyche for the worse. We heard of criminal people suddenly making a change for the better and remaining on that better course.

There is the story of Saul, a Roman military official, who when he was encountered by the apparition of Jesus Christ, changed permanently for the better and was renamed Paul. He was later canonized as Saint Paul. It happens. In his case because of the divine energy of Jesus Christ, his political nature was gutted and replace by a saintly package-energy.

People call such things inspiration but they do not understand how it happens. Some say that it is the Holy Ghost. Otherwise, when it is to the contrary, they say it is the influence of the devil, the Unholy Ghost.

After the energy was changed, some other energy was infused into my psyche through the *sushumna nadi* which at the time was like a lit tunnel going downwards from the head. I went through it. At the bottom there was a flowing river of dark blue-brown water. As soon as I got to that river, at the bottom of the *sushumna nadi* the river converted into a divine woman who was buxom looking. She stood on a place like standing on land. As soon as she touched me, my body converted to that of an infant of about two months old.

Then her top fell off. She nursed me. First one breast, then the next breast, then the first one, then the second one again, her breast were shaped like full mangoes. The milk was creamy. After she felt that I had sufficient, she threw me into the air. I found myself back in an adult astral form out of that place but in another place in the psyche.

I realized that there was an approaching and departing movement through the third eye chakra with a dark blue color of energy, moving in and moving out about the center of the eyebrows.

The goddess was Mother Ganga, the personification of the river Ganges. She is one of Lord Shiva's consorts and is a mother to some student yogis.

This may happen because today I struggle with one illustration for the *Kundalini Hatha Yoga Pradipika* book. I did an illustration of Shiva, who is the patron deity of the book.

By sucking that milk into my subtle body, I got the energy to finish the publication in the months ahead, all by the grace of Goddess Ganga, Lord Shiva and my yogaGurus.

Trusting of a yogaGuru

Yesterday (August 16, 2014), I had an energy surge from Buddha. This was energy which was supposed to be used by some Buddhist monks but which they were unable to utilize for one reason or the other.

The energy surged down through my *sushumna*. Then it disappeared. There was no trace of it. It was put in through the gutted kundalini-less *sushumna* passage for storage to be used later by someone, not necessarily by me.

I may or may not use the energy but for the time being it is put in storage in my psyche because some monks were unable to keep it in theirs, or Buddha decided not to award it to them for some reason or the other.

In such cases, a yogi like myself will keep the energy and then later transfer it to someone as instructed. I will not interfere with it. I will not pry it to know its content.

This is like when one is asked to keep a sealed package. One complies to keep the container without opening it and with no concerned for the contents.

We can assume however that it has energy in regard to the process of meditation which Buddha pioneered. That is his only concerned with people on the earth plane. If a wealthy banker asks one to carry a brief case to another place, or to keep that container, one can assume that it has to do with money or with financial securities. But that does not mean that one should dwell on that and keep thinking about it, or make any effort to pry the container. It is not necessary to know everything, even everything which is in the psyche. A student should be discretionary and trusting of a yogaGuru and should not always land a barrage of questions and pry in what the guru does, says or even stores in the student's psyche.

Buddha's Extreme Detachment

Examples of the degree of detachment required on the Buddhist path are there in the life of Buddha in many instances but there is one particular description which is striking.

Once when speaking to monks, Buddha described the noble and ignoble search. This is in *Bhikkhu Bodhi's "In the Buddha's Words."* (page 54)

The ignoble search as described by Buddha is when one who is subjected to birth, aging, sickness and death, to sorrow and defilement and seeks the same. The technicality of this, he explained, was that one needs to know what is subject to these features which are wife, children, men and women slaves, goats and sheep, fowl and pigs, elephants, cattle, horses and mares, gold and silver. He said that these acquisitions are subject to birth, aging, sickness and death, to sorrow and defilement, and one who is tied to these things, infatuated with them, and utterly absorbed in them, being himself subject to birth to sorrow and defilement, seeks what is subject to the same.

This description leaves no doubt as to the degree of detachment required on the Buddhist path, because if Buddha had not listed the features which are subjected, it would be left to anyone to speculate what he meant.

Further, Buddha explained the noble search as completed by one who is himself subjected to birth, danger, sickness, death, sorrow, and defilement and to the danger of these features but who seeks the undefiled supreme security from bondage, *nibbana*.

He said that earlier on when he was an unenlightened *Bodhisatta*, he too sought what was subjected to aging, sickness, death, sorrow and defilement. But he questions himself as to why he did so. He considered seeing the undefiled supreme security from bondage, *nibbana*. Then later, while still young, a black-haired youth, endowed with the blessing of youth, in the prime of life, though his mother and father wished otherwise and wept with tearful faces, he shaved his hair and beard, put on the ochre robe, and went forth from the home life into homelessness.

This is interesting because he admitted that it was painful to his parents and still, he did it in the interest of seeking the opposite of what his parents recommended which was for him to remain in the home life and do duties.

Can it be concluded here that he was a hard-hearted person?

What about his Middle Way?

What is it the middle of?

Part 6

Thought-Desire-Motivation Control

Even though it is difficult to control, suppress and completely eliminate a thought pattern of energy, a desire force or a motivation which arises in the mind or in the emotions, still these features actually begin with an energy that is smaller than the smallest of seeds. I noticed this in meditation, that when a thought, desire force or motivation develops, it becomes larger than life, even larger than the observing personSelf (*atma/purusha*), and then the self cannot control it but is controlled by it, made into its pawn.

What can be done about it?

Since once the idea, feeling or impulsion develops, it becomes like a tidal wave and the observing self is then like a human on a beach, helpless and not having the power to turn the wave back, what should one do about it?

At what stage in the development of the idea, feeling or impulsion, should one turn it about with the magic of one's willpower or one's energy of disinterest?

Before we give magic solutions, let us be real in actually observing that a thought, desire force or motivation may be realized after it developed somewhat and not at its original point. The mind is such an apparatus that it has secret operations which are unknown even to the observing self (*atma-purusha*). This means that if the self cannot see the early stages of development of idea, then that self, if it realizes these developments when the ideas are well-developed, may be unable to do anything about it, and must submit to these motivations.

Suppose I live on a small island somewhere in the Pacific. If there is an earthquake which produced a tsunami, and if I did not feel it, and it is heading for the island, then certainly I cannot get out of the way of the water. I will be destroyed by it.

In this example, there is no possibility that I could stop the wave but in the example in the mental development of idea and in the development of traumatic emotional applications, my awareness early on would result in complete suppression or elimination of the idea.

How then can I develop the sensitivity to be aware of the beginning of a thought, desire force or motivation, because without that sensitivity I am doomed to fall under the influence of these motivations, to be affected by them, to submit to their plan of action and then to struggle with the ensuing circumstance?

B.K.S Iyengar Apparition

Strangely today, after afternoon breath infusion and just at the end of the meditation after it, I had an apparition of B.K.S Iyengar where he said that even though Krishna clarified the issue clearly in the *Bhagavad Gita,* people still do not get it about the body being temporary.

He also said that in his next human life, if there is one, he will be aiming to be a *pranayama* yogi rather than an *asana* posture yogi.

There was no heavy astral energy in his subtle body, only energy like sunlight where he used a transparent astral body. It showed no signs of astral disease. He was in a happy mood.

Kundalini-Prana Loop-Pull

This diagram below shows what happens when the reproduction energy was reformed in the subtle body. It does not affect the global system of material nature for reproduction but only the personal psyche of the yogi on a particular level of the subtle body which is out of range of nature's operations for reproduction.

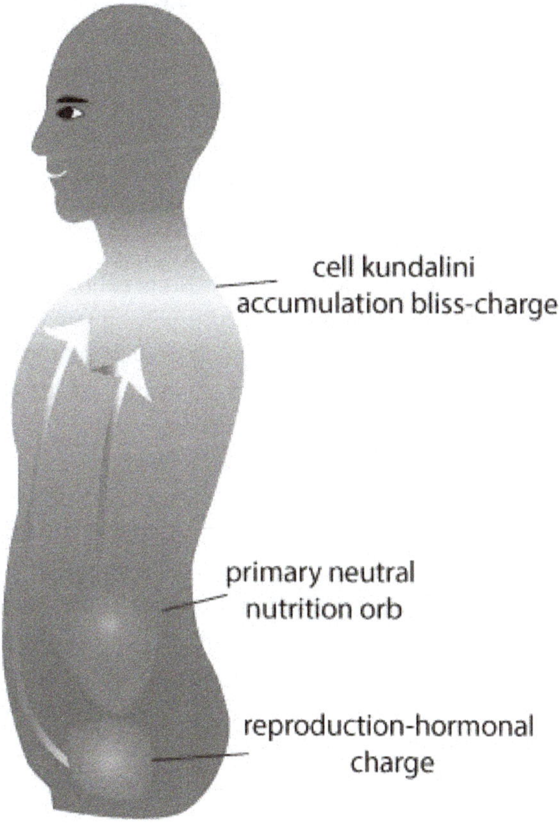

Getting a psyche to change in this way may take years of effort, or lives even, but it is worth it for those students who are dead serious for transiting to the spiritual world.

Getting rid of the idea of the sex organ chakra, and reproductive means, is the key to this but one must also eliminate the idea of nutrition for the very purpose of perpetuating an existence, surviving in that existence and reproducing to survive by jumping to a new body.

Many ascetics, who feel that they are celibate, become stymied because of a failure to understand nature's perspective as being reproduction and not sexual pleasure. Nature runs its own show in its own way without regard to the considerations, reasoning and common sense of the ascetic. At some point an ascetic should break from that and look at nature, see what it does, how it operates, what its priorities are and then work in a practical way to abandon its supports.

Abandoning its supports never means that nature will cease its operation. That must be understood. In fact, nature will continue its operations even in the body of an advanced ascetic. It will act as if his/her austerities mean absolutely nothing. Some ascetics mistake a lull in nature's behavior to be a cessation of the same but this is a costly error.

Whatever we desire which coincides with what nature does, has nothing to do with nature, because when nature is good and ready it will flip anything on its own time scale. A coincidence with nature should not be taken seriously by an ascetic. One should keep one's desires to one side, and keep a separate account with nature's operations. The two systems should not be confused, unless one wants to experience dire frustration.

What is the trick?

It is to change yourself, your interest in this creation, and agree to leave nature as is. The obsession to change nature will be frustrated. Hence one should agree to leave nature as is and to extract what little of the energy one contributed. It has to do with interest, the removal of interest in nature's operation. This is different to the removal of nature's operations. Leave nature's operations as they are and work ceaselessly for the removal of one's interest in its operation. Pull out your interest but leave nature to itself to do as it pleases. This is the ultimate practical way to extract the self from nature's existential layout.

Initially a student begins this by the effort to change nature. That is a necessarily step because of an inherent confusion where the student cannot sort the coreSelf from nature. Hence the student feels the compulsion to stop nature. A similar discussion occurred in the *Bhagavad Gita,* early on, when Arjuna did not understand how he could be involved in a battle and also apply yoga expertise. One begins with the confusion and the desire to stop nature dead in its tracks even though that is not possible. But once a student progressed sufficiently, he sorts his interest in this and that. He can leave aside the nature which is assigned to him or glued to him. He can extract his interest in it as it proceeds.

Extraction of one's interest in nature does not cripple nature. It continues because it is not reliant on one's contribution for its operations. One self, if extracted from nature, does not budge nature even an iota, no more than a teaspoon of salt water if removed from the Pacific would result in any change in the ocean force.

A bit of this is the realization that one has no significance to nature. It will not suffer if one is extracted from it. This realization is great once the student becomes advanced because it releases the person from an innate arrogance.

Buddha: Package of Desire

During meditation this morning, there was a flash of insight which came from Gautam Buddha about his idea of dependent arising. Because of the way his philosophy is described and because of the schematic plan for the monks to follow to be liberated, it is difficult to sort the methods uses. These methods go under the name of *jhanas* which are procedures for analytical mystic analysis into the causes of trauma.

About a week ago, I got an inspiration energy stored into my psyche. This was an energy from Buddha. It was a sealed energy. Today he opened that package of energy and showed me some of the content. It had to do with explaining his teachings in the modern English.

In that package which he opened, there was a bright light like an electric lighting system. The location of it was down in *sushumna nadi* at about the third chakra on the spine. There was a leveled dimension there like the floor of a large skyscraper. He showed that the ascetic should disable all causal-energies which, if left as is, would cause rebirth somewhere in some zone or dimension which has a trauma content.

The ascetic has to correctly anticipate what a specific desire energy will result in, in terms of his/her future birth. Any energy which will cause the assumption of a future birth in a trauma content environment, which will cause coming into being, getting a physical body or even getting a subtle form as a precondition for getting a physical body, should be abandoned forthwith.

Buddha said that this may be considered like when a beggar wanders through a city looking for a meal. Sometimes he sees something wrapped in a paper which he thinks may be the lunch of a rich man which that wealthy person discarded. The beggar eagerly goes to that parcel. He gets it. However, when he opens it he finds that it is something else. It is a dead rat which was deceased for over a week. Or it may be the stools of that wealthy man. The beggar then throws that away in disgust with his hopes dashed to pieces.

An ascetic must have the mystic insight so that he can sense what is in packages of desire, packages of potential desire, packages of offerings of fate, so that he can leave aside and not handle anything which will cause him to appear in the future in a trauma-content environment.

When one takes a haphazard rebirth for instance, one has to endure that life and may become entangled further in the history of the time, in the political circumstances and also in the social upkeep of the family and friends. Worse yet is the situation if one takes birth in an animal species. Hence unless the ascetic can recognize the desire packages and can side-step the ones which will prove to be negative in the long run, he will inevitably, because of a lack of spiritual insight, meet with ruin.

The problem with this information from Buddha is that he did not say how the ascetic develops such insight. Usually, human beings are not born with such insight as a given perception. Therefore, how should that be developed?

Buddha: His Phony Yoga Practice

One nice thing about Buddha is his honesty which was related to posterity in the Pali cannon literature which was written by his disciples after his demise. In the book, *"In the Buddha's Words,"* (page 56) *Bhikkhu Bodhi* wrote of the first yoga teachers of Buddha, persons to whom he submitted for training.

After callously walking away from his grieving and very concerned parents, Buddha went in search of what he considered to be wholesome, seeking the supreme state of sublime peace. He went to a spiritual master named *Alara Kalama* and said, "Friend *Alara Kalama*, I want to lead the spiritual life in this *Dhamma* and Discipline."

Alara Kalama replied, "The venerable one may stay here. This *Dhamma* is such that a wise man can soon enter upon and dwell in it, realizing for himself through direct knowledge his own teacher's doctrine."

Buddha soon quickly learned that *Dhamma*. As far as mere lip-reciting and rehearsal of the teaching went, he could speak with knowledge and assurance. He claimed, "I know and see," and there were others who did likewise.

Buddha then considered that it was not through mere faith alone that *Alara Kalama* declared that. Buddha thought that by realizing it for himself with direct knowledge, he could enter upon and dwell in that Dhamma, because certainly the teacher dwelled knowing and seeing that *Dhamma*.

Buddha went to the teacher and asked him. Buddha questioned: "Friend *Kalama*, in what way do you declare that by realizing it for yourself with direct knowledge you enter upon and dwell in this *Dhamma*. In reply the teacher declared that it was from the base of nothingness.

After this Buddha meditated and attained the realization. Then to be sure he checked with the teacher and the teacher confirmed that indeed he realized that level of consciousness. The teacher then made Buddha a co-teacher. But after a time, Buddha felt that he should go to a higher stage. He left that teacher.

This is interesting how at first Buddha did phony yoga practice with this teacher where he has no realization of what the teacher explained but he acted as if he did by mere lip-reciting and rehearsal of the teaching. He spoke with knowledge and assurance, and claimed that he knew about it and realized it, even though he did not.

It is wonderful that he later admitted this, and set an example about such honesty as one progresses on a spiritual path.

Married in the Next Life

Have you ever wondered about whom you would be married to in the next life? Have you ever desired to marry a specific person in the next physical existence, perhaps the same person you are married to in this life or someone whom to your mind would be more compatible than the person you are currently espoused to?

I had an astral encounter with an elderly relative who in the dimension was dressed in a white shirt, black pants and black tie. He is from the Catholic Christian tradition. His attire may be interpreted as an omen of his death. For me however it was a night of astral encounters with elderly persons who think of their upcoming demises and some persons who were already deceased.

When we appeared together in the astral lands, the relative spoke to me. He urged me to go to a place where he could speak to one of my children. The specific child was in another dimension. Even though he made efforts to switch his subtle body to that place, it could not transfer. Still, he was happy to be with me, thinking that I could help him to get a body among the relatives, and that I would select a birth circumstance which would favor him.

Just then another relation, his wife, appeared. She was well dressed as if going to a church service. She was just as upbeat as him. She looked at me and asked about the possibility of marrying him in the next life.

"What do you think," she said, "will I marry him in the next life? I feel that if there would be a next life, I should marry him again. What do you think? How to arrange this?"

I smiled because I did not have an answer which would satisfy her. In her mind, she already designed what would happen. She was not interested in getting the answer which I would provide. She interpreted my smile as approval of what she visualized.

Sun Father Glorious Radiance

During an afternoon meditation, I took the opportunity to absorb some satisfaction energy from the sun-god. Interesting, is how we neglect the sun-god and chase after many other supernatural and divine personalities. Just as parents maintain a child but are neglected by the infant who takes the parents for granted and who praises others who do not render the daily upkeep, the sun-god maintains the physical and subtle bodies on a daily basis.

One cause of unhappiness in this world is the feature of not being satisfied and always hankering for satisfaction here or there with this or that person, and neglecting basic objects of satisfaction like the air we breathe and the charge of energy which abounds on the earth. If these two features are taken away, suddenly our situation would change so drastically that perhaps we would not recognize ourselves, and our talk about this and that would turn to nothing.

From India, we got the gift of how to formally worship the elements; the sun, moon, planets and the earth, the water, wind, sky. There are worship ceremonies for each. In the West this is mostly regarded as superstition. From the Jews we got the idea of worshiping one God, monotheism. The instruction is that polytheism is detrimental. However, during the meditation, I used the *Savitur* (sun) *gayatri* mantra and imbibed sun energy from the sun into the subtle body. It is a satisfaction-energy.

Someone may think, “This yogi is happy because he does this or does that or because he is with this person or with that person.”

What about what one cannot see of a yogi’s actions.

What about a yogi’s mystic connections?

Can there be happiness coming from what one cannot see?

Nourishment also comes from the sun. In fact, the subtle body would vanish if it did not get energy from the sun. Sun-god is the immediate supreme father to us.

The incarnations and special agemts of God come and go, flashing through human history like lightning in a sudden rain storm, but the sun-god gives satisfying energy from moment to moment for the entire duration of all the life cycles on the earth. The one sun does that.

After saying Sun *Gayatri*, I communicated with the sun-god like this:

> *Father, we sometimes forget that you nourish and support from moment to moment. You constantly act as a dutiful caring parent. You supply*

energy from moment to moment. We have everything to gain by looking to you, seeing you and getting in touch with your subtle energy. When we open our psyches to your glorious radiance, our subtle bodies are cleared of heavy astral energy.

Failed Meditation Session

There are numerous reasons for becoming disappointed over a failed meditation session or over a partially successful one which is ruptured by one incidence or the other. There are numerous physical and psychic means of disrupting a meditation session. Some of these are beyond the control of the meditator. Some can be adjusted so that future sessions are not interfered with by whatever caused the disruption.

If a physical disruption is within the control of the student, he/she should do something about it but if it is without the range of control, then she/she should abide with it, accepting it as providence.

Psychic interferences are the worse. These are subtle. Sometimes the student cannot figure the cause. Or he/she may miscalculate it. Some psychic disturbances cannot be removed by the student but recognition and proper identification is still important because the student when given the opportunity in the future to escape from a pressure, could avoid it if he/she knows what it is.

If deer know that lions are the enemy, the deer can run if there is a chance but if the deer have no idea and regards lions as harmless friends, that will ruin the deer. All the same even if the deer recognize the lions for what they are, that still does not mean that every deer will escape from the grasping claws of lions. Some deer will still be victimized by lions.

I found that even after years of meditation day after day, consistently, making progress to advanced stages and actually getting somewhere in deep meditation, still from time to time, there are some sessions which are riddled with trivia based on intentional or whimsical association with media, with other persons who are yogis, and with other persons who are non-yogis, with the living people and the deceased ones whom I encounter in the astral world and who reach me psychically even when I am focused on physical existence.

What to do when this happens?

For every yogi, for every lineage of yogis, there is a solution for this. Every Swami, every person with *Ananda* as a suffix to his name, every New Age guru, every *vipassana* authority, every yoga blogger, every certified yoga teacher, has a cure for this which they will swear by. This is, if anything, the Age of Opinion; my opinion, your opinion, his opinion. There is someone who gives opinions and then state that he/she is egoless and has no opinion or that his/her opinion embraces all opinions.

I got a technique from Lahiri, that of allowing a switch aspect to operate which moved my focus from the realm where the interference played to a place where there was sheer quiet in the mental environment, a place where there was a soothing satisfaction energy which the self could imbibe and be happy in its association, a place like a cooling breeze flowing through a dessert.

The location of this is such that it is so close to the realm of interference that it may be missed by the meditator, who may switch the self from that interference to some other meditation obstruction.

What comes to mind in describing this is the tuning of a radio, where the listener is at one noisy station which blast musical sounds which hijack his attention. Then he turns the knob but instead of going to a quiet place where there is no broadcast, it goes instead to another noisy station which is worse or which is about the same or which is less noisy.

But between one broadcast frequency and the other, there is this blank place, where no sound is heard where there is no broadcast, where the radio is quiet as if it was switched off.

Perhaps the meditator needs to get a new tuning mechanism installed, one which allows for very fine tuning, so that it does not skip from one noisy broadcast to another but remains at those blank places on the dial.

Then when there is interference, the meditator can immediately hold the knob and move the focus to one what supports and reinforces the aims of the meditation.

There is something from the Yoga Sutras.

तस्य प्रशान्तवाहिता संस्कारात् ॥१०॥

tasya praśāntavāhita saṁskārāt

tasya – of this; praśānta – spiritual peace; vāhita – flow; saṁskārāt – from the impressions derived.

Concerning this practice of restraint, the impressions derived cause a flow of spiritual peace. (Yoga Sutra 3.10)

सर्वार्थतैकाग्रतयोः क्षयोदयौ चित्तस्य समाधिपरिणामः ॥११॥

sarvārthatā ekāgratayoḥ kṣaya udayau
cittasya samādhipariṇāmaḥ

sarvārthatā – varying objective; ekāgratayoḥ – of the one aspect before the attention; kṣaya – decrease; udayau – and increase; cittasya – of the mento-emotional energy; samādhi – the continuous effortless linkage of the attention to the higher concentration force, object or person; pariṇāmaḥ – transforming effects, change.

The decrease of varying objectives in the mento-emotional energy and the increase of the one aspect within it are the changes noticed in the practice of continuous effortless linking of the attention to higher concentration forces, objects or persons. (Yoga Sutra 3.11)

ततः पुनः शान्तोदितौ तुल्यप्रत्ययौ चित्तस्यैकाग्रतापरिणामः ॥१२॥

tataḥ punaḥśānta uditau tulya pratyayau
cittasya ekāgratāpariṇāmaḥ

tataḥ – then; punaḥ – again; santoditau = śānta – tranquilized, settled, subsided + uditau – and agitated, emerging; tulya – similar; pratyayaḥu – conviction or belief as mental content, instinctive interest; cittasya – of the mento-emotional energy; ekāgratā – of what is in front of one aspect before the attention; pariṇāmaḥ – transforming effects, change.

Then again, when the mind's content is the same as it was when it is subsiding and when it is emerging, that is the transformation called "having one aspect in front of or before the attention". (Yoga Sutra 3.12)

Dogs' Distress

I was never in the habit of keeping animals but I grew up in a circumstance where I supervised a dog name Ricky. Once the animal was crushed by a car and was incapacitated for weeks. Miraculously it walked again. When it was hurt, we heard the scream of the animal and knew that it belonged to our family. I was sent to get it. When I tried to lift the animal, it bit me because the movement was painful for it.

I remember getting cardboard under it and pulling that to get the dog to its kennel which was a small construction near the house. My duties with this animal were to feed it daily and to bath it once per week. That bathing was a horrible job because the animal had a smell as dogs do. When it was bathe, it would immediately bristle shiver its body to shed the water. I ran from it to prevent the water from sprinkling on my body, which meant in that environment that one has to take a bath and sometimes depending on the strength of the odor in the water, even a bath did not remove the smell.

When I came to the United States, I was exposed to a totally different human culture with dogs. While in Guyana dogs were not allowed in the house with the humans but had to stay in the yard. They were kept for the protection they offered from thieves and unwanted strangers, I found that in the USA, dogs were kept mostly for companionship. They lived in the house with the owner. The body odor was tolerated; In fact, it is not noticed even by most persons who keep the animals indoor.

Once I left my childhood environment, I had no interest in keeping dogs. For one thing in the USA where I lived there was no need to have dogs for protection because usually people did not prowl at night prying into business premises and houses. No one is interested in stealing fruits from the neighbors at night and in fact in most residential places there are no fruit trees even in the subtropical part of the USA

I used to look on in wonder at why people need dogs in the USA being that their society was not plague with thieves in most areas, and people get jobs or government assistance if they are in need of food and basic amenities. After sometime I began to understand that dogs were kept for companionship. In the developed countries some people are scared of progeny. As soon as someone gets pregnant or if there is the threat of a pregnancy, people are against it unless the pregnant mother is married and unless she has sufficient income.

People ask questions like:

- Is she married?
- Who is the father?
- Will they be on welfare?
- That is another mouth to feed?
- How many rooms are in her house?
- Does she have a job?
- Is she getting child support?
- How old is the man?
- Why is he begetting children?
- Why is she pregnant for a married man?
- She could have used contraceptives. These are not the days of being forced to carry children.

Pregnancies are carefully checked. People spend sleepless night worrying about it.

Since there are fewer children, since children are so undesirable, it seems that nature caused the humans in the developed country to substitute domestic animals like dogs and cats so that people can have affectionate relationships with animals instead.

In my travels over the years in the USA since 1972 and also in recently in South Korea which is a developed country, I found that dogs become terribly stressed when their owners are absent. They fuss and fume about it because they think that they should be with their owners at all times to enjoy the company of the owners and to share in their activities. The animals become stressed also if they are not allowed to eat with the owners.

Even if the animals are given more than enough food, they still desire to eat from the plate of the owner. They stand and look in eagerness to get a morsel and are happy to get something, anything or they become despondent.

The real way to gage this is to remain in the home of the owner when the owner leaves and to watch the antics and expressions of the animals. A dog will make loud sounds to announce its disfavor with the situation and will ignore the visitor when the owner is gone but will show the visitor its dissatisfaction for being left behind.

Cats on the other hand are more detached. They also suffer from the owner's absent but they are not as expressive of emotions of frustration as dogs are.

Cats and dogs sometimes sleep in the same bed with the owners or become distressed if they are not allowed to do so for one reason or the other.

Non-Interference

In kriya yoga there is a special feature of sentiency which must be suppressed and then be deleted from the individual psyche. This is the tendency for interference in nature's affairs. There is this urge we have as sentient creatures, not just as human beings, but as every life form which displays sentiency in the slightest, where we feel that we can and should adjust the situations of nature, that we have better ideas than what nature displayed long before we got into her environment.

Over the years, I found that the elimination of this tendency is difficult to achieve. I know of many students whom I clearly failed to convince of this. Still, it is necessary for success in kriya practice. The reason is that the energy of the self is just sufficient for its self-concerns. If that energy is used to tamper with nature's affairs or her supervisory powers, there would not be enough for self-upliftment. Once the student understands that to interfere in the lives of others is to deprive himself/herself, I no longer have to convince the person about non-interference.

The problem is that one feels a benefit when one interferes. When I say that there is no benefit; that the accounting is off, the student harbors doubt even though superficially he/she may agree with me because I happen to be the teacher.

Every time one interferes in the life of another person, and this means any other creature because there are person-selves in other life forms, full person-selves, then there will always be kickback energy. There will be in the near or distant future, a reaction to the interferer. It may be delayed for the next life. It may be immediate in this life. For sure there will be a reactive energy.

When should one interfere?

One should do so only when one has a commission by the Universal Form of Krishna, and only for so long as that commission is assigned. One can safely assume that any such commission will not run forever. Hence, one should always keenly listen for the instruction to desist, to be unconcerned about what one was instructed to be involved in.

I was a parent in this life. With that authority I interfered in the lives of the entities who were the progeny of my body. Now however I am no longer commissioned as the parent except superficially. I relinquished my interference tendency, withdrew it and have little or no concern.

Interference is a way of saying:

I do not want to fix myself. I find more excitement and pleasure in fixing others. The sad part of this is that it may the truth. It means that we feel better with ourselves if we remain as we are as spiritual misfits.

This above is an introduction to a meditation which I did under the supervision of Lahiri, where he has me test some levels of consciousness which are very close to the chatter level of the mind. These levels are close but if the student can tune into them, he/she can make substantial advancement and cross chasms to reach the transcendence.

In a particular practice, the student is in mediation but he/she finds that the usual mental considerations begin or are continued, despite the fact that he/she does not desire for these to be the focus of attention.

He ignores this and keeps focus on the meditation but when he is reinstated, that does not last, and immediately he finds that he is drawn into another stream of ideas of mundane origin coming in his mind like a movie. He realizes that this is a grievance energy, a corrosive psychological force, an unfavorable social kickback, a wash of tidal energy coming from someone who feels that he has an obligation.

He sees its origin and reverses it into its cause. This is like when there is movement of an athlete at a ballgame. The movement is so fast that human eyes cannot perceive how it was done. But the people who videoed it has the technology to slow it all down, to reverse it so that one sees the entire movement in reverse back to its origin when the athlete first began.

The ascetic reverses the energy. It reenters the person of origin. This action is like when there is something written on a dry-erase board and then the duster for the board is moved across it and the writing disappears.

No interference in the energy of others, even when that penetrates into the mind of the ascetic, no handling of that energy, no interest or curiosity into it, no checking to see what it is, to get the satisfaction of knowing what it is and the passionate need to analysis, consider and criticize that person, there is none of that, no interference.

The ascetic approves of nature's handling of the lives of others. His confidence in nature is sound. He does not need to check and double check how nature conducts the lives of others or how nature allows others to conduct themselves in its environment. He sleeps at night knowing that by the grace of nature, everything happens as fated, everything is within the perfection and completion of what is. Everything is beyond his control. He is happy for it.

In the advanced stage this same method is used but in reference only to interference energies which arise in the psyche of the yogi and which is from the yogi's psyche itself and not from others whose energies penetrated or invaded the yogi.

In this method, during meditation, suddenly the yogi will notice an interference energy arising from within the mindscape. It will usually arise from the left or right side of where the coreSelf is located during a non-image non-sound meditation session. It may also seem to come from behind or from underneath but it will be like a meteor gaining speed as it entered the atmosphere of a planet.

The yogi will notice the energy coming to him like a missile which moves rapidly. Before it gets to the core, the yogi, because of having integrated disinterest in the affairs of nature and because of sincerely adopting the non-interference posture, will see the energy-package moving to him. With a smile, he will cause it to retract into its source point. It will begin moving backwards away from him. He will know what was in the energy but he will have no interest in it. He will not ponder, inquire or be curious about it. He will not try to get information from it. He will not care if it was a concern energy for some other person or if it was a good energy which would help that person. No type of justification for being involved will arise.

It will retract itself into the source-point within his psyche. His meditation will continue. He will know that if he tended it, if it developed, it would produce interference energies in reference to someone somewhere whom he knew before, and who did things which were against spiritual realization.

Now that the yogi developed full confidence in nature, knowing that it handles this situation perfectly and that it is qualified and empowered to supervise entities, the yogi is relieved by not interfering, just as one would be relieved if one ceased doubting someone whom one should surely trust.

The yogi will conclude:

It is wonderful how without my contribution or with my partial insignificant contribution, nature conducted this creation before. It is also wonderful how through ignorance I interfered, thinking that my contribution was vital. It is by the grace of the yogaGurus and deities that I am detached enough to appreciate nature's wonderful supervision. What a fool I was when I felt that it was my contribution which made a difference and that I could reform this or become the caretaker of this. Wonderful! Wonderful! Was my massive ignorance!

Astral Rainstorm

Last night in the astral, I found myself in a parallel world where there was a forty-year rainstorm. It was a hurricane but it lasted for years. Nearly all land creatures were wiped out.

I endured the whole forty years of it with full astral perception of what happened but in a body which was invisible, even though it had eyes and feelings which sensed and responded to the storm.

In that world we passed the forty years in about half hour of the earth time but actually it was forty years there because of the reference of time to the specific astral body used.

Nothing could withstand the rain and wind. Everything was lashed about as if each was a straw.

Suddenly it was over. The sky cleared. I saw some astral people. One man was at a hut. Another man had a stall where he sold produce. One acted as if the storm never took place. No one discussed it.

Then I was with a young woman who was in another dimension and who told me to go with her to inform some persons who were in a submarine. We traveled as desired, by thought, with no machine device. The astral body traveled through the air as willed. When we got to the sea there was a submarine which was battered by the storm. It floated with its top surface above water. The woman took an invisible piece of astral iron and hit the escape chute making a loud noise. Then she disappeared. I was left there. After five minutes, the same woman came out of the chute with another person. Somehow, she had dimension transit powers and could shift into various dimensions effortlessly.

More sailors came out of the submarine. They were in it during the entire storm. They survived.

When I looked down in the water, I notice that the sub was in water which was no more than about twenty feet deep. There were fishes swimming. One sailor, a female crew member, threw crumbs overboard. Some small fish greedily devoured it.

It was then that I considered reporting this when I would return to my physical body. I was inspired to explain that even though so many people died to the astral place in the storm. The death of an astral body is not like the death of a physical form where there is something remaining which decomposes. What happens it that the person disappears from that dimension and enters some other vibrational frequency or the person's existence may be suspended for a while where the person is not aware of itself in any place. Then later that person becomes aware of the self in some other place but usually with no memory of being in the previous location.

The astral body of the person merely disappears without a trace. There is nothing left to decompose. To get some idea of this, consider what is left after say a cellphone message is deleted or after a radio signal is no longer present in the atmosphere soon after it was broadcasted.

Yogi to Help Relative to Reach Heaven

Last night in the astral world, I was with a relative who asked me to assist with the passage out of the physical body. It is a crazy proposal because I too have to deal with being evicted from my physical form. Death stalks me from day to day.

As a child in South America, one thing which was common with children, was this idea that one may die in one's sleep. Some elderly people died while sleeping. At the funeral people would state that the person died peacefully. As children we thought that such a death was not such a good idea because one has no idea where one may awaken on the other side. Of course, this is silly but it begs the question as to if there is a difference between dying in one's sleep and dying while wide awake.

The relative who consulted me had this idea that since I am a yogi, since I write books about spirituality, since I am familiar with books like the *Bhagavad Gita*, since I was always preoccupied with mysticism, I should know something about it and should advise and assist relatives to get a passage hereafter to heaven.

When the person requested assistance, I said nothing in reply. I can do nothing. I checked my psyche and then checked the person's subtle body to see its condition. There was a little wholesome energy (subtle force) in that person's subtle body but it oozed through that subtle body into the feet where it disappeared when it was absorbed by polluted astral energy. Even if I transferred energy from my subtle form into that person's form that would be a waste, because the energy transferred would be absorbed by the polluted astral energy.

As for going to heaven?

That can only be done if the subtle body is compatible with the vibrations in the specific heavenly world.

Patanjali Mahamuni gave this guideline.

जात्यन्तरपरिणामः प्रकृत्यापूरात्॥२॥

jātyantara pariṇāmaḥ prakṛtyāpūrāt

jātyantara = jāti – category + antara – other, another; pariṇāmaḥ – transformation; prakṛiti – subtle material nature; āpūrāt – due to filling up or saturation.

The transformation from one category to another is by the saturation of the subtle material nature. (Yoga Sutras 4.2)

How could I saturate this person's subtle body with energy from my own, if the pollutions in that person's form destroys my energy when it enters that person's form? A blood transfusion is effective only if the antibodies in the recipient are not hostile to the donated plasma.

Lahiri Mahasaya: *Shaktyatma* Meditation

Shaktyatma is a combination of *shakti* and *atma*, which are psychic energy and the individual coreSelf. Lahiri introduced the term in a practice which I did under his direction.

The reason for these notations is to share this with others and to show the progression of blindly following a legitimate yogaGuru. Some question my advisories. Nearly everyone wants guarantees. Some want to know the ins and outs, and want to be sure that I have the whole method. However, despite the risks in following yogaGurus, still the yogic system is one of having confidence in a teacher and following his direction even though one cannot make head or tail of it. It is very similar to that of children who follow the direction of parents while the children have no idea where that instruction will lead. The infants cannot understand what will happen in their adult years and how the training will be of use then. It is for this reason that we regard the yogaGurus as fathers.

This *Shaktyatma* (shak-ti-aat-muh) procedure is used after a breath infusion session when the student sits to meditate. It may be used without breath infusion even though I cannot vouch for that because I always use it after breath infusion.

This practice is used in cases of advanced students whom when they sit to meditate have a blank mind where they do not have to work in meditation to produce an idealess-imageless blank mind. If the student endeavors for that in meditation, this practice is of no use.

Once the blank mind is noticed, the student should check for naad sound at the back of the head or to the right or left, wherever it would be. Naad sound is the permission to proceed. It is the assurance that the student is in good graces and is approved by the yogaGurus.

The student should then look ahead to the frontal part of the subtle head. If when doing so some disturbance arises, the student should do what he/she usually does to rid the mind of the interference. If successful the student should proceed.

The next step is to note the type of energy which is in the frontal part of the head.

- Is it a glow light?
- Is it like a spot light?
- Is it totally dark?
- Are there twinkling little stars?
- Is there a chakra energy?
- Is it like indistinct subtle patterns?

Once the energy is identified in some way, the student should remain as is, and absorb the energy.

This energy is shakti. The one who absorbs it is the atma or coreSelf.

In my experience this energy has a mild, very mild, bliss aspect to it. It will not be exciting. It will not be pleasurable but it will be pleasant and fulfilling nevertheless.

The self should absorb that energy and feel fulfilled doing that, just as a hungry child feels fulfilled while it quietly sucks its mother's breast.

According to Lahiri, this is an advanced technique. It is one that makes him smile when a student does it. They lose the hankering for various things even for divine vision. They become patient. Without being hasty and demanding of the yoga process and the yogaGurus, they practice and wait for spiritual perception. This is a wonderful attitude of a student which makes him/her compatible with the advanced teachers and deities.

Thought Control Failure

As a meditation instructor, one difficult process to teach is thought control technique. I raked and scraped my brains over the years and made very detailed study in my mind about the initiation, development and illustration of thoughts in the mind, as to how the mechanism operates.

First of all, I wrote books and instructed students individually. What happened over the years, is that I cannot point to one single student and say, "He knows the technique." Or, she mastered it."

After years of reviewing this and looking at the failure of students, I determined that the cause of the failure is the inability of students to slow the rapid production of ideas in the mind.

- Should the mind be blamed?
- Should I as the teacher be criticized?
- Should the student be held responsible?

I will let you decide who/what is faulty in this case. Blame must be placed somewhere somehow because we are sentient beings and laying the blame is our habit.

To ease my way out of the court room before the guilty verdict is made, I will explain the following and then exit.

The reason for students' failure to stop thoughts dead in their tracks is the students' lack of a checking psychic mechanism which is as rapid as the mind itself. In the history of predators, we hear that they are successful because of rapidity. A cheetah on the African savannahs would starve to death if it did not have speed. A hawk which flies after a rabbit must use speed. A cat catches a mouse because of speed. But that is not all. You may have the speed and still you may fail to capture whatever you wish to arrest.

Unless the student has a speedy glancing mechanism in his/her mind, there can be no apprehension of thoughts because thoughts usually occur so rapidly, that the student cannot stop their production.

An example can be two trains which run on parallel tracks. If one train is faster than the other, the slow train will not be in a position to observe the faster one. But if both travel at the same speed, the observations can be made because they will move side by side. To see the front of one train, the other train must move at a faster speed.

With thoughts this speed analysis is necessary if the student is to stop the ideas. If one sees thoughts after they are well-developed and if then they move at a rate which is so rapid that one cannot perceive how they are formed, one cannot restrict those thoughts.

Sequence of Events in Thought Formation and Display:

- tiny thought energy, begins invisibly in the mind
- it gets bigger
- it is perceived by the observing self when it reaches an illustrative state
- in that illustrative state it has a compelling power
- this compulsion energy grasps the observing self and hypnotizes it
- the observing self becomes enthralled by the illustrated thought

- the observing self is compelled to view the scenes of the thoughts and to endorse associative memories and ideas which surface in the mind
- the observing self does not have the power to stop the thought and must allow it to run its course

The method of the self gaining power over the thought displays, lies in the self being able to see the thought when it first arises as an invisible minute thought energy or just after it appears and begins to develop.

Can the self gain this insight?

Which meditator can honestly say that he/she perceives the tiny thought energy before it expands in the mind and that he/she usually arrests that idea and extinguishes it?

Bliss Energy / Battle with the Subconscious

There is a development when doing *bhastrika/kapalabhati* breath-infusion, where there is a burst of bliss energy in the torso of the body. This burst Is as concentrated as when kundalini shoots through the spine and enters the brain.

This development is important as a step in the direction of developing a *yogaSiddha* body and later becoming aware of a spiritual body. While initially one gets the experience of bliss consciousness essentially in the head of the subtle body during kundalini yoga practice, and while in the physical body, by the grace of nature, one gets bliss consciousness of another quality in the genitals during sex experience, in this practice, what happens is that the quality of bliss consciousness in the head is felt in the lower torso but it is not centered on the genitals. It does not have the feeling quality of the bliss energy of sex experience. Instead, it has the bliss energy feeling of when kundalini burst into the head of the subtle body.

The attachment one has for bliss consciousness of sex pleasure experience in the genitals is a huge impediment in the advanced stages of kundalini yoga practice because it remains predominant in the consciousness in the form of almost non-erasable memory which surfaces repeatedly. This means that despite the rises into the head, there will be a situation of the psyche not releasing itself from the sex pleasure need which was based on the natural kundalini system.

An example of this, something ordinary, is a student's attachment to sweet foods. If for instance a student grew up eating many sweet foods, it will be difficult to get that habit gutted. Even after it is removed, there may be a ghost of it in the psyche. This ghost will rest for a while and will not present itself but it will be resurrected at a later date. The student will find that he/she will return to it and again cherish the sweet foods.

In the *Bhagavad Gita*, Lord Krishna spoke about this, where he stated that the memory of previous indulgences. emerge again to motivate the yogi/yogini.

विषया विनिवर्तन्ते
निराहारस्य देहिनः।
रसवर्जं रसोऽप्यस्य
परं दृष्ट्वा निवर्तते॥२.५९॥

viṣayā vinivartante
nirāhārasya dehinaḥ
rasavarjaṁ raso'pyasya
paraṁ dṛṣṭvā nivartate (2.59)

viṣayā = viṣayāḥ — temptations; vinivartante — turn away; nirāhārasya — from(without) indulgence; dehinaḥ — of the embodied soul; rasavarjaṁ = rasa — memory or mental flavor of past indulgences + varjaṁ — except for, besides; raso = rasah — memories (mental flavors); 'pyasya = apyasya = apy (api) — even + asya — of him; paraṁ — higher stage; dṛṣṭvā — having experienced; nivartate — leaves

The temptations themselves turn away from the disciplinary attitude of an ascetic, but the memory of previous indulgences remain with him. When he experiences higher stages, those memories leave him. (Bhagavad Gita 2.59)

यततो ह्यपि कौन्तेय
पुरुषस्य विपश्चितः।
इन्द्रियाणि प्रमाथीनि
हरन्ति प्रसभं मनः॥२.६०॥

yatato hyapi kaunteya
puruṣasya vipaścitaḥ
indriyāṇi pramāthīni
haranti prasabhaṁ manaḥ (2.60)

yatato = yatataḥ — concerning an aspiring seeker; hyapi = hi — indeed + api — also; kaunteya — son of Kuntī; puruṣasya — of the person;

vipaścitaḥ — of the discerning educated; indriyāṇi — the senses; pramāthīni — tormenting; haranti — seize, adjust; prasabhaṁ — impulsively, by impulse; manaḥ — mentally

Concerning an aspiring seeker, O son of Kuntī, concerning a discerned educated person, the senses do torment him. By impulses, the senses do adjust his mentality. (Bhagavad Gita 2.60)

An appreciation for non-sweet foods cannot be had fully so long as those memories are in the psyche and lurk in the background like hidden ghosts. It does not matter if the person stopped the sweet foods craving unless the subconscious agreed to get rid of the ghost-memories and hidden secret desires for those pleasures. The observing self has so much power in the psyche. Its accomplishments fall apart because of a lack of support of the subconscious which has its agenda. It eventually takes command of the psyche and reinstates its policies.

Thus, even if that person spent millions of years at an ashram where the sweet foods were not available or were effectively discouraged, if the sweet-food desires remain as a ghost in the subconscious, the person will return and support that at a later day.

Dormant hidden desires are future desires. They will rule the psyche in the future. These are like when a ruler conquered the territory of an opposing king where that opposing monarch escaped and went to another territory. We can know for sure, that the loser will return with a more powerful army to fight another battle.

Those silly yogis, who feel that they defeated the enemy and that he is done forever because he ran away, will be crushed by the enemy in the future.

Any type of evolutionary pleasure experience is a downslide for the yogi because if the yogi is trained in how to leave that aside, the subconscious mood if it retains the experience of that pleasure, will undermine the efforts at some other time. It will bring the psyche back into compliance with its desire. Of course, a serious student will handle this in a way which will not erase his/her advancement but still it shows that the conscious observing self may not be absolute in the psyche. It must calculate how to deal with that part of the self-composite.

Patanjali gave an important hint when he said to cultivate what is opposite. It seems like such a simple instruction but actually it is more than we think. In this case, say in the incidence of the memory of biological sex desire, the opposite may seem to be no sex desire. It is that for beginners who have a simplistic view and who naturally do not grasp the complexities.

The actual opposite is another type of bliss burst, one that has nothing to with the passionate energy, with the sex-charged hormonal energy. That bliss burst happens in the lower torso which includes the reproductive organs.

The opposite is not the absence of sex pleasure, or pleasure, but a pleasure which is devoid of the biological hormonal charge, one which is similar to the bliss burst in the head when kundalini goes through *sushumna nadi* central passage into the subtle head. When that type of pleasure happens during kundalini practice but when it occurs in the lower torso and when it is exactly like when it happened in the head previously, that is when the yogi can know that the sex pleasure memories in the subconscious are being erased.

Eventually when this happens repeatedly for a long time, those memories of biologically charged-sex pleasure will be erased. The subconscious will no longer have that in its reserves. It will not undermine the progress because it will not have that reference to oppose the yogi.

The evolutionary pleasure experiences are awarded by nature free of charge but at nature's convenience and according to how a spirit is accommodated in any species and in specific environments which are designed by physical nature. There is deity supervision of many of the activities of nature but the particulars rest with nature, which ultimately designs the environments with very little interference from the deities.

Without getting these evolutionary experiences, a self would not make the progression to understand what it is not and what its preferences should be. Thus, the selves need to appreciate the contributions of evolutionary experiences, even though the same features are problematic for it.

If one continues appreciating nature for its evolutionary urges and opportunities, one is condemned to being nature's victim but if one does not get those urges and opportunities, one cannot progress in the mundane evolutionary cycle. One will stagnate somewhere in a mediocre position which is not to one's liking.

Thus, one should appreciate nature and at the same time, reduce one's interest in its urges and their related opportunities, so that eventually one can squeeze the self out and make the exit.

Bliss Under-Aspect Location

Lately I reported on finding bliss energy in the psyche. Of course, nature has its own course of instruction in this regard, which begins in the infant body and then gradually changes or is upgraded by nature as the body ages. The meditation process is totally different but since we began this life with the nature process, with nature's way of introducing the various pleasures, we are stymied by the free offering of nature. It will be a task to change the attitude in this regard.

The change must be made by someone somehow, by a deity, by a yogaGuru, or by the student himself/herself, if the said person can manage such a shift in perspective

During one meditation which was conducted under Lahiri's supervision, with a method which he asked me to pioneer and take abstract notes about, he transmitted a message which read:

> *Each of those has a bliss aspect which should be located and used as soon as anything disturbing manifests. While absorbing on that bliss aspect, the student will escape from the traumas and be reinstated to chit akash either directly or through a jump process.*

When he said this, I tried to reach the bliss aspect but at first, I was unable to. However soon after, within moments, I reached it miraculously. I transmitted a reply stating that his instruction was verified in the affirmative.

Soon after when I was in that bliss aspect, another trauma thought content arose. I found myself involved in that, like a man who was in a violent sea and was switched to a calm lake and then found to his dismay that he was in another violent sea.

Now however I immediately switched to the calm bliss aspect of that level. After this I decided to keep testing to make sure that it happens for every type of traumatic mento-emotional energy which I would find myself in. It kept working one after the other.

I must however test this again.

The problem however is to describe how the switch happens.

As I tested this repeatedly, I could not find a way to describe how it worked. then I got a message from Lahiri.

> *Let them use naad. Those who cannot locate naad, cannot do it. Let them use naad initially. In time, they will do it without even finding naad. Each of those trauma levels has a bliss aspect under-basis, just as every disturbance on the surface of a deep lake has calm water under it.*

I then decided to try naad. That worked as well as finding the local bliss aspect.

Regrettably at this time, I can give no other method even another method which I do. This is because of not verbalizing the abstract techniques.

Buddha's Limited Originality

One may get the idea that everything about the path Buddha introduced was originally conceived by him but on a close inspection of the data in the

Pali Cannon, it should be admitted that some aspects of the path were taught to him by others when he first went into India to do the austerities which he felt would relieve him of being subjected to the traumas of having a physical body.

Certainly, much of his path was practically invented by or discovered by him but some of it was not. There is in Buddhism a system of realizations one after the other, in an upward progression. These are called *jhanas*. *Bhikkhu Bodhi* in the glossary to "In the Buddha's Words," gave *jhana* as states of deep meditative concentration by the one-pointed fixation of the mind upon its object. The *sutras*, he wrote, distinguish four stages of *jhana*.

However, in these stages some of the accomplishments are exactly what Buddha was tutored in by the teachers whom he practiced under before he struck out on his own.

There are at least two of these accomplishments which are:

The meditative objective of Teacher *Alara Kalama* which was to the base of nothingness

The meditative objective of the Teacher *Uddaka Ramaputra* which was of neither perception nor non-perception

Interestingly these teachers died just before Buddha attained the enlightenment which he pursued. Buddha regretted their demise when he heard of it from some supernatural beings because Buddha felt that these persons would be fit recipients of what he discovered which was beyond what they attained and shared with him prior.

The conclusion is that some of his realizations were gained under the instruction and with the help of other teachers even though the high end of his accomplishments were either pioneered outright or discovered by him.

Does it matter that he took help from others? Should any other teacher be given credit for part of what he attained?

Lahiri Baba / Bunch Focus

Yesterday Lahiri Baba introduced me to a *bunch focus* kriya. This is an important process for those who try to reach the *chit akash* sky of consciousness. It concerns a bliss aspect but one which is neutral more or less, hardly discernable, which makes it hard to recognize it as being valuable.

Because we were conditioned to the pleasure aspect by the natural energy, we are stuck with a dead-end type of consciousness in reference to bliss where we feel that it has to be similar to what we experienced from infancy. No one, or say hardly a soul, has any idea of any other type of bliss energy except the pleasures we are familiar with, which were introduced to us in the present physical body, from its infancy through its growth into adult status. This makes it difficult to cut loose from this and go for yoga full-out, because the full course requires forgetting and then completely erasing from one's psychology what nature introduced.

What would it be like if I totally forgot sweet foods for instance?

How would it be if I were to relocate into a body in an environment where there was nothing sweet-tasting. Obviously, I would not miss sugar because I would not have its memory reference. I would appreciate other flavors and would not be depressed because I did not have sugar. So much of what we are, and what we desire, is based on memory of what we experienced. We are restricted by memory.

Apart from kundalini rises into the brain, the most sensation bliss experience in these bodies is sex experience but that along with the other pleasures have to be forgotten to make progress on the high end of yoga. If it is not forgotten, the mind will use it as a reference. This will cause failure in the practice, because the mind will silently evaluable some very important meditation experiences as being insignificant or as being void states.

What is the *bunch focus* kriya?

Simply stated it is when the meditator finds himself/herself in a blank state of mind, in a mind without thoughts or images, where in that condition there is no effort to maintain the blank state, where it is experienced spontaneously.

When the meditator is in the blank state, he should check to see if a part of his attention latches to a general location in that state, If it does he should grasp that area which will seem like when one grasp bread dough where the pastry bunches in one's grip. The student should hold that steadily.

According to Lahiri, this is the beginning of what is termed as *singular focus*. It will prepare the student for penetrating into *chit akash* sky of consciousness.

In some meditations the student will feel this grasp. In others he will see the grasp. In some it will be like bread dough. In some others it will be like grasping water in an ocean. The hold will be stable and the student should note that, keep holding and wait.

This will cause stability of focus.

The pre-stages to this are:

- full naad absorption
- attainment of blank state of mind which is spontaneously maintained
- shift from ideas and thoughts instantly to blank states where neutral bliss is absorbed as psychological nourishment

Lahiri / Steady Focus Achievement

Lahiri instructed in various kriyas for the purpose of students reaching the *chit akash* by a definite reliable method. Just as using *kapalabhati* and/or *bhastrika pranayama* breath infusion, a student can on a daily basis raise kundalini without fail if he/she persists in the practice, there must be a system of steady focus which the student can practice daily.

The problem is a reliable method.

Recently I experimented and tried various systems which Lahiri introduced. My conclusion is that a method cannot be acquired using something which the student does not have or something which the student hopes to have. In other words, the student cannot have a steady focus on something which he/she visualizes or imagines or something which the student hopes to have because he/she was told about it by a reliable source.

This of course seems gloomy and hopeless because if the student never reaches the *chit akash*, this would mean that there would never be a time when the student would succeed.

However, Lahiri has an idea which is that the student should use what the student has, which is the mind's level of consciousness during meditation. The student should, with that, find a steady focus and apply that as the meditation. This he says will eventually lead to *chit akash* meditation.

Even though it is perhaps the most frequently recommended focus, the method of staring between the eyebrows is an unreliable one. Unless the chakra is visible there that focus does not work. If, however there is a light there which is different to the chakra, that light can be used as a reliable focus but only if the light is not momentary, if it persists. Until there is either a steady light or the chakra appearance which remains there of its own accord, that location is useless for this practice. Imagining a light or chakra there is counterproductive and is not part of this practice.

For the process which I can vouch for, breath infusion is an absolute must. It is the reliable method of reaching a higher plane during the meditation session. If there is no breath infusion the meditator may reach a higher plane, but with breath infusion that will definitely happen because the subtle body will be infused with fresh subtle energy which will displace stale energy which sponsors lower awareness.

Since I use breath infusion prior to these meditation practices, I make assurances based on that usage even though I admit that without breath infusion, one may be successful. There were ascetics who were successful in various types of transcendental achievements without doing breath infusion.

Lahiri gave a system of steady focus this morning where the interval between one idea and another is lengthened. This interval is for the most part in most people a split second of time. However, if one does breath infusion thoroughly, that interval is lengthened so that it may last for seconds or even minutes. It is a blank interval. If the student can locate it and focus on it, that causes it to lengthen.

This will eventually result in switching to the *chit akash*.

How long would it take?

How many meditation sessions must be practiced?

That I cannot give a reply to at this stage. It would depend on the particular student, the quality of energy in the subtle body and the student's category as a limited living entity.

What is it like when the interval is extended? It is like a blank space where there is the relaxed contraction of mental force. Then there is an attempt for the mind to move on to the next slide, the next idea, but then there is no movement to that impression, the tick-tock psychic machinery stopped. It stands still, the grasp holds. Then after a little more time, the machinery continues to the next idea.

Because of the grasp of the ascetic, that idea comes out only partially developed and with no compelling force and the next interval starts again. This interval or blank space is grasped and the same thing is repeated.

The partial developed idea seems like when an insect change from a larvae stage into its adult body and something happens so that the insect dies in the larvae stage and falls to the ground out of it cocoon, done for, not developing, stunted. This is a victory for the yogi. It is a relief for the yogaGuru in finding a student who progressed and achieved meditation.

Lahiri / Lifting Nectar

Lifting nectar is a procedure in kundalini yoga. It is also used as an observation for changes in the attitude of the subtle body, in the yogi's effort to develop a *yogaSiddha* body, which is the precursor for going either to the highest of the subtle material worlds or to the spiritual world.

Lahiri gave a procedure. After practicing for some months, I am in a position to recommend it to others because of getting evidence that it does work and is not a hope or fantasy. There are prerequisites. If these are completed, then definitely this will work, just as if there is water trapped on a mountain, if a person digs at the edge of the water, that water will flow out. Because of the laws of nature regarding gravity, it flows. Due to a law of psychic nature, if the prerequisites are met, this procedure will work. This does not depend on anyone's willpower or imagination. If you dig the edge of a lake which is situated high on a mountain, the water will flow even if you do not want it to do so.

The lift nectar procedure is done long after a person did kundalini yoga practice using breath infusion to motivate kundalini through the spine into the brain on a daily basis for some years, at least to the time where *sushumna nadi* central passage remains open during the day when the person is not doing the exercises even.

This open *sushumna* causes constant release of sexual energy hormones so that the accumulation of that energy is no longer taking place, where the energy is released and expressed continuously in such a way that it does not form a reservoir in the pubic area. It is important to understand that there may be a reservoir and also continuous release of the energy but this is the removal of the reservoir with the same continuous release.

The different is that if there is a reservoir the released energy will have a particular type of sexual charge which it cannot have if there is no reservoir. The reservoir causes a charge to accumulate and to empower the energy for sex expression in one way or the other, openly or covertly. The open type is the simplest type to identify while the covert type stymies many ascetics who think that they are advanced and who rate themselves as being better than anyone else, while in fact, they are in a worse position because of the hidden power of the energy which even they cannot detect.

There are many covert forms of sexual energy expression which assail sannyasis, the so-called celibate monks and nuns. Unfortunately, they do not understand how this happens. Nature is so psychically subtle that even the ascetics themselves are fooled by it.

The kundalini laid out this body in such a way as to cause all cells of the body to be like heavily taxed citizens of a country. Each cell is required to produce concentrated polarized energy. This energy is then confiscated and routed to the sexual glands. Kundalini routs it there for its survival upkeep but the coreSelf, small-minded as it is, considers that the routing is for sexual pleasure fulfillment.

Lahiri's system is for all cells which are above the genitals in the body, to donate their concentrated polarized energy in an upward direction. For the cells which are located below the genitals, like in the thighs for instance, the concentrated polarized energy should be release upward but with no interest in the genitals. It passes by the genitals but does not go towards the genitals, to be processed there.

The attractive pulling force of the genitals is effectively terminated. The cells process their energy so that there is no attractive interest in the genitals. This is experienced by the yogi during breath infusion practice where the energy in the thighs veers away from the genitals when it rises as contrasted to the way kundalini designed the system which is that the energy released goes rapidly to the genitals.

During sleep, many cells work to create and store the concentrated polarized energy. Therefore, upon awakening, a yogi should do *pranayama* practice and instruct the cells to yield the energy in the desired way. This is done by the breath infusion up-draw. After doing this for months or years as is necessary, one will notice that the cells changed their attitude and routes the energy upwards as desired.

Because the kundalini is hell-bent on reproduction (not sexual pleasure enjoyment), it will continue its interest into that but a yogi should work side by side with it for his/her aims as instructed by the yogaGuru. At some point a yogi must part ways with kundalini because it will never yield itself fully to anyone. A yogi should realize that nature will remain as it is but he/she has to find a way to transcendd or de-energize it.

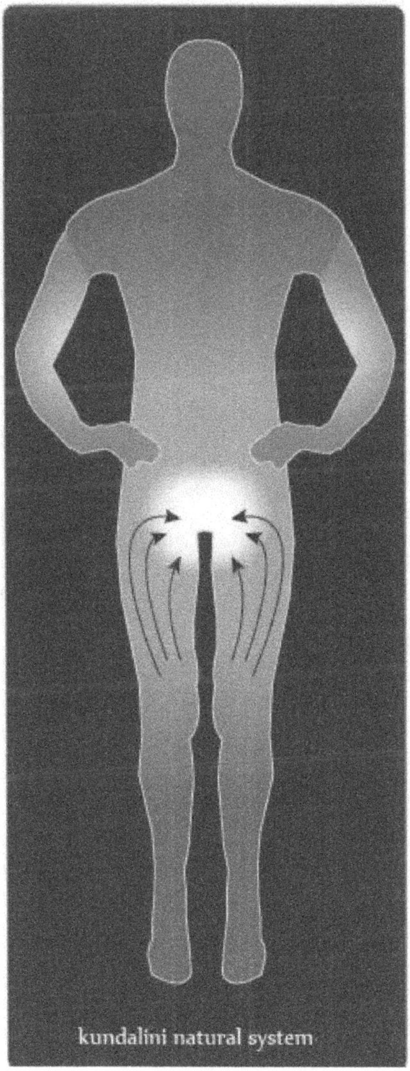

kundalini natural system

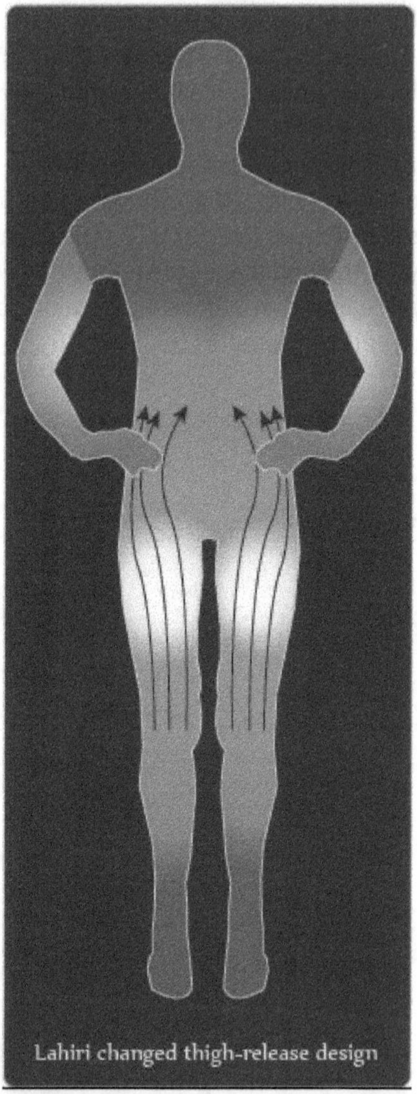

Lahiri changed thigh-release design

coreSelf as Target

This is a report on the use of the coreSelf as a target in meditation. Initially in the inSelf Yoga™ course, the core is offered as the only target in the *pratyahar* sensual energy withdrawal practice, which is the fifth stage of yoga.

The *Meditation Pictorial* book has the diagrams for this practice. It is further explained in the *CoreSelf Discovery*. However, that is just the beginning of the inSelf Yoga™ meditation process.

Once the student consolidates the *pratyahar* sensual energy withdrawal, the next step is to get the mind space in order and to reform the adjuncts one by one. The main facilities to be brought under subjugation are the intellect analytical orb and the kundalini lifeForce.

When these are harnessed somewhat, the student will know because the mind space will not be dominated by images and ideas which the mind presents to the core. The self will be free to roam in the psyche without being a captive of the mind's impressions which are created by the intellect and which were sponsored by the lifeForce and its accessories like the senses and memory.

The target used after the coreSelf was used as the target in *pratyahar* sensual energy, is for the most part the naad sound resonance. In other words, the coreSelf does not use itself as a target in this case. It uses naad as an object.

When that is completed, the core wIll again use itself as a target but not as before in the fifth stage where it was the target of sensual energies, target of the extrovert energies. This is because at that advanced stage, there are no extrovert energies to deal with, or stated more precisely there are negligible extrovert energies to handle.

What then are the energies at this stage?

Those energies are the inner introvert energies which surround the core in psyche, in the subtle body. This practice begins with pulling into the core. It also uses higher astral energies from higher planes of consciousness which occur in the psyche. It pulls into itself those energies and uses itself as the focus of that. These are introvert energies as compared to the extrovert or outward-bound energies in the *pratyahar* sensual energy practice.

What is the value of this practice?

It is the preliminary stage before becoming stabilized in the *chit akash* sky of consciousness. It may take months, years or even lives to complete.

Let me clarify this:

When the self finds itself to be an extrovert unit where its energies are pouring out of the psyche into the environments beyond, it should practice the *pratyahar* sensual energy withdrawal and retract that outward bound energy. This type of energy is recognized because it punctures through the membrane of the psyche in a rush to detect and locate objects in an external environment either in the physical or psychic world, but particularly the physical one.

Conversely when the self finds itself to be an introvert unit, where there are no energies pouring outward but the energies experienced are within the psyche without any eagerness to go outward, and there are no thoughts and images arising from this side of existence, then the self may become a target of its own focus for cultivating steady focus in preparation for being exposed to the *chit akash* sky of consciousness. The yogi cannot command that he/she be exposed to the *chit akash*. He/She must wait patiently for that to happen, but should while waiting develop stability of focus, otherwise when the *chit akash* is accessed, it will be access for a split second. The yogi will not remain in the experience.

Beauty-Bath of a Yogi

Since having a childhood body, I was amazed at the length of time some people spend before a mirror. I used to watch some elders stand before a full-length mirror. and twist this way, and that way, to see the looks of features and clothing. I still have not figured as to why we humans do this.

Once I decided to know if most animals were obsessed with mirrors. I realized that they were, even though on occasion, an animal will stand before a mirror and be marveled at its image, usually mistaking it for another of its kind.

During the teen years, the idea surfaced that I should observe what I saw when I looked in a mirror. From then onwards into young adult years, I tried to heed this urge which nature graciously gave me, something which I naturally lacked but which nature felt that I should acquire if I wanted the approval of humanity.

Later however, as the teen years ended, I lost interest in mirrors. My interest was transferred into the subtle body, where I felt that if anything I had to get that in order. I had to fix that, not the physical body. However, I realized that if I did not give attention to physical reality, my life with other earthlings would be a living hell. Understanding this, I decided to do the very minimum in a mirror on the physical side.

Recently I translated and commented on the *Hatha yoga Pradipika*. I was amazed to find that the author, Swatmarama, stated that a yogi should not be concerned with baths.

The secret to this statement is that a yogi should be concerned with bathing but not with baths of the physical body only baths of the subtle one.

How should a yogi clean the subtle body?

He should do so with breath infusion (*pranayama*).

But should a yogi use cosmetics? When I was a teen, it was required that a man should use cologne and powders.

Again, we should consider how to fix the looks of the subtle body, how give it an agreeable odor.

To do this a yogi must set his psychic adjuncts in order. Just as people trim the eyebrows carefully and add mascara, a yogi should carefully trim the influence of his intellect, kundalini lifeForce, senses and memories, so that he looks sweet when he appears in the astral world.

Messing Up the Kundalini

This post is an alert for those yogis who struggled with sex desire and who realize that for the most part they fight a losing battle with a recurring principle of existence which is survival through reproduction.

This is for advanced people who understand that sex pleasure has nothing to do with it and is a diversion from the issue. For some reason and it does not matter what the reason is, because it is nonsense, we think that sex pleasure is the problem but that is not the issue because the kundalini is not concerned with that. We are concerned with that but that is still not the issue. The issue is survival which is the kundalini's primal concern. To do that it must reproduce bodies and then hop into a new body which is reproduced.

To run the operation for survival, the kundalini issued a franchise license to the sex organ to collect taxes from all other cells of the body. This is a cruel system but it works because it provides a pleasure to the coreSelf which that self becomes enthralled in and which causes the self to approve the real plans which are for survival through reproduction. The bribe in this case which the coreSelf accepts is the sexual pleasure part of the system. Being bribed like that, it turns a blind eye to everything which the kundalini does for its obsession of survival through reproduction.

Stopping sexual indulgence has nothing to do with this, because the kundalini is not concerned with the actions taken by the coreSelf because the kundalini has its own program and could care less about the plans made in the head of the subtle body. These plans can be upset under certain conditions. Thus, the kundalini does not have to worry about being deprived of anything because it knows that as soon as the tide of events change, the plans in the head of the subtle body will be scrapped.

For instance, say that I am a celibate monk by whatever definition my religious sect gives, still can I, or my sect, guarantee that I will remain celibate hereafter or that I will remain like that when and if I take another physical body. Unless such a guarantee is solid, the celibate definition, no matter what it is, will fall apart. In other words, the kundalini does not have to bother about the aspirations and definitions, because I do not have full control of the developments of various environments and body changes.

For instance, in youth before puberty one is not motivated by sex desire, neither by the positive or negative features of it. As soon as puberty develops one must deal with it. The person cannot control when the body will mature at puberty. In fact, the control of that is in nature's hand according to the genital ability of the body. In the Puranas, there was a case of four persons who remained in prepubescent forms perpetually but these were supernatural beings who were great yogins. They were known as the *Four Kumaras* who were mind-born sons of the creator-deity Brahma.

In summary, in the short range, celibacy is a grand achievement. It is recommended all the way through the Vedic literature with only a few exceptions. In the long range it is uncertain because the ascetic cannot guarantee that he will remain in control of his psyche in the future. He does not know which body he will take and where it will be. He does not know how his subtle body will act because of the uncertainty in reference to which level of consciousness it will experience hereafter.

Essentially the sex mechanism runs a dictatorship where all cells of the body pay taxes to it in the form of hormone concentrate. This is on the physical level. On the astral side the same principle holds where subtle vital energy is contributed on demand by the subtle sexual mechanism. However, the kundalini is the ruthless overlord behind the operation. Targeting the immediate culprit is only the beginning. The ascetic needs to do some more prying to see what really happens and to get to the real boss of the operations.

If somehow one can understand what is explained above, that would be a major breakthrough. Then there is the problem of carefully studying the system in one's body and psyche.

Sun-Deity Companions

According to the *Bhagavad Gita* there are two types of passing away of the souls using physical bodies. One is under the influence of the sun. One is by the influence of the moon. Krishna recommends the sun type and states that those who pass under lunar influence will return for a physical body, while those under solar dominance will go to the worlds of the gods.

Recently with yoga becoming a trend in the developed countries, a series of poses which were termed as *Surya Namaskar* became popular as a sun worship. This is interesting because many Western people who follow yoga, usually rejected deities. Some feel that they are just as good as a deity. How is it then that they do obeisance (*namas*) to *Surya*, the sun god. Perhaps they have no idea of the meaning of the terms *Surya Namaskar*.

Surya is the name of the sun-god. *Namas* means obeisance. *Kar* mean to do or it means an action committed.

Based on some instruction from yogaGurus and also from an instruction from the sun-god, I did a meditation to make contact with the sun deity and his energy. This was not the *Surya Namaskar* set of yoga postures which are so popular. This consisted of using the *Savitur gayatri* mantra after doing a full session of breath infusion. The worship or *namaskar* began with the breath infusion where the sun energy in the air, was infused into the subtle body. This caused a shift in level of consciousness, where when I sat to meditate, I made contact with the deity.

This is a different kind of *namaskar* obeisance which consists of working to extract low energy from the subtle body to replace that with the sun's energy. After sitting to meditate within ten minutes, there was a burst of light of sun energy which left the sun planet and pierced the subtle body. It settled in the center of chest. This was bright flashing gold energy. It eroded the birth energy impressions which were in the subtle body. These are the impressions which were there for the creation of this physical body.

After this happened, the subtle body changed. It travelled to the sun but it grinned from ear to ear. It traveled. In a short time, it was near the sun deity who rode a gigantic chariot. On either side of him were micro people, *valikhilas*, who were the size of about two inches. I was drawn to be with those small people. My subtle body assumed that two-inch size.

Buddha: Individual Divine Eye

There was an episode in Buddha's life where he described the realizations in meditation which culminated in enlightenment.

First, we should understand clearly what that enlightenment was. It should not be lumped with everything we conceive of as enlightenment. For each of the successful ascetics, there were special experiences which were termed as enlightenment or liberation. The tendency is to assume that each is the same, that Jesus's realizations were the same as Krishna's, which was the same as Buddha's, whose was the same as Rajneesh's, which was the same as Ramakrishna's.

Buddha told his monks about using a divine eye. Was this an individual perception or is the divine eye, one eye which every successful or near-successful ascetic accesses. Is it like each man buying a telescope and peering at distant stars from his backyard. Or is it like a government observatory, where each citizen can see distant stars using one huge mechanism after paying an entrance free.

Part 7

Divine Eye

In the "In the Buddha's Words," *Bhikkhu Bodhi* described that when Buddha's mind was concentrated, purified, bright, unblemished, rid of imperfection, malleable, wieldy, steady, and attained to imperturbability, he directed it to knowledge of the passing away and rebirth of beings.

Then with the divine eye, which is purified and surpasses the human, he saw beings passing away and being reborn, inferior and superior, beautiful and ugly, fortunate and unfortunate, and he understood how beings fare on according to their actions thus:

These beings who behaved wrongly by body, speech, and mind, which reviled the noble ones, held wrong view, and undertook actions based on wrong view, with the breakup of the body, after death, have been reborn in a state of misery, in a bad destination, in the lower world, in hell.

But these beings who behaved well by body, speech, and mind, who did not revile the noble ones, who held right view, and undertook action based on right view, with the breakup of the body, after death, have been reborn in a good destination, in a heavenly world.

Thus, with the divine eye, which is purified and surpasses the human, he saw beings passing away and being reborn, inferior and superior, beautiful and ugly, fortunate and unfortunate, and he understood how beings fare on according to their actions.

There are two special observations here. Buddha claimed to have perceived, actually seen with mystic vision. beings who passed on. He saw that they got certain results hereafter on the basis of the lifestyle in the last body.

Conditions Hereafter

The second observation is that even though Buddhism has the no-self, no-soul, *anatta (anatma)* doctrine, still there is repeated talk by Buddha about beings. The word self is not used in the translation but beings is used continually. What does that mean? If there is no self and person who will persist beyond the death of the body who will face punishment or favorable reward on the basis of actions from the past life?

We may query if those hellish and heavenly conditions which Buddha saw with the divine eye, were merely figments of his imagination. Are there really astral hells or heaven hereafter? Who or what agency enforces who is sent to either place?

Does this operate like gravity where we see no personal agency, no sentient being enforcing anything, but we feel the enforcement like when an object drops from the roof of a building and falls by a non-personal law of gravity which is evident even to the most skeptical person.

God Answers Prayers

Last night I have an astral encounter with my deceased mother, who began to explain that another relative who is not deceased, hounded people in the astral existence with grievances for what happened on the physical side.

And what can the deceased do?

That depends on the leverage influence of the deceased, on how the deceased can influence the living. There is a verse in the Srimad Bhagavatam where it says that the dead are more powerful than the living. It is a fact however that this statement is not always applicable because sometimes the dead are unable to exercise ancestral authority over the living. A dead person's priority is to get another body in a status part of the family of those relatives who are alive. Sometimes the living ones resist the influence of the dead, depriving them of birth opportunities for many years.

Living people who find deceased relatives and file complaints about disagreeable situations of the family, who are left behind on earth, fail to realize that the deceased have problems, such as the worrisome problem of becoming an embryo.

Imagine if you are shut out of physical existence and someone who is on the physical side comes to you with a description of his/her real or imagined crisis, what should you do?

You are in crisis and cannot get a physical body. This other person has one and complains about not getting this and not getting that. You explain to the person that when you were alive you did not get much of what that person has. What should you do to help that person?

As my deceased mother explained the complaints of that living relative, my mother said this,

"We, on the dead side, rely on you. We are hopeful that if we do not get bodies soon, then at least you will be deceased soon. You will be on this side with us and can help to better use the astral state. You are expert at yoga mysticism.

"If no one likes you in the physical existence, that is his/her concern. Being that we are on this side our priorities are not over petty disagreements on the physical side. We have real problems here just living on the astral side, not being fulfilled here and also not getting to come over into physical history.

"To many of us on this side, being in a physical body even one in poverty, is much desired because then we are a part of the earth's glorious history. We want to be on the physical side and are unfulfilled in the astral existence. We do not know how to use the astral existence in the same way that we would have challenges to meet in the physical world."

After she said this, I remembered my childhood life in Guyana, where I lived surrounded by women of African racial stock, descendants of slaves brought to the South America by the British. These women were Christian. They believe that whatever went amiss in their lives would be fixed by Jesus Christ, the Son of God, or God Himself as God was defined in the Bible.

What was the subject of their prayers? Mostly it was money, making others confirm to their wishes, resolving their hard feelings and resentments to others.

When the person lives on the physical side, God fits in as the person who should compensate all wrongs, fix all grievances, provide for every need, and set the entire universe in order.

When the person lives on the astral side, the need for God diminishes.

It begs the question:

Does God really answer prayers?

Is that a superstition?

I got an email this morning from a relative. It was a photo of my deceased mother, Agatha Clementina Grant. She looked exactly like this in the astral encounter last night, except the body was a semi-transparent astral one. It has no physical solidity.

Love of Resentment

One of the tastiest psychological delights in human existence is resentment. It also surfaces as grudge and assumes other behavior formats. It may remain hidden for a time, and considering reincarnation, it may remain dormant for centuries in the nature of a living being and then suddenly burst like a volcanic eruption.

In many incidences the cause of the burst has nothing to do with the initial formation of the resentment energy. For instance, in a previous birth, I had resentments for a certain person but was unable to properly vent it to that someone. I passed on. I took another body. In the new life, when something happened which was similar to what happened in the previous body, the old resentment energy erupted, just as a volcano which simmered for centuries may erupt because of a depression in the atmospheric pressure, thousands of years after the initial up-thrust of magna force from the crater.

Due to the tastiness and delicious aspect of the resentment a person cannot understand the previous motivation and usually we take it for granted that the resentment is due to a current incidence only.

The pleasure of it, is the fulfillment and reverse enjoyment which is derived. As humans we fool ourselves into thinking that we only enjoy what is pleasant and what is sweetly desirable but that is not true. What is true is that we have a need to deny when we enjoy things which are disagreeable. For some reason in our consciousness, we have this judging system which sorts good from bad, desirable from undesirable to where it cordons what is approve and what is disapproved according to cultural orientation and intution. It is a haphazard and unreliable system but it is the only system one has. One must use it.

Each person has to use whatever he/she has as mental equipment, even if it is faulty and error prone for the most part.

inSelf Yoga™ gives insight into the distortions of judgment and into the denial necessities within nature, where we can face whatever chaos or inadequacies we discover in the psyche.

Resentment is tasty, that is the first thing we need to admit. Unless we understand and face this, we cannot possibly manage. It is delicious to say the least.

If I like something, it is my vice, no matter what it is. To get rid of it will not be easy. It would be to deprive myself of what I desire. That is austerity.

Resentment and grudges; these are relishes of human existence. Can I admit that?

Lahiri Baba / Focus Cultivation Necessary

Lahiri stated that focus cultivation is absolutely necessary for advanced students. He said that the idea that one can sit to meditate and pierce into the chit akash or see the star at the third eye, is a false claim for most students. It certainly is that for those who have not spend years cultivating focus.

What is this focus?

It is when the student established in the mind space, total calm during meditation, when the student honored Patanjali's second *sutra* about the absence of the fluctuation in the mento-emotional energy *(yogah cittavritti nirodhah - Yoga Sutra* 1.2), when naad is present and the student is attracted to it, and when the student with naad has no chatter or images in the mind space even in the frontal part of the subtle head, and the student then focuses or attempts to do so.

Lahiri asks the question:

What is the focus when the yogi is in a chatter-less imageless mind?

Some students meditate on the space between the eyebrows. Some meditate on the heart region. Some on this. Some on that.

Lahiri challenged like this:

Whatever it is that you meditate on, be sure that it is in your possession, that you have it as your property?

Then he said:

If it is something you have to imagine, the practice is a farce.

If it is something which is not there but which you hope will be there, the practice is a farce.

If it is indistinct where it changes at every moment, so it is one thing now and then something else a moment after, it is a farce.

Know what is in your possession for sure. Then I can direct you to use that as the steady focus. Do that for some years for proficiency. It must be something in your possession.

Lahiri / Chit Akash Focus

I still practice some procedures which Lahiri engaged me to test and perfect. Right now, on the edge of reaching the *chit akash* consistently, I practice on the inner focus which causes a gap to open from this side of existence. A yogi on this side of the existential divide, cannot force his/her way into the *chit akash*, divine sky, but he/she may set a condition on this side that causes a puncture from the other side.

A yogi can learn how to raise kundalini daily using breath infusion. Similarly, there is a way to cause a burst from the *chit akash* to the yogi but it is not as easy as focusing between the eyebrow.

Method:

- silence the thought-image display operation of the mind
- be fully absorbed in naad sound resonance
- with naad as the background contact, focus on the interest of the self either by itself as interest energy alone or with one of the senses

The question of how to silence the thought-image display operation of the mind is answered simply:

Do whatever is effective for you which actually gives the result of the mind not producing thoughts or images.

The question of how to be fully absorbed in naad sound resonance is answered simply:

- Locate naad which is usually in the back of the subtle head. Stay absorbed or pinned in it. If you cannot hear naad, be in the blank black space in the back of the head. Remained pinned there.

The question of how to be with naad or blank blackness in the back of the head and simultaneously focus on the interest of the self either by itself as interest energy or with one of the senses is answered simply:

- First learn what the interest energy of the self is. This energy is in the sense of identity which surrounds the coreSelf spherically. It is the sense of identity in focus either though a sense or in focus by itself without application through a sense.

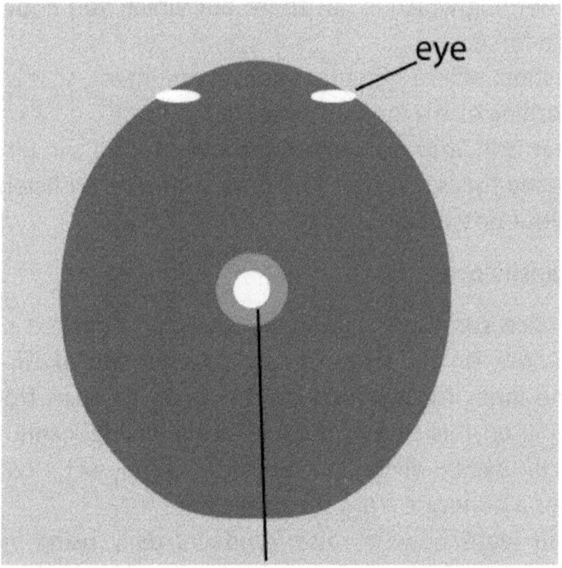

coreSelf in white surrounded by unfocused sense of identity

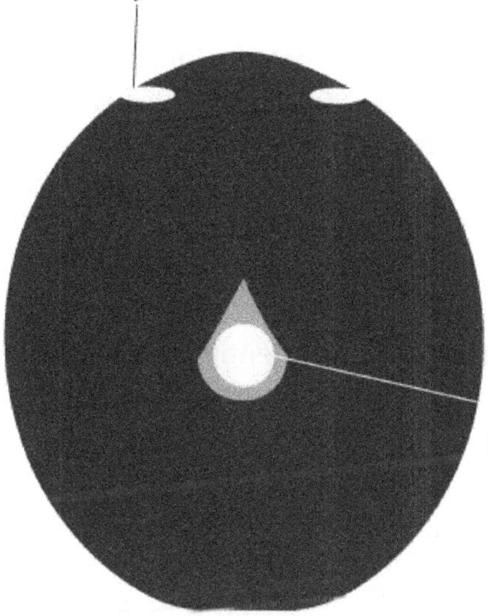

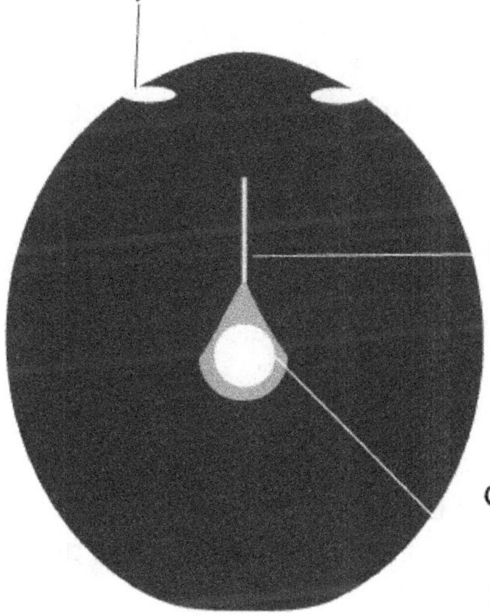

To understand this, one should be in naad and then develop an interest in naad. As soon as an interest is developed, one will feel a psychic instrument like a tongue in the mouth. It will lay there without moving like when the tongue is relaxed in the mouth and has no tasting or touching interest.

When this is achieved, the yogi should turn to the front side of the subtle head. Then a sense will adhere to the interest. This will usually be the visual sense but it may be the hearing sense which was used in naad absorption.

This will be like when the tongue has a feeling which produces the urge to touch or taste.

Lahiri says that this interest energy must be developed by the yogi by focusing on it steadily in meditation while keeping in touch with the naad sound. The yogi will see through this interest energy into the *chit akash* sky of consciousness. This is even better than using the *buddhi* intellect orb for the vision, because the sense of identity is higher than the *buddhi* intellect orb. The sense of identity is closer in vibration energy to the coreSelf than is the intellect.

It is really wonderful when the sense of identity turns into a vision perception instrument, into a divine eye. This is magic in the subtle head of a yogi.

I tried this to note its functions. It works to cause *chit akash* punch through but for a short period. It required hours of meditation to make it steady.

There are two incidences which I noticed which is that one can focus in the interest energy. That is easier to do except that it requires a subtle mind. Students usually do not have such high psychic sensitivity.

They can focus on the sense and the interest energy together. That is easier except that the sense has a tendency to escape and to begin hunting its pursuits which ruins the meditation and puts the student back into a struggle with images and thoughts during meditation.

I will practice this and report developments. I am not in a position to explain this to students because I have to be sure that I have a fool proof method which works time and time again. I was to develop this practice within six months but years passed. I still am unable to complete it. I will report if I find anything definite.

However, I herewith declare that meditation at the third eye is unreliable for getting to the *chit akash*. It can happen but it is infrequent. Ancient yogis recommended the third eye. It is mentioned in the *Bhagavad Gita* but in the modern situation, it is unreliable, perhaps because our psyches are in disorder.

Buddha: Insight Vision of Actions/Reactions

During his phase of enlightenment, Buddha said that he developed the divine eye where he could see the actions of the living beings and the reactions which nature imposes. At the time he did not explain what he saw as being the agency for enforcing the good or bad reactions. He explained that:

> *When his mind was concentrated, purified, bright, unblemished, rid of imperfection, malleable, wieldy, steady, and attained to*

imperturbability, he directed it to knowledge of the passing away and rebirth of beings.

With the divine eye, which is purified and surpasses the human, he saw beings passing away and being reborn, inferior and superior, beautiful and ugly, fortunate and unfortunate, and he understood how beings fare on according to their actions thus: 'These beings who behaved wrongly by body, speech, and mind, who reviled the noble ones, held wrong view, and undertook actions based on wrong view, with the breakup of the body, after death, have been reborn in a state of misery, in a bad destination, in the lower world, in hell; but these beings who behaved well by body, speech, and mind, who did not revile the noble ones, who held right view, and undertook action based on right view, with the breakup of the body, after death, have been reborn in a good destination, in a heavenly world.'

How should this information about lower worlds, hells, heavens be considered?

Are these real places or states of mind?

Astral Underwater Cities

This morning, I was urged to go to the Gulf of Mexico. I was about ten minutes late for the engagement. When I got there, I sat down and did a Shiva call-mantra and meditated on reaching the Gulf of Mexico deity.

The deity was all smiles when he came to the surface. He approached on the beach where I sat. He said, "See this!"

I saw some astral cities under the water way down in the deep. Then the water deity disappeared. Some spirits came from the water-cities. They approached me. Most were women who used bodies in places which lined the Mississippi River.

They showed me some astral pollution energy which came from the river and spread through the bottom of the Gulf which blighted many parts of their astral cities. I told them that there was nothing I could do because I had no position to create or enforce pollution regulations. They said that they needed me for another reason which was to voice astral energies which would affect the situation of the people who were involved in the pollution.

At that time, suddenly much energy from these persons entered into the bottom of my central spinal passage and vented through the top of my head. This was like when there is wood burning in a stove, where the smoke of it leaves through a chimney. As the energy left through the top of my head it went into a north westerly direction.

After this I left that place, knowing that the purpose of the call from the deity was fulfilled. Those departed souls, astral entities, needed to release reactionary energies through someone who used a physical body and who had psychic perception.

Lahiri / *Chit Akash* Pre-Focus

This diagram comes after years of meditation beginning since around 1970. That is over 40 years ago. It may look simple but it took years of meditation to develop the ability to do this. I publish this to give insight. This was developed as a meditation process for reaching *chit akash* by a definite method. It was done under the direction of Lahiri.

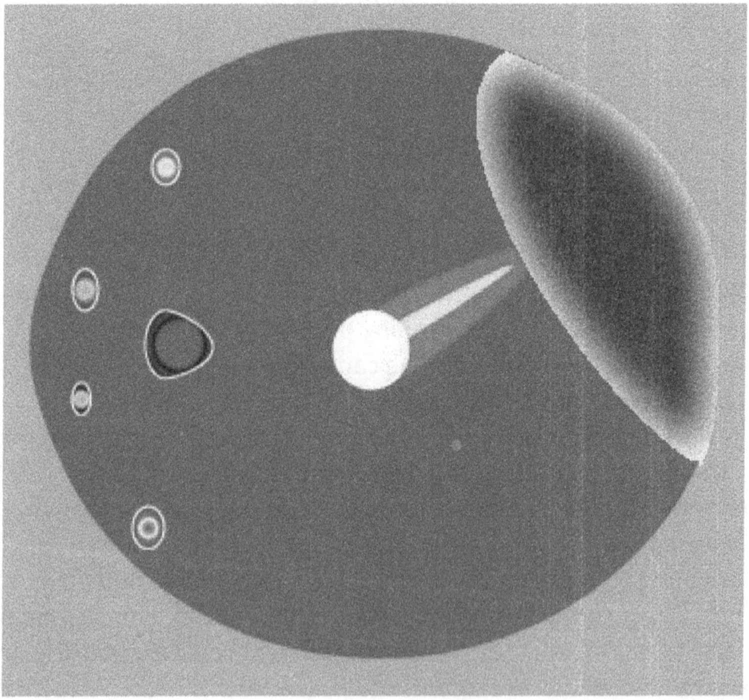

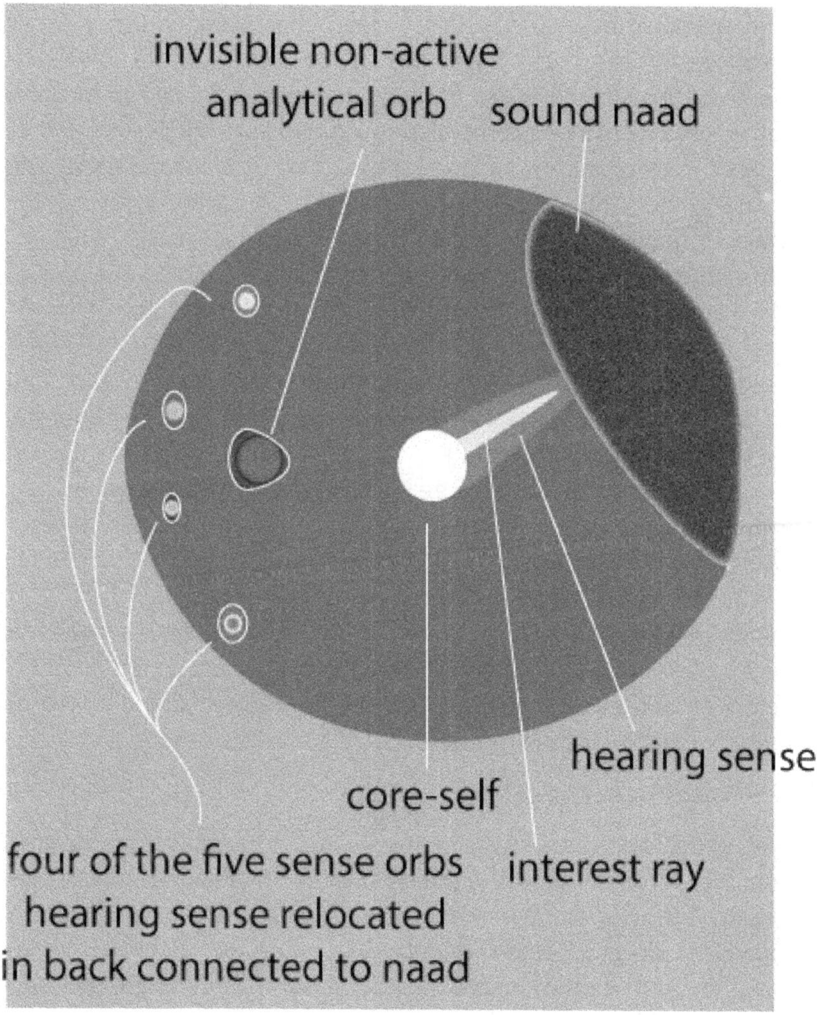

In the diagram there are four sense orbs in the front of the subtle head. This is because the hearing sense vanished from there to be used in the back part of the subtle head. It is present in the back, sheathing or surrounding the interest energy of the coreSelf. This is similar to a leather sheath which holds a knife, or a glove which shields fingers.

The coreSelf is not distracted by thoughts and images in the frontal part of the head because the analytical orb in the front part of the head is invisible. It ceased operating. This orb is rarely seen even by advanced yogis.

The intellect is represented because it is existent. A student should realize that and always bear that in mind. It is seen indirectly by its activity which is thinking and imaging in the mind. Whenever an image or thought is illustrated in the mind, that occurs on the screen of the analytical orb. As soon as the images or thoughts cease, the screen goes blank and invisible and is not seen.

Because the analytical orb is silent and does not display images, the coreSelf is freed from being compelled to look through the frontal part of the subtle head. It can focus on naad resonance or on a blank darkness which is in the back of the subtle head.

When it focuses or even tries to focus, it emits an interest energy. This is not from the coreSelf. It is from the energy which surrounds the core which is the sense of identity. This energy forms into an interest ray.

Lahiri asked me to investigate the probability of focusing on naad and holding that focus to see how long a student may do that.

To complete this practice and report to him, I have to separate the hearing sense from the interest energy to see how it would be to focus on the interest energy alone and also to see what happens in comparison when the hearing sense surrounds the interest energy.

Ultimately the purpose of these practices is to develop the coreSelf focus so that the *chit akash* can be facilitated easily by the students.

Lahiri, the great father, feels that one must first cultivate a steady focus, and then if that is attain one can peer into the *chit akash*. Otherwise, one will wait and wait and make mystic actions in the subtle head which will never allow vision into the divine atmosphere.

Lahiri: Sense of Identity Escaping

It seems that continually the sense of identity escapes from the grasp of the core. This sense of identity is the subtlest of the adjuncts. It is so close to the core in vibrational frequency as to be indistinguishable from it.

How then can the students find it?

Most students cannot locate the intellect orb which is grosser, so how can they get a whiff of the sense of identity.

One way to detach the sense of identity is to sit silently and then to suddenly try to develop an interest in something, anything, even if there is nothing coming into the mind, just make that mental effort to develop an interest. As soon as one does this, one will expose the sense of identity. The urge to develop that interest is itself its invocation. This is abstract. Most students will be at a loss to identity that urge as being something, as being anything.

However advanced students, if they do this repeatedly, will get some idea that the sense of identity is a psychic adjunct. It is difficult to grasp. Try grasping water with your fingers. It cannot be held in that way. Try grasping air with your fingers. The same inability will be displayed.

Unless the self has keen psychic perception it cannot perceive much less grasp the sense of identity. The more the self is in tune with physical matter and with the lower astral levels; the more it cannot in any way grasp the sense of identity.

Lahiri said that the verse in the *Bhagavad Gita* about *prajñā pratiṣṭhitā* pertains to the yogi who can grasp the sense of identity and remain with it for the duration of the meditation. Here is a verse.

तस्माद्यस्य महाबाहो
निगृहीतानि सर्वशः ।
इन्द्रियाणीन्द्रियार्थेभ्यस्
तस्य प्रज्ञा प्रतिष्ठिता ॥२.६८॥

tasmādyasya mahābāho
nigṛhītāni sarvaśaḥ
indriyāṇīndriyārthebhyas
tasya prajñā pratiṣṭhitā (2.68)

tasmād — therefore; yasya — of the person who; mahābāho — O powerful Arjuna; nigṛhītāni — retracts; sarvaśaḥ — in every interaction; indriyāṇīndriyārthebhyas = indriyāṇi — sensual feelings + indriyārthebhyaḥ — of the attractive objects; tasya — his; prajñā — discernment; pratiṣṭhitā — remains constant

Thus, O Arjuna, concerning the person who, in every interaction retracts the sensual feelings from the attractive objects; his discernment remains constant. (2.68)

His explanation is solid. If everything but the sense of identity is stabilized (*sthita*), the effort will fail because that is the adjunct which is nearest to the coreSelf.

If the whole world is at peace but there is war in your home, that is as good as hell.

Yogi / Falls Back to Earth

I had an astral experience that reminded me of how a yogi may, after leaving the body for good, be recaptured by the influence of the history of the earth. He would mannifest again as a human being somewhere, somehow, on the planet earth and will again endure childhood, youth, adulthood and elderly years.

It can happen easily by a chance association with someone. The other person does not have to be dead or departed either. The yogi once he is departed if he remains sensitive to anyone who is earth-bound would be susceptible.

Imagine a rocket going up and up through the sky. Just before it reaches beyond the gravitation pull of the earth, something goes amiss so that its booster ceases firing.

What will happen?

It matters that it was within 100 feet of escaping from the earth's gravity.

If he/she becomes influenced by energy from any earth-bound soul, a yogi can take another body. It could be a friendly influence or a hostile one. What would it matter?

I was in an astral encounter where my astral form was pulled to some people whom I knew when my body was in infancy. The deceased father of my present body was there and so was a woman who in my infancy was about fifteen years of age.

In reviewing my relationship with the woman at the time, I surmised that at the time my senses were irresistibly attracted to the woman. For some strange reason, the woman's senses were attracted to me. The result of this is that now some fifty years after, this mutual attraction is still operative and caused this person to find my father hereafter and to use his ancestral rights to contact me.

The woman wanted to look into my eyes. She got satisfaction from doing that. It was then that I considered what would happen hereafter, if this association prevailed. It would cause me to be doomed to taking another body in some other place, having some other parents, in some other type of political and social circumstance, in the flow of the earth's history.

Pre-Meditation Check

What do you do during the first moments after sitting to meditate?

Honestly, what do you do?

I suggest that at first one should check the condition of the mind. Know how the mind is engaged. Instead of sitting to meditate and then instituting your meditation procedure or practice, how about first checking the mind's condition.

- Is the mind thinking?
- Is the mind showing images or scenes?
- Is the mind attentive to external sensual stimuli?
- Is the mind attentive to inner sounds within the head space?
- Is the mind obsessed with seeing lights or supernatural objects but is unable to perceive any of these?

- Where is the observing self located?
- How much power does the observing self have over the rest of the mental space?
- Does the observing self have to struggle with the mind to make it adopt the meditation procedure?
- On the average what is the general condition of your mind, when you first sit to meditate?

Guru Liabilities

In some spiritual societies/institutions there is this belief that the guru of the sect, and/or the deity of the religion, will absorb the liabilities, once a person moves into the ashram, or surrenders completely to the guru or mission.

Is this a fact?

What is the proof that the guru can take all liabilities for all persons who move into the ashram and becomes subjected to the rigors of ashram life with its early wake up, its restrictions on what to eat and think, its mandatory menial services, compulsory respect or worship of the guru, his deputies and the deity?

Last night (October 12, 2014), I was in an astral discussion with an old pal, a friend with whom I served in an ashram many years ago. He and I served as gurukula teachers in the institution. At one point he abandoned his wife and took to a semi-swami status, meaning living a life with no sexual connection with a woman. He was not an avid preacher. He was not charismatic. More or less, he was in the background of everything, because mostly the charismatic persons became the leaders of that institution.

During the discussion, the subject of the liability of people in the ashram surfaced because it was later discovered and proven that many boys in the boarding school were sexually abused (sodomized) by some teachers. Some children got a raw deal in the name of religious education of the sect, where when they entered adult status, their knowledge was not on par with the average child who did not live in ashrams. They knew everything about the guru and the deity of the sect but nothing about how to get a job, make an income and manage a family. They were handicapped so they could not function outside the sect.

On one hand the guru of the sect claimed that he would absorb all the reactions of a person who entered the ashram fully as well as the children of such persons who were born in the society or who came into the society and were in the program fully.

Later people began saying that the errant teachers who abused the boys were deviant and that it has nothing to do with the guru. Diehards who could not tolerate the guru being blamed for anything , said that the deviant teachers were to blame because they did not adhere to the moral conduct prescribed by the guru.

However, this argument is invalid because initially the guru did not say that he did not cover persons whom he appointed. He gave guarantees for the entire society about its purity and about its disinfectant influence on a member.

My friend inquired as to what happened to the family which I had at the time when I was in the ashram. He spoke of his ancestors and the fact that he failed in this life to assist any of them because of the guru's influence in his life which caused him to abandon his wife and make no effort to beget children. He said this,

"Just imagine I could have had two or three children and help my ancestors in that way. Instead, I did not realize that I should do this. Who knows where my ancestors are? I know for sure that the guru did not produce a single body for anything of them. That situation is still pending. That much I know."

Yoga Practice Completion

One of the things which evade modern yogis, is completion of practice methods. Most modern yogis are fakes. The sincere ones do not have the required supportive environment for success. Unfortunately for full completion of any part of yoga practice, one must have certain supports. If those factors are not present, one is out-of-luck and will not complete it.

Apart from supports one must have a certain strength of will. If that is absent, no amount of imagination or visualization will replace it. The lifeForce will not be interested in responding to imagination or whimsical visualization. If the willpower is weak, the lifeForce will simply disregard the instruction and continue doing whatever pleases it.

Sometimes when I introduce a student to a yogic method, that person may take ten weeks to put that practice into place into his or her lifestyle. However, another student may take ten years to complete it. And yet another student I may see ten lives hence, and still he/she may not complete it.

The time one takes to complete a practice may be an eternity but nevertheless whenever one completes it that is appreciated by the yoga teacher. Even if that teacher is not present in the universe at the time of completion still an energy will be released and some other yoga teacher will sense it and express appreciation.

For my part, I express appreciation for any student who took ten weeks, ten years or even ten lives to complete a practice which I introduced.

Yoga can be incremental, meaning that it can be mastered in bits and starts with very little progress or none even at times, but it accumulates over time. Eventually, if one hacks away at it, one will reach the culmination of a specific part. This is vital for developing self-confidence and having faith that yoga can be completed given enough contribution of practice in sufficient time according to the rate of the student.

Is a Yogi Practicing?

Recently I was slow in publishing reports. One may wonder if I practice even. Someone may think that I digressed.

Many yogis decrease their *asana* and breath practice as the body gets older, as they make more and more disciples, as their reputations increase. They sit back and meditate, enter samadhi, gave lectures and are served by their disciples who are all too ready to indulge the teacher as being a great yogi who is famous and should be served.

However, in my case, I was instructed by two yoga teachers not to stop doing the *asanas* postures and *pranayama* breath infusion until the body just cannot do any of it, which could be tomorrow or in a few years or near its death.

If I practice, why am I not reporting?

First of all, if one practices, if one is a yogi or even a fake one, why is one not reporting?

I do not report because right now the practice is subtle even the postures with the breath infusion. This means that verbalizing what happens is difficult. This occurs in an abstract domain. Even if I understand what it is, telling others about it is difficult especially when the experiences do not have a reference to what we experience on the physical level.

In some instance, I may have to wait days, weeks or months before I have enough experience and can develop a vocabulary and give reference to a meditation experience. That is reason why I may not report.

In some experience one has a hint of what happened but when it happens again and again, then over time one gets more and more perception in that dimension and can give an informative report. One must develop the vision to see in the new dimension. That development may take days or weeks or even months.

Recently I develop two aspects.

- cell kundalini
- *chit akash* pre-focus development

These aspects are subtle and difficult to master but progress is made.

In the area of cell kundalini, I cleared the thighs and make progress down to the toes even. There is a block-energy in the lower trunk of the subtle body.

This was removed. Once that is removed one can access the thighs and work on clearing that. The energy which blocks in the lower trunk is sex hormone energy and dense astral energy which stagnates in that area.

A strong up-pull when doing breath infusion causes this blocked energy to be lifted from the trunk. If enough of it is done, that removes it completely. Once it is removed one can target the thighs which are the support for the sexual hormonal situation of a body. The strong up-pull develops when one masters *bhastrika pranayama* which is the advanced stage of *kapalabhati* breath infusion. In *kapalabhati* one focuses on the exhale only and then when one masters that it switches so that one can focus on both the inhale and exhale. Eventually however one has to take help from a yogaGuru to really pull that inhale in strongly where it will lift the heavy astral energy from the lower torso.

Today I notice that in the trunk, through the lower part of it, the blocked energy was absent. The area was transparent instead of being cloudy or opaque. Reaching into the thighs was easy as a result.

With the *chit akash* pre-focus, somehow today a strange thing happened when I sat to meditate after breath infusion, where I found that the energy in the subtle head coursed outwards but did not leaving the psyche. This is another type of *pratyahar* practice. It occurs as a result of doing a thorough session of breath infusion just before meditating.

Usually, the energy in the head of the subtle body is stilled with none of it coursing around. In this experience it boiled without heat like a sun with nuclear energy churning around and around, except that the energy made no attempt to go outside the psyche. It boiled without heat. It had a golden color like inside the sun but it did not leave the psyche.

I realized that this was a meditative *pratyahar* state. I focused on it.

After a time, it ceased moving. Naad sound keyed in immediately. I focused on that.

This was the first time I experienced this version of *pratyahar*. The key aspect of this is that of its own accord the energy does not leave the psyche, not even a tiny bit of it does. It moves rapidly like in the center of a fiery nuclear explosion but without heat. It does not leave the subtle edges of the psyche. It does not course outwards beyond the edge of the yogi's psyche. After it boils for a while, it suddenly ceases of its own accord, and one hears naad sound resonance streaming, while everything else is absolutely silent with no images, ideas, sounds or thoughts.

Religion and Pedophile Behavior

What we define today as pedophile behavior was not always defined in that way. In some societies it was not a disapproved behavior. In some previous societies, men were neutered just as we neuter animals today in the developed countries, and we feel that it is the right thing to do. The neutered males or eunuchs were used in various ways, even sexual ways which were approved but which today is illegal.

I was in one ashram of an institution which began by a Swami from India where one of his leading school teachers was discovered to have sexually abused a boy who was under his care in the institution's boarding school. The person who did the abuse was the principal of the school for many years.

This happened in a developed country in which such behavior of adults is considered to be illegal and is punishable under the law.

When the abused boy told his parents of it, they confronted the leader of the ashram who was a primary disciple of the Indian Swami. This leader who was also a Swami but who was not of Indian (India) descent, explained that it was of little consequence and that it should be overlooked. The parents who were senior disciples in the same institution could not stomach the explanation and left that place forthwith.

They departed sometime in the 1980s. Last night (October 14, 2014) I met the abusive teacher in the astral world. I use the term abuse in its modern application. It is not my term or my opinion but rather how the term is used today in the developed countries, particularly in the USA.

I met this person in the astral world, where he stayed with the Swami who was the leader of the ashram (not the Swami who founded the whole institution), the person who excused the abusive behavior and told the parents of the boy to overlook what happened.

The abusive teacher began to smile as he did when we were on good terms during the period I taught at the boarding school. But as happens in the astral existence, he suddenly without saying a word, shifted to the topic of his pedophile behavior. He said mentally that he wanted me to understand what happened, that he was not a homosexual male nor a person who liked to have sex with minor boys.

Please note that at the time I got to the ashram when this happened, that boy was about nine years of age. I never saw the teacher in sexual position with this boy but I did see him periodically in questionable affectionate positions with the boy. The way it was set up we used to have to sleep on the floor on sleeping bags or narrow foams in classrooms with the chairs and desks pulled aside to give sleeping space.

Each teacher had a group of boys. At the time when I first go there, I was put in charge of about 8 boys whom I supervised for sleeping, waking, bathing, getting dressed and teaching. This was the all-male part of their boarding school. There was a total of about five teachers but only three of these lived as boarding teachers who had jurisdiction over the sleeping and cleaning of the boys. The others came to teach according to the courses they tutored. I was the only resident teacher who had sexual access to a woman (married or unmarried).

The way the place was set up, the nature of their social values was that having sexual access to women was a downgrade, a sign of not being advanced spiritually.

This abusive teacher explained why he sodomized the boy. This is what he said below but I asked you to give your opinion on this as to if it makes sense and as to if you feel that he will get grievous reactions for the behavior. I would like to know who shares in the responsibility of what he did, if he will carry all of it, or if the Swami who began the society and the one who established this boarding school system will bear the responsibility.

Here is what that teacher said to me:

"I did not deliberately do it. What I mean is that it just happened because I used to sleep on the floor with the boys as you know. I was fond of that boy. He slept close to me.

"I had erections. Gradually over time I began to have sex with this boy. But to be clear it was not something I planned. It was not my habit before I came into the society. I was not a homosexual even though perhaps I did have an affinity for men more than for women. I mean I did not practice sexual entries with men before even though I knew others who did that.

"I want to tell you this however, that I feel that I did this because I had no sexual access to a female. In other words, I feel that if I had access to a female, I would not have related to that boy or any other boy for that matter in that way. Something happened to me I feel because I did not have access to women in the society. You know that it was taboo to be with women. If a man was with a woman, it was shunned by the senior people and even by the leading Swami.

"In private meetings, sex between a male and female was rediculed. The preferred idea was celibacy meaning no marriage, no sex with women at any time. If you could do that you were considered senior. You were rated as being advanced.

"You were there so you know what I mean. You know how it was."

As he said this he smiled, knowing that I knew what happened. He felt that I would help him with this terrible act which may bring him bad consequences.

I looked at him with detachment. Why should I interfere? What have I to do with it? Nature will react in its own way and who knows what the past life of the boy or of this teacher was and why they were pushed together by fate in a situation from which such behavior was made possible.

After a few moments of silence, the teacher again addressed me. He said,

"Madhva, I got this feeling somehow that you know about this and that you can help me or should have assisted me but then I see that you could do nothing because of the the rules of the institution about not doing yoga. But I heard that this yoga you do helps with containing and safely using sexual energy. Perhaps if I learned your method and practice it from the onset, this would not happen. What do you think? Do you think that I can learn this yoga?"

After he said this, I said nothing to him. We parted from that astral place.

The truth is that I could not guarantee him anything. I could not say for sure that sometime in the future I would be his teacher. I could not say for sure that he would learn the method.

So much hinges on providence, which is something I do not control. And to booth there is no question that I would exert pressures on fate to allow me to be his teacher. I would not twist my providence to become his teacher, to save him from acts of sodomy or whatever. What business is it of mine to be involved in the destiny of any entity, just like that, just by their desire or by my own or whatever? Who is that crazy?

Buddhism: No-Self / A Composite of a Self

I searched for some time now to get to the bottom of the no-self concept in Buddhism. First of all, I found no solid evidence that Buddha discussed it much or was particular about it and had it as part of his doctrine. I found no focus on a self or a non-self but mostly only methods of jumping away from trauma and its potentials.

In any system if there is no self, the teacher will be hard pressed to explain who he is and who everyone else is especially if the said teacher singles himself out, as the unique enlightened one, as Buddha repeatedly did.

After looking over reliable translations of the Pali canon literature, I came to the conclusion that the use of the word *atta* (Sanskrit *atma*) was not trendy in the area where Buddha was.

It seems to me now that the term he used regularly to denote a person was *satta* which in Pali means creature or living being. Buddha did not deny this creature or living being as being individual. In fact, he explained the individuality of this creature or living being especially in relation to the fated reactions or consequences which such a creature or living being would face in the future and also in the potential of this being for liberation. Just after the enlightenment he claimed that he ranged over the world with the divine eye and saw only a few beings who could become enlightened all depending on the amount of what he termed as dust in their eyes.

Is the term *satta*, which is translated by reliable Buddhist authorities like *Bhikkhu Bodhi*, as being, a composite of a self?

Buddha / Operation of Fated Consequences

Gautam Buddha described what he perceived with the divine eyes in terms of the operation of karmic consequences which a person faces on the basis of social behavior. This was explained in *Bhikkhu Bodhi's* book; *"In the Buddha's Words"* (page 66).

Just before his enlightenment when Buddha meditated, he got the perception of how karmic consequences are flung back into the life of someone on the basis of the positive or negative actions performed.

Buddha said that when his mind was concentrated, purified, bright, unblemished, rid of imperfection, malleable, wieldy, steady, and attained to imperturbability, he directed it to knowledge of the passing away and rebirth of beings.

With the divine eye, which is purified and surpasses the human, he saw beings passing away and being reborn, inferior and superior, beautiful and ugly, fortunate and unfortunate, and he understood how beings fare on according to their actions thus:

> *Those beings who behaved wrongly by body, speech, and mind, who reviled the noble ones, held wrong view, and undertook actions based on wrong view, with the breakup of the body, after death, have been reborn in a state of misery, in a bad destination, in the lower world, in hell.*
>
> *Those beings who behaved well by body, speech, and mind, who did not revile the noble ones, who held right view, and undertook action based on right view, with the breakup of the body, after death, have been reborn in a good destination, in a heavenly world.*
>
> *Thus, with the divine eye, which was purified and surpasses the human, he saw beings passing away and being reborn, inferior and superior, beautiful and ugly, fortunate and unfortunate, and he understood how beings fare on according to their actions.*

It is clear from this that *Gautam* Buddha believed in heaven and hell but on the basis of mystic insight into astral circumstances hereafter. He did not think that heaven and hell hereafter were just states of mind but that their manifestation to any person would be based on that person's behavior during the earthly life.

The other important issue is that even though in Buddhism there is mention of *anatta (anatma)* or no soul, no self, here we get the idea of Buddha about a continuum being who performed the acts and who faces the reactions hereafter.

Flash of Heaven

This morning (October 19, 2014) in meditation I had a flash of large persimmons. There were five of them, being offered to me by someone from a heavenly world. This occurred through *buddhi* analytical orb vision. That kind of perception usually occurs within the head about two inches or so behind the center of the eyebrows. It is different to third eye vision which occurs at the center of the eyebrows. Third eye vision is more objective, while *buddhi* vision is mostly subjective.

The five persimmons were luscious fruits but, in the perception, I did not taste them because there was no taste perception. I did not see the hand even of the person who presented these.

Patanjali instructed that yogis should not accept anything from angelic beings who make offerings because that usually carries an energy whereby the yogi will be restricted to the level of the angelic person who makes the offering. After being trapped like that the yogi will spend some time in that astral paradise, then he will again find that he is among astral human beings with the result being that he will again be someone's infant, being pushed out of a woman's channel. It is a routine of nature.

Once a yogi takes the invitation, he is captured. Once he takes the invitation, it is like a roller coaster ride, where he is strapped in and can only come out at the end of the ride when the equipment is turned off by the operator. He will not be in a position to leave it but it will of its own accord deliver him to the earthly existence, with him having no control over how that happens.

Think of it in this way. Suppose you are invited to go on a ship cruise. You accept the offer thinking that this would be great. You get on the ship. It moves from your home port. You are taken to a beautiful island where you are entertained as if you were a celebrity. But then a storm begins. Your life is threatened. At that point what can you do? Can you command the captain of the ship to erase the experience and to make it so that you never left the home port?

However, in following this instruction of Patanjali one has to be careful that one does not offend a supernatural being, because to do so presents another danger into the life of a yogi. In the story of Mudgal, we find that when he was offered to go the Swarga angelic world, he refused to go on the celestial conveyance but Mudgal did so in a respectful way. He did not insult or offend the angelic being who presented the opportunity. Mudgal simply explained that he was not interested in the upside to such paradise life because it has an accompanying downside which he preferred to avoid. He also explained that he wanted to do more yoga austerities and research. Subsequently, his life span was extended so that he could finish the austerities.

In the case of King *Nala* however that was not the case, he acted against the supernatural people. For that he endured difficulties for many years. Therefore, one should be careful in following Patanjali because Patanjali cannot protect one from a supernatural being if one offends the deity.

As for King *Nala* when requested by the supernatural rulers to abandon his love for the beautiful woman *Damayanti*, he refused to comply. Subsequently the woman and *Nala* were put into serious misfortune. Hostility or offence, arrogance or plain ignorance when dealing with the supernatural people could hurt a yogi. In following Patanjali one has to use commonsense otherwise one may be ruined.

The stories of *Mudgal* and *Nala* are in the *Mahabharata*.

The important part of the experience with the persimmons is that I saw the fruits; which means that the vision perception to see these celestial objects is operative. I did not experience the taste of the fruits which means that in that experience, the tasting sense on that level was inoperative.

On some levels of the celestial world, where one may appear, one may find that one gets there but does not have all the required sensual means to experience the place. One may have one or two or more of the senses required but not all. Others who live there permanently will have all senses required. This is similar to life on earth, where on occasion a child is born with one or more senses not functioning properly. Someone may be born with eyes which do not see or with ears which do not hear. It happens.

Here is the instruction from Patanjali:

स्थान्युपनिमन्त्रणे सङ्गस्मयाकरणं पुनरनिष्टप्रसङ्गात् ॥५२॥

sthānyupanimantraṇe saṅgasmayākaraṇaṁ
punaraniṣṭa prasaṅgāt

sthāni – person from the place a yogi would then attain if his material body died; upanimantraṇe – on being invited; saṅga – association; smaya – fascination, wonderment; akaraṇaṁ – non-responsiveness; punaḥ – again; aniṣṭa – unwanted features of existence; prasaṅgāt – due to association, due to endearing friendliness.

On being invited by a person from the place one would attain if the body died, a yogi should be non-responsive, not desiring their association and not being fascinated, otherwise that would cause unwanted features of existence to arise again. (Yoga Sutra 3.52)

It may be argued that King *Nala* was not invited to a heaven by the supernatural people, but the argument does not hold, because it was an indirect invitation. If for instance the King agreed to leave aside his love for the beautiful woman, the supernatural people would give him a favorable result. The other more important factor is that *Nala* did not know who the woman really was or where she was in her previous existences.

Psyche Grip / Naad Support

This is a kriya which is part of naad focus development. After securing naad sound vibration shelter consistently where after doing breath infusion the yogi finds the coreSelf to be in or near naad automatically, without special efforts to locate naad, the yogi should develop a close relationship with naad just as if naad is a person.

This causes the development of various relationships with naad, like that of a dear friend, that of a lover, that of a beloved, that of parents with naad always in the more nurturing position towards the core.

When this is developed, the yogi can find naad even when he does not do breath infusion but as a matter of course, as the practice dictates. He does not abandon breath infusion because otherwise how will he infuse the subtle body with fresh energy. Reliance on imagination and visualization is for those who cannot do breath infusion. Any yogi who can do the infusion would be foolish to neglect it because even if one reached naad without doing it, still that will be on a lower plane than if one did it.

Once the yogi secured this intimate relationship with naad, he should regularly check during the meditation to be sure that there are no thought-images in the frontal part of the subtle head. If there are thoughts this practice is not proficient. The yogi should practice more. He should do whatever is necessarily to curtail the displays.

Actions to curtail would be one or more of the following:

- Restrict physical and psychic association with others even with other yogis.
- Do a more thorough breath infusion, even do double sessions to be sure that more negative subtle energy is extracted from the subtle body.
- Service pending responsibilities because those may splice into the meditation session and undermine progress.

Responsibility is the bane of a yogi but that does not mean that he can successfully neglect it. He must have the intelligence and organization to properly sort and service it. If he is unable to do this, because of being a sloppy person, or because he does not have the insight to manage it, he cannot be successful in this practice.

There is the added danger with responsibilities where people whom the yogi has a duty towards will make excessive demands. The yogi should have the intelligence to side-step such requests and still do the needful for the satisfaction of the Universal Form of Krishna. It does not matter if others feel that the yogi has a certain duty. The concern is that the duty is his assignment by the Universal Form of Krishna. A yogi should not shift focus from the Universal Form or he will become a pawn of duties which the form does not sanction. He will deviate from the path of yoga to his ruination.

Suppose a doctor treated tuberculosis patients. How would it be if he forgot the medical training and begin taking advice on treatment from the patients? A yogi should not fall under the influence of students. The doctor should stick to his medical training and should serve the interest of the people who licensed him. Any shift from that is a mishap.

When the yogi developed the close very intimate relationship with naad sound vibration, he should on occasion while he is absorbed in naad, check to be sure that the front part of the subtle head is not involved in images and thoughts. Once he sees that it is not involved and that no effort was made on his part to control, restrict or suppress thoughts, he is ready for the next stage which is to lift the rest of the psyche. Getting a grip on the psyche which is outside of the subtle head, which is below the neck, is the next achievement. Usually, yogis neglect the parts of the psyche below the neck but that is mistake.

If there is anything amiss below the neck, if a vibration below is not of the highest, the yogi will find that his progress is checked by that heavy astral energy.

If the yogi is lucky, if while in naad resonance, he looks downward into the rest of the psyche below the neck and perceives a gold glow light which is similar to the light one sees at dawn just before the sun creeps above the horizon. This glow light will not flicker or disappear but will remain in the view of the yogi. The yogi may find that his focus on this glow shifts but when he resumes, it will be there as it was before in exactly the same way as when he first saw it.

The yogi should keep a mild focus, not a sharp pin-point focus, on that gold glow light. Gradually, he should feel the rest of the psyche which is below the neck. He should clasp and lift it.

Hariharananda Meditation Procedure

Hariharananda (October 25, 2014) appeared in my head this morning while I meditated. He explained his meditation procedure saying that it was simple. I concluded the breath infusion session prior to the meditation and was located in the naad sound resonance in the back of the subtle head. I was also focused forward into a glow light. This is a gold glow light which is all pervasive except that it is not in the naad sound itself but is everywhere else in that dimension.

This is a special focusing kriya which I practice at this stage of meditation.

Hariharananda said this,

"Think of something"

Before I could even think, a woman's figure appeared. It was someone I knew some years ago when I was in Guyana. She was there for a split second only but her form was distinct which gave positive identification.

Then Swami instructed this:

- Now do you see light?
- There is no light.
- Now go back into naad, become naad absorbed again.
- Now see light again.
- That is it.
- Now go deeper into naad absorption. Now pull light from the brow chakra.
- That is what he taught us.
- Very easy - see it is easy.

After this he disappeared.

I pondered his process. My conclusion:

It will not work if the student cannot reach a deep state of naad. It will not work if the student does not begin with a mind which is cleared of images and ideas. After the instruction to think of something when the woman appeared, I reestablished the coreSelf in naad but all the same the glow light did not appear as he said. Instead, there was a greyish light which is not suitable for this meditation. After I noticed that I went deeper into naad. The glow light appeared but it was not as brilliant as before.

This means that the intrusion of any thought, image or idea into the mind from any source will degrade the meditation. The student will lose the footing on the higher level and will fall back to the usual mental plane where there is no light but only speckled darkness or greyness in the mind.

After this happened, I sent a mental query to the Swami. He left my psyche already. I could not confront him directly. This was that question:

What is the process for reaching the high level of naad absorption?

He replied promptly with this,

"It used to be various types of *pranayama* as recommended by the teachers before. I can reach naad absorption without doing that."

My conclusion about that answer is that it lacks a set process. That is a loophole in his process. This is my opinion based on my years of meditating where I find that in my case, I was unable to reach a high naad absorption state without first doing the breath infusion through *kapalabhati* or *bhastrika*. I did on occasion reach naad state without doing breath infusion but that was infrequently. I could not rely on it to happen on every occasion.

Sleep / Meditation

Patanjali mentioned sleep as having nothing to do with yoga. He listed it as one the five unwanted *vritti* functions of the mental and emotional energy. Unless there is banishment or total suppression *(nirodhah)* of sleep, yoga, according to Patanjali cannot be practiced.

However, sleep cannot be eliminated entirely. According to the *Puranas*, even the cosmic god, Brahma, sleeps, even on a daily basis but on his time schedule.

Since sleep cannot be eliminated not even for the cosmic god, what does Patanjali means by his suggestion that sleep should be totally suppressed? After practicing meditation for over forty years, I feel that I am in a position to explain what Patanjali suggested.

For sure he could not mean the total suppression of sleep for all time because that is not possible even for the gods up to the level of Brahma. His meaning has to be that there should be such suppression during the meditation session for say between twenty minutes to two hours or more.

I can say definitely that during meditation I achieved the no sleep stage but only because of doing proficient breath infusion before the session. The breath infusion has to be thorough where one can extract carbon dioxide even from the thighs down to the knees. With the removal of that energy, the sleep potency is disrupted and cannot assert itself in the subtle body during meditation. It may assert itself on the physical form but it should not control the subtle body. Then one will experience a new-ness, a new sense of sleeplessness during meditation.

Shrinking of Identity / Next Body

Before one can get another body, one must assume a shrinking down of one's social identity. Seniority, which is ingrained, must be scaled down before one takes a new body. One can either do the scaling oneself or one can let nature do it. Any which way, it has to be done before the next embryo develops.

I was with my deceased father in the astral world a few nights ago when this topic came up. He is in the process of acquiring an embryo and wanted to chitty chat about it, asking if I could render assistance.

Looking at his subtle form, I could see that it is scaling down his social identity. Psychologically this means that the person loses the footing as a senior, as an elderly body. The person loses seniority and must adapt the demeanor of someone who is to be someone's child.

As soon as the astral time runs out for a person, this begins to happen where he/she feels that the seniority from the past life disappears. It happens gradually. Before nature would apply it, a yogi can trigger this change himself.

Lahiri / Double *Bhastrika*

Lahiri suggested that in the advanced stages, the student should do a double *bhastrika* practice. This does not mean to repeat every posture with breath. It means to achieve a complete clearance of the *apana* carbon dioxide. On some days a repeat of every posture with breath infusion may be necessary. But on other days, some postures or even other postures would be necessary.

There is no set rule. The student should be psychically sensitive enough to know what to do on any given day. The best way to achieve this is to do a thorough session while using a blind fold. Because any distraction takes away from the effort, the blindfold will assist in the effort to keep the mind within the psyche.

Once a complete session is done, the student should begin a new session and be attentive to do whatever is intuitively supportive within the psyche. Having the intention of doing a new session, the student should begin and should complete that second session without expectation or preconception of what it should be.

This approach will accelerate practice and cause the student to reach the success of yoga earlier.

Thigh Clearance / Celibate Practice

Students who work on celibate practice should monitor the thighs, down to the knees. Initially one should be concerned with the thigh area which is close to the trunk of the body, close to the genitals and buttocks regions. If the thighs are not subdued, the celibate practice will fail. *Asana* postures which target the thighs are valuable in this practice but these must be done with breath infusion, otherwise the energy released in the thigh stretches will simply be re-absorbed into the fleshy tissue, tendons and bones just after doing the posture.

Breath infusion is the way to pull this energy from the thighs. It may be proposed that a person can do this merely by visualization or by will power. That is fine for those who can achieve that. However, I do recommend a very aggressive *asana* and breath infusion method for extracting this energy and clearing the thighs of sexually charged blood on the physical side and sexual charged lust energy in the astral body.

This practice was not shown to me by a yogi. I discovered this in the quest for changing the subtle body. After dealing with the groin area, one discovers that the thighs are the background energy and support system for that. One is then confronted with the task of curbing the thigh which is a *hard to reach* area. Until one can get the pubic area cleared of stale stored energy on a consistent basis, one cannot tackle the thigh.

In one practice recently, when gutting the energy in the thigh there was a cool twinkle bliss force which was released. This energy passed up into the abdomen bypassing the groin as if that area did not exist. It gave a twinkling shifting bliss potency. This experience is valuable to let the ascetic know of his/her progress where he/she can gage what happens to change the subtle body in a definite way.

Students doing these practices, should make keen observation of what happens, as to where, how, and in which direction, energies are released. These observations give confidence that the practice is productive.

Food Problem / Yogis

I was questioned a few days ago about diet, in regards to yoga practice and what I think is the best food to consume.

Here is a list of the important facets of my meals:

- main meal in the morning before 9.30
- no solid heavy foods or main meals after 5 pm.
- no meat, fish or eggs
- use organic dairy products
- use very little cheese
- greens, carrots or squash, potatoes or light beans.
- use whole wheat.
- avoid white flour breads and pastries
- do not use sugar
- use very little salt less than 1/8 of a teaspoon per day
- do not use chips or dried foods
- do not use hot pepper
- do not use strong condiments like onions, garlic or spices
- do not use black pepper
- do not use garbanzo beans, chick peas or channa

- do not use canned foods
- do not use red kidney beans
- use about three bananas daily with milk
- use organic fruits
- use citrus fruits mostly as medicines for helping body immunity and for producing digestive enzymes
- do not use pineapples because farmers usually use strong herbicides and also other chemicals on the plants in the tropics

What do I do for intoxication?

That is better explained by stating what I do not do:

- do not use marijuana, cocaine, heroin, LSD, ayuasca, mushrooms etc.
- do not use tobacco
- do not use alcohol
- do not use vinegar
- do not use fermented drinks
- do not use coffee

Do I prohibit people from taking substances?

The answer is no. I could care less what you take. We are all in this together on this great tourist ship called Mother Earth. If it sinks, we go down with it?

Yoga Success Unlikely

I came to the conclusion to day that full success in yoga, is unlikely at the present time, in the cultural situation which humanity is currently bogged with.

Looking back over the years at what I had to do for practice and at the slow rate of progress despite my determination and application, which far excels many students, I concluded that it will not be possible for most students to succeed.

There are too many impediments, too many social hassles, too many diversions, too many stops and starts, for a consolidated cumulative practice to succeed at present. I state this to inform students.

During a meditation this morning when I followed a procedure given by Lahiri. I considered the detailed and very minute abstract adjustment which he required me to make. I cannot see how most students could do it. I remember the incidence reported from Buddha's austerities where after his enlightenment, he surveyed in his mind if he could teach what he discovered. He concluded that there was hardly a soul anywhere who could do what he did. It was too difficult, he concluded, for others to practice.

Buddha was convinced by the Brahma deity to explain it anyway. I am not Buddha. I explained everything I do as I practice. So as not to cheat anyone, as not to give anyone false expectations, I declare that it is hardly likely that one will succeed because of the abstractness of the process.

With that however, I encourage every student to practice.

Index

K

Kaitabha, 158
Kalama, 170
Kalyani, 50
kamma, types, 112, 117
kanda, 43
karma, types, 112, 117
karmic fly backs, 115. 117
killing of the body, 100
kleem, 46
Krishna,
- instruction, 139
- Satyabhama, 89
- supreme person, 61
- time, 105

Kumaras, 200
kundalini,
- bribe, 199
- coils, 64
- component, 158
- defined, 63
- franchise, 199
- goddess, 55
- stub, 51
- powerful, 56

Kundalini Hatha Yoga Pradipika, 163
Kusinara, 80

L

learn alone, 62
liberated person, 38
liberation, attainments, 95
Licchavis, 70
lifespan, 119
lift hormone, 14
lift nectar, 193
lift suction, 43
light green energy, 42
lineage guru, 100
lion pose, 81
lions, 173
locks, 16, 148
loop around system, 53
Lord, 78
love, 123
lust free bliss, 56
luxury, 48

M

Madhu, 158
Mahamaya Devi, 89
Mandana Misra, 158
mandarava, 81
mango woman, 70
mangoes, 123
mantra,
- bestowal, 154
- body change? 69
- confidential, 47
- free, 13
- usage, 45

Mara, 162
marijuana, 40, 66, 136
marriage next life, 171
mascara, 198
Matsyendranath, 19
meat, 66
medication, 136
meditation,
- God, 31
- objective, 37
- types, 129

memory,
- Arjuna, 157
- coreSelf access, 78
- restrictive, 191

mental fog, 56
merchandising, 69
method, 6, 14
milk, 74
mincemeat, 71
mirror, 198
mission change, 163
mission, fulfilled, 100
Mississippi River, 211
modesty, 134
Moggallana, death, 71
money, 48

Q, R

S

T

About the Author

Michael Beloved (Yogi *Madhvāchārya)* took his current body in 1951 in Guyana. In 1965, while living in Trinidad, he instinctively began doing yoga postures and tried to make sense of the supernatural side of life.

Later in 1970, in the Philippines, he approached a Martial Arts Master named Arthur Beverford. He explained to the teacher that he was seeking a yoga instructor. Mr. Beverford identified himself as an advanced disciple of *Śrī* Rishi Singh Gherwal, an Ashtanga Yoga master.

Beverford taught the traditional Ashtanga Yoga with stress on postures, attentive breathing and brow chakra centering meditation. In 1972, Michael entered the Denver, Colorado Ashram of *kundalini* yoga Master *Śrī* Harbhajan Singh. There he took instruction in *bhastrika* pranayama and its application to yoga postures. He was supervised mostly by Yogi Bhajan's disciple named Prem Kaur.

In 1979 Michael formally entered the disciplic succession of the Brahmā - Madhava-Gaudiya Sampradaya through *Swāmī* Kirtanananda, who was a prominent sannyasi disciple of the Great Vaishnava Authority *Śrī Swāmī* Bhaktivedanta Prabhupada, the exponent of devotion to Sri Krishna.

However, yoga has a mystic side to it, thus Michael took training and teaching empowerment from several spiritual masters of different aspects of spiritual development. This is consistent with *Śrī* Krishna's advice to Arjuna in the *Bhagavad Gītā*:

Most of the instructions Michael received were given in the astral world. On that side of existence, his most prominent teachers were *Śrī Swāmī* Shivananda of Rishikesh, Yogiraj *Swāmī* Vishnudevananda, *Śrī Bābāji Mahasaya* - the master of the masters of *Kriyā* Yoga, *Śrīla* Yogeshwarananda of Gangotri - the master of the masters of *Rāj* Yoga (spiritual clarity), and Siddha *Swāmī* Nityananda the Brahmā Yoga authority.

The course for kundalini yoga using pranayama breath-infusion was detailed by Michael in the book *Kundalini Hatha Yoga Pradipika*. This current book was composed from meditation and breath-infusion notes which were originally shared in staple bound booklets as Yoga Journals.

Michael's preliminary books relating to this topic are *Meditation Pictorial, Meditation Expertise*, and *Meditation ~ Sense Faculty* (co-author). Every technique (kriya) mentioned was tested by him during pranayama breath-infusion and *samyama* deep meditation practice.

This is a result of over forty years of meditation practice with astute subtle observations intending to share the methods and experiences. The information is published freely with no intention of forming an institution or hogtying anyone as a disciple.

Publications

English Series

Bhagavad Gita English

Anu Gita English

Markandeya Samasya English

Yoga Sutras English

Hatha Yoga Pradipika English

Uddhava Gita English

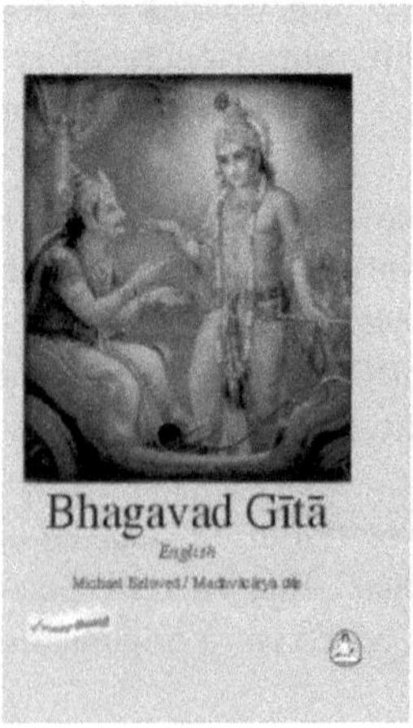

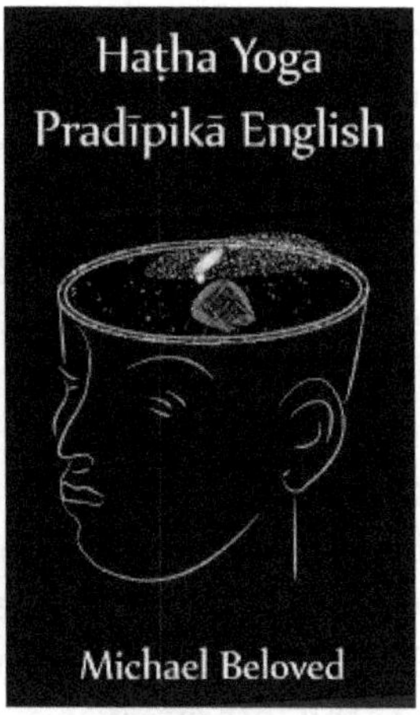

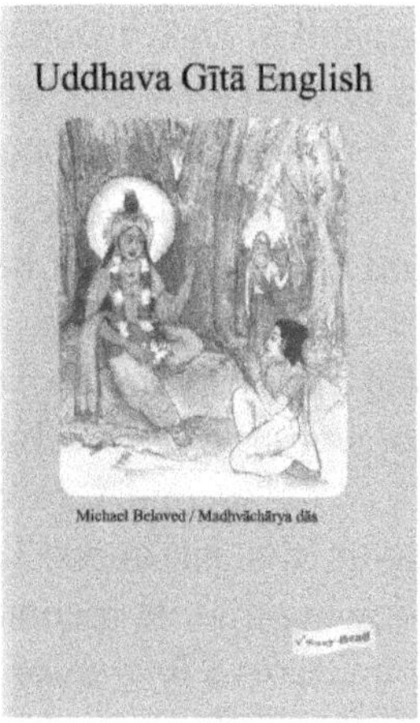

These are in 21st Century English, very precise and exacting. Many Sanskrit words which were considered untranslatable into a Western language are rendered in precise, expressive and modern English.

Three of these books are instructions from Krishna. **In *Bhagavad Gita* English** and **Anu Gita English**, the instructions were for Arjuna. In the **Uddhava Gita English,** it was for Uddhava. *Bhagavad Gita* and Anu Gita are extracted from the Mahabharata. Uddhava Gita was extracted from the 11th Canto of the Srimad Bhagavatam (Bhagavata Purana). One of these books, the **Markandeya Samasya English** is about Krishna, as described by Yogi Markandeya, who survived the cosmic collapse and reached a divine child in whose transcendental body, the collapsed world was existing.

Two of this series are the syllabus about yoga practice. The *Yoga Sutras* of Patañjali is elaboration about ashtanga yoga. Hatha Yoga Pradipika English, is the detailed information about asana postures, pranayama breath-infusion, energy compression, naad sound resonance and advanced meditation. The Sanskrit author is Swatmarama Mahayogin.

My suggestion is that you read ***Bhagavad Gita* English**, the **Anu Gita English, the Markandeya Samasya English,** the ***Yoga Sutras* English,** the **Hatha Yoga Pradipika** and lastly the **Uddhava Gita English**, which is complicated and detailed.

For each of these books we have at least one commentary, which is published separately. Thus one's particular interest can be researched further in the commentaries.

The smallest of these commentaries and perhaps the simplest is the one for the Anu Gita. We published its commentary as the Anu Gita Explained. The *Bhagavad Gita* explanations were published in three distinct targeted commentaries. The first is *Bhagavad Gita* Explained, which sheds lights on how people in the time of Krishna and Arjuna regarded the information and applied it. *Bhagavad Gita* is an exposition of the application of yoga practice to cultural activities, which is known in the Sanskrit language as karma yoga.

Interestingly, *Bhagavad Gita* was spoken on a battlefield just before one of the greatest battles in the ancient world. A warrior, Arjuna, lost his wits and had no idea that he could apply his training in yoga to political dealings. Krishna, his charioteer, lectured on the spur of the moment to give Arjuna the skill of using yoga proficiency in cultural dealings including how to deal with corrupt officials on a battlefield.

The second Gita commentary is the Kriya Yoga *Bhagavad Gita*. This clears the air about Krishna's information on the science of kriya yoga, showing that its techniques are clearly described for anyone who takes the time to read *Bhagavad Gita*. Kriya yoga concerns the battlefield which is the psyche of the living being. The internal war and the mental and emotional forces which are hostile to self-realization are dealt with in the kriya yoga practice.

The third commentary is the Brahma Yoga *Bhagavad Gita*. This shows what Krishna had to say outright and what he hinted about which concerns the brahma yoga practice, a mystic process for those who mastered kriya yoga.

There is one commentary for the **Markandeya Samasya English**. The title of that publication is Krishna Cosmic Body.

There are two commentaries to the *Yoga Sutras*. One is the *Yoga Sutras* of Patañjali and the other is the Meditation Expertise. These give detailed explanations of ashtanga Yoga.

The commentary of Hatha Yoga Pradipika is titled Kundalini Hatha Yoga Pradipika.

For the Uddhava Gita, we published the Uddhava Gita Explained. This is a large book and requires concentration and study for integration of the information. Of the books which deal with transcendental topics, my opinion is that the discourse between Krishna and Uddhava has the complete information about the realities in existence. This book is the one which removes massive existential ignorance.

Meditation Series

Meditation Pictorial

Meditation Expertise

CoreSelf Discovery

Meditation Sense Faculty

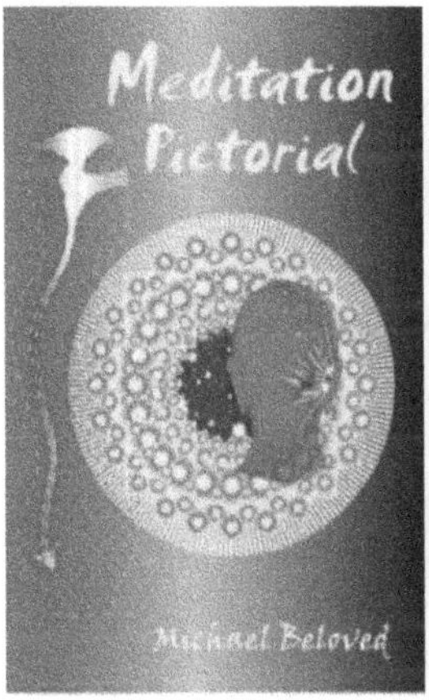

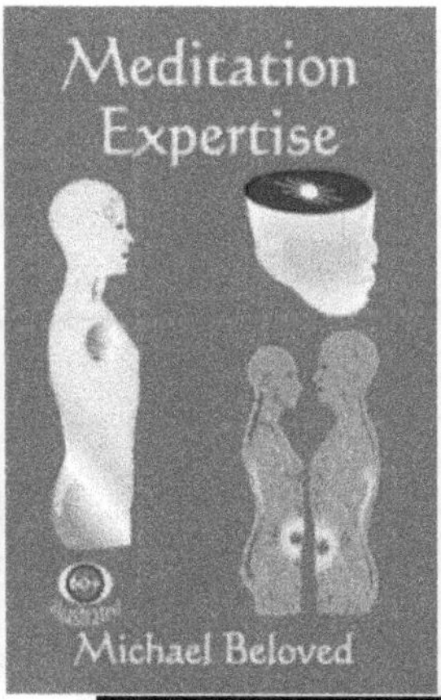

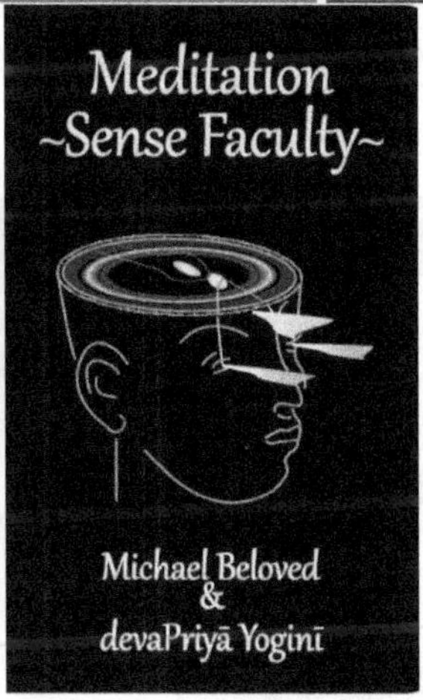

The specialty of these books is the mind diagrams which profusely illustrate what is written. This shows exactly what one has to do mentally to develop and then sustain a meditation practice.

In the **Meditation Pictorial**, one is shown how to develop psychic insight, a feature without which meditation is imagination and visualization, without any mystic experience per se.

In the **Meditation Expertise**, one is shown how to corral one's practice to bring it in line with the classic syllabus of yoga which Patañjali lays out as the ashtanga yoga eight-staged practice.

In **CoreSelf Discovery**, (co-authored with *devaPriya Yogini*) one is taken though the course of *pratyahar* sensual energy withdrawal which is the 5th stage of yoga in the Patañjali ashtanga eight-process complete system of yoga practice. These events lead to the discovery of a coreSelf which is surrounded by psychic organs in the head of the subtle body. This product has a DVD component.

Meditation ~ Sense Faculty (co-authored with *devaPriya Yogini*) is a detailed tutorial with profuse diagrams showing what actions to take in the subtle body to investigate the senses faculties. The meditator must first establish the location and function of the observing self. That self must be screened from the thoughts and ideas which usually hypnotize it.

These books are profusely illustrated with mind diagrams showing the components of psychic consciousness and the inner design of the subtle body.

Explained Series

Bhagavad Gita Explained

Uddhava Gita Explained

Anu Gita Explained

The specialty of these books is that they are free of missionary intentions, cult tactics and philosophical distortion. Instead of using these books to add credence to a philosophy, meditation process, belief or plea for followers, I spread the information out so that a reader can look through this literature and freely take or leave anything as desired.

When Krishna stressed himself as God, I stated that. When Krishna laid no claims for supremacy, I showed that. The reader is left to form an independent opinion about the validity of the information and the credibility of Krishna.

There is a difference in the discourse with Arjuna in the *Bhagavad Gita* and the one with Uddhava in the Uddhava Gita. In fact, these two books may appear to contradict each other. In the *Bhagavad Gita*, Krishna pressured Arjuna to complete social duties. In the Uddhava Gita, Krishna insisted that Uddhava should abandon the same.

The Anu Gita is not as popular as the *Bhagavad Gita* but it is the conclusion of that text. Anu means what is to follow, what proceeds. In this discourse, an anxious Arjuna request that Krishna should repeat the *Bhagavad Gita* and again show His supernatural and divine forms.

However, Krishna refuses to do so and chastises Arjuna for being a disappointment in forgetting what was revealed. Krishna then cited a celestial yogi, a near-perfected being, who explained the process of transmigration in vivid detail.

Commentaries

Yoga Sutras of Patañjali

Meditation Expertise

Krishna Cosmic Body

Anu Gita Explained

Bhagavad Gita Explained

Kriya Yoga Bhagavad Gita

Brahma Yoga Bhagavad Gita

Uddhava Gita Explained

Kundalini Hatha Yoga Pradipika

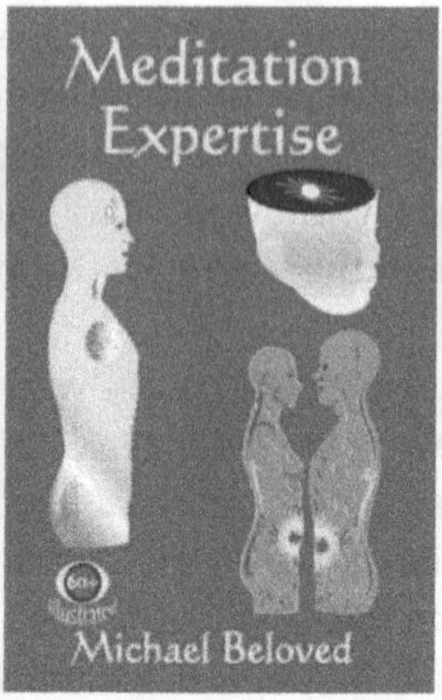

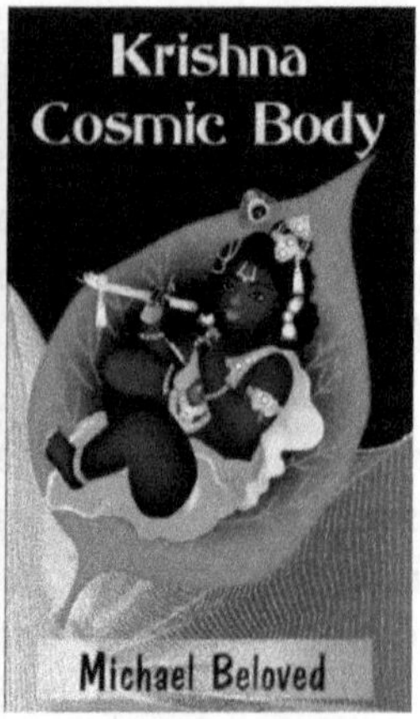

***Yoga Sutras* of Patañjali is** the globally acclaimed text book of yoga. This has detailed expositions of yoga techniques. Many kriya techniques are vividly described in the commentary.

Meditation Expertise is an analysis and application of the *Yoga Sutras*. This book is loaded with illustrations and has detailed explanations of secretive advanced meditation techniques which are called kriyas in the Sanskrit language.

Krishna Cosmic Body is a narrative commentary on the Markandeya Samasya portion of the Aranyaka Parva of the Mahabharata. This is the detailed description of the dissolution of the world, as experienced by the great yogin Markandeya who transcended the cosmic deity, Brahma, and reached Brahma's source who is the divine infant, Krishna.

Anu Gita Explained is a detailed explanation of how we endure many material bodies in the course of transmigrating through various life-forms. This is a discourse between Krishna and Arjuna. Arjuna requested of Krishna a display of the Universal Form and a repeat narration of the *Bhagavad Gita* but Krishna declined and explained what a siddha perfected being told the Yadu family about the sequence of existences one endures and the systematic flow of those lives at the convenience of material nature.

Bhagavad Gita **Explained** shows what was said in the Gita without religious overtones and sectarian biases.

Kriya Yoga *Bhagavad Gita* shows the instructions for those who are doing kriya yoga.

Brahma Yoga *Bhagavad Gita* shows the instructions for those who are doing brahma yoga.

Uddhava Gita Explained shows the instructions to Uddhava which are more advanced than the ones given to Arjuna.

Bhagavad Gita is an instruction for applying the expertise of yoga in the cultural field. This is why the process taught to Arjuna is called karma yoga which means karma + yoga or cultural activities done with yogic insight.

Uddhava Gita is an instruction for apply the expertise of yoga to attaining spiritual status. This is why it explains jnana yoga and bhakti yoga in detail. Jnana yoga is using mystic skill for knowing the spiritual part of existence. Bhakti yoga is for developing affectionate relationships with divine beings.

Karma yoga is for negotiating the social concerns in the material world. It is inferior to bhakti yoga which concerns negotiating the social concerns in the spiritual world.

This world has a social environment. The spiritual world has one too.

Currently, Uddhava Gita is the most advanced and informative spiritual book on the planet. There is nothing anywhere which is superior to it or which goes into so much detail as it. It verified that historically Krishna is the most advanced human being to ever have left literary instructions on this planet. Even Patañjali *Yoga Sutras* which I translated and gave an application for in my book, **Meditation Expertise**, does not go as far as the Uddhava Gita.

Some of the information of these two books is identical but while the *Yoga Sutras* are concerned with the personal spiritual emancipation (kaivalyam) of the individual spirits, the Uddhava Gita explains that and also explains the situations in the spiritual universes.

Bhagavad Gita is from the *Mahabharata* which is the history of the Pandavas. Arjuna, the student of the Gita, is one of the Pandavas brothers. He was in a social hassle and did not know how to apply yoga expertise to solve it. On the battlefield, Krishna gave him a crash-course on yogic social interactions.

Uddhava Gita is from the *Srimad Bhagavatam (Bhagavata Purana),* which is a history of the incarnations of Krishna. Uddhava was a relative of Krishna. He was concerned about the situation of the deaths of many of his relatives but Krishna diverted Uddhava's attention to the practice of yoga for the purpose of successfully migrating to the spiritual environment.

Kundalini Hatha Yoga Pradipika is the commentary for the Hatha Yoga Pradipika of Swatmarama Mahayogin. This is the detailed process about asana posture, pranayama breath-infusion, complex compressions of energy, naad sound resonance intonement and advanced meditation practice.

This is the singular book with all the techniques of how to reform and redesign the subtle body so that it does not have the tendency for physical life forms and for it to attain the status of a siddha.

These books are based on the author's experiences in meditation, yoga practice and participation in spiritual groups:

Specialty

Spiritual Master

sex you!

Sleep Paralysis

Astral Projection

Masturbation Psychic Details

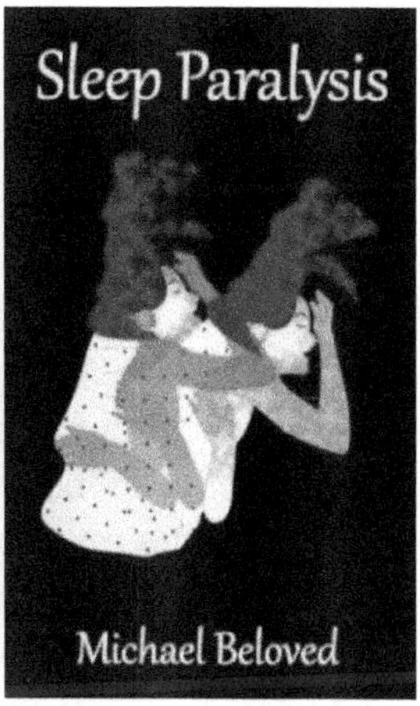

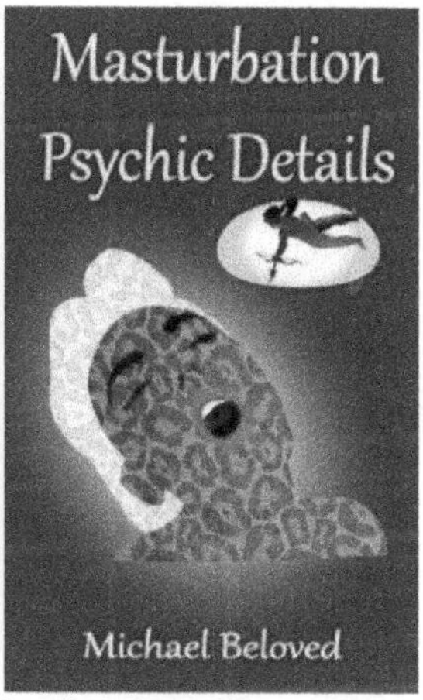

In **Spiritual Master**, Michael draws from experience with gurus or with their senior students. His contact with astral gurus is rated. He walks you through the avenue of gurus showing what you should do and what you should not do, so as to gain proficiency in whatever area of spirituality the guru has proficiency.

sex you! is a masterpiece about the adventures of an individual spirit's passage through the parents' psyches. The conversion of a departed soul into a sexual urge is described. The transit from the afterlife to residency in the emotions of the parents is detailed. This is about sex and you. Learn about how much of you comprises the romantic energy of one's would-be parents!

Sleep Paralysis clears misconceptions so that one can see what sleep paralysis is and what frightening astral experience occurs while the paralysis is being experienced. This disempowerment has great value in giving you confidence that you can and do exist even if one is unable to operate the physical body. The implication is that one can exist apart from and will survive the loss of the material form.

Astral Projection details experiences Michael had even in childhood, where he assumed incorrectly that everyone was astrally conversant. He discusses the lifeForce psychic mechanism which operates the sleep-wake cycle of the physical form, and which budgets energy into the separated astral form which determines if the individual will have dream recall or no objective awareness during the projections. Astral travel happens on every occasion when the physical body sleeps. What is missing in awareness is the observer status while the astral body is separated.

Masturbation Psychic Details is a surprise presentation which relates what happens on the psychic plane during a masturbation event. This does not tackle moral issues or even addictions but shows the involvement of memory and the sure but hidden subconscious mind which operates many features of the psyche irrespective of the desire or approval of the self-conscious personality.

inVision Series

Yoga inVision 1

Yoga inVision 2

Yoga inVision 3

Yoga inVision 4

Yoga inVision 5

Yoga inVision 6

Yoga inVision 7

Yoga inVision 8

Yoga inVision 9

Yoga inVision 10

Yoga inVision 11

Yoga inVision 12

Yoga inVision 13

Yoga inVision 14

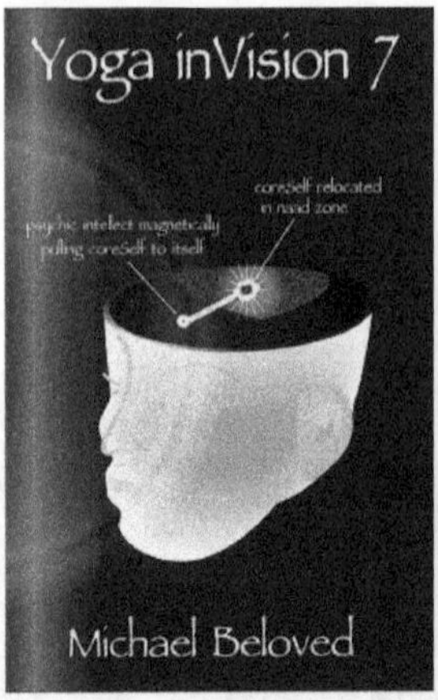

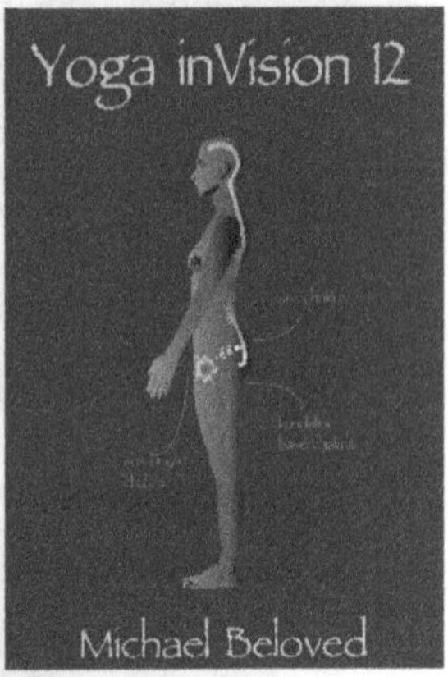

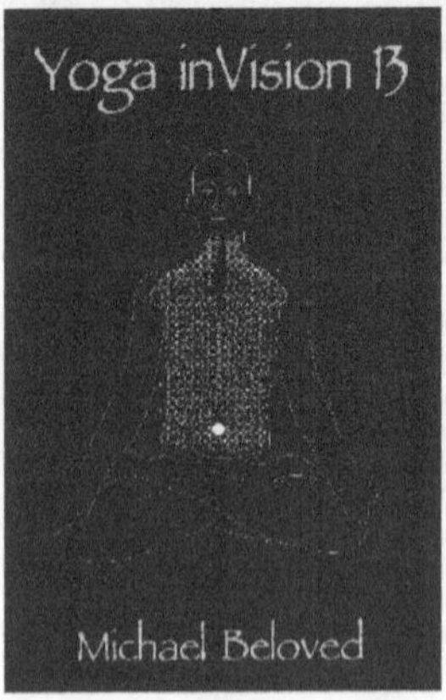

Yoga inVision 1, the first in this series, describes the breath-infusion and meditation practices during the years of 1998 and 1999. There are unique, once in a lifetime as well as recurring insights which are elaborated. inFocus during breath-infusion and the meditation which follows is an adventure for any yogi. This gives what happened to this particular ascetic.

Yoga inVision 2 reports on the author's experiences from 1999 to 2001. Each day the experience is unique, illustrating the vibrancy of practice. Many rare once-in-a-lifetime perceptions are described.

Yoga inVision 3 reports on the author's experiences from 2001 to 2003.

Yoga inVision 4 reports on the author's experiences from 2006 to 2009.

Yoga inVision 5 reports on the author's experiences from 2006 to 2008.

Yoga inVision 6 reports on the author's experiences in 2010.

Yoga inVision 7 reports on the author's experiences in 2011.

Yoga inVision 8 reports on the author's experiences in 2011.

Yoga inVision 9 reports on the author's experiences in 2012.

Yoga inVision 10 reports on the author's experiences in 2012.

Yoga inVision 11 reports on the author's experiences in 2012.

Yoga inVision 12 reports on the author's experiences in 2012-2013.

Yoga inVision 13 reports on the author's experiences in 2013-2014.

Yoga inVision 14 reports on the author's experiences in 2014.

Online Resources

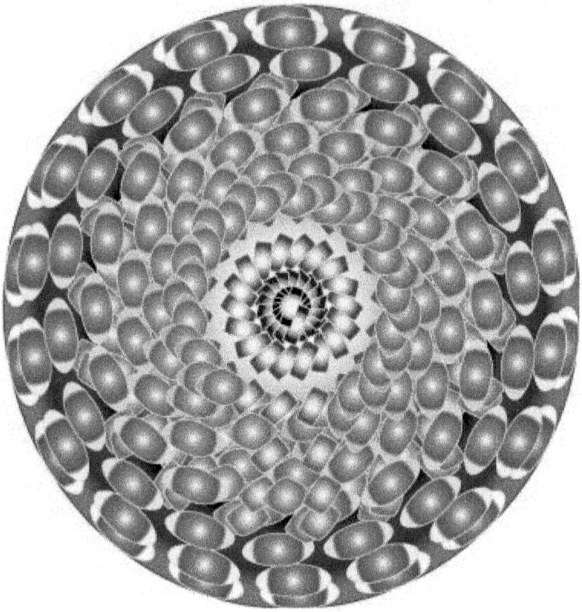

Email:	michaelbelovedbooks@gmail.com axisnexus@gmail.com
Website:	michaelbeloved.com
Forum:	inselfyoga.com
Posters:	zazzle.com/inself

www.ingramcontent.com/pod-product-compliance
Lightning Source LLC
Chambersburg PA
CBHW072341090426
42741CB00012B/2873
9781942887362